Paul, Women Teachers, and the Mother Goddess at Ephesus

A Study of 1 Timothy 2:9-15 in Light of
The Religious and Cultural Milieu of
The First Century

Sharon Hodgin Gritz

UNIVERSITY
PRESS OF
AMERICA

Lanham • New York • London

Copyright © 1991 by
University Press of America®, Inc.
4720 Boston Way
Lanham, Maryland 20706

3 Henrietta Street
London WC2E 8LU England

Library of Congress Cataloging-in-Publication Data

Gritz, Sharon Hodgin, 1954-
Paul, women teachers, and the mother goddess at Ephesus :
a study of 1 Timothy 2:9–15 in light of the religious and
cultural milieu of the first century / by Sharon Hodgin Gritz.
p. cm.
Includes bibliographical references and indexes.
1. Bible. N.T. Timothy ist, II, 9-15—Criticism,
interpretation, etc.   2. Women in the Bible.
3. Ephesus (Ancient city)—Religion.   I. Title.
BS2745.2.G75   1990
227'.83067—dc20   90–24216 CIP

ISBN 0–8191–8110–2 (alk. paper)
ISBN 0–8191–8111–0 (pbk. : alk. paper)

TO PAUL

TABLE OF CONTENTS

v

FOREWORD

Having read the research of Dr. Sharon Gritz in its dissertation stage at Southwestern Seminary, I am glad to commend it to a wider circle of readers. She addresses a theme that is significant both for current discussions in the church on the role of women in ministry and also for the illumination of the mission of the apostle Paul in the ancient city of Ephesus.

Dr. Gritz wisely gets beyond the nineteenth-century theory of F. C. Baur, which read 1 Timothy as a pseudo-Pauline letter written long after the Apostle's death, and rightly interprets it within the context of Paul's own mission and lifetime. The prevailing assumption of nineteenth-century scholarship that Paul sat down on a Sunday afternoon and wrote a letter and that, consequently, his authorship could be tested by internal criteria of a common style, idiom and vocabulary has now been shown to be mistaken.[1] Fatally flawed in at least two respects, it failed to take into account both (1) the variable role and influence of the secretary in the writing of his letters[2] and also (2) the presence of preformed traditions, some of which were non-Pauline pieces used by Paul but created by other pneumatics in his and other apostolic circles. Literary analysis has now shown the importance of these factors for understanding the composition of the Apostle's letters.[3]

1 Timothy contains a high percentage of preformed pericopes, a number of them apparently not composed by Paul.[4] Indeed, 1 Tim. 2:9-15, which has affinities with both 1 Cor. 14:34f. and 1 Pet. 3:1-7,[5] also shows signs of being such a piece. If so, it had a relevance and usage beyond the immediate Ephesian audience of 1 Timothy. However, the Artemis cult had

a presence in many cities of the Mediterranean, including Rome.[6] Thus, it may still be the case, as Dr. Gritz argues,[7] that 1 Tim. 2:9-15 reflects in part a situation in which Christian women remained under the influence of their pagan background.

While not every reader will be persuaded by all the points made in this book, everyone can profit by careful consideration of them. By her study Dr. Gritz has rendered a valuable service both to New Testament specialists and to the Christian community generally.

E. Earle Ellis

NOTES

1. Even on this assumption the pseudepigraphal hypothesis concerning 1 Timothy has remained unconvincing to many. E.g., A. Kenny (*A Stylometric Study of the New Testament*, Oxford, 1986) finds "no reason to reject the hypothesis that twelve of the Pauline epistles are the work of a single, unusually versitile author" (100). Only Titus stands stylistically at a great distance from the other Pauline letters (95).

2. Cf. E. Randolph Richards, *The Secretary in the Letters of Paul*, Tübingen, 1990.

3. Cf. E. E. Ellis, "Traditions in 1 Corinthians," *NTS* 32 (1986): 481-502; idem, *The Making of the New Testament Documents*, forthcoming, and the literature cited.

4. About 41% of 1 Timothy can be identified as preformed material. For Titus it is about 46%. Cf. E. E. Ellis, "Traditions in the Pastoral Epistles," *Early Jewish and Christian Exegesis*, ed. C. A. Evans, Atlanta, 1987, 237-43, 247.

5. As Dr. Gritz has observed; see below, 125, 158. Cf. E. E. Ellis, *Pauline Theology: Ministry and Society*, Grand Rapids, 1989, 71-75; idem (note 4), 242.

6. See below, 36. Cf. G. H. R. Horseley, *New Documents Illustrating Early Christianity, Volume 4*, Sidney, Australia, 1987, 79f.

7. See below, 43, 115-16.

PREFACE

My interest in the role of women in the church is a personal one. When I arrived at Southwestern Baptist Theological Seminary in Fort Worth, Texas, in 1977 for theological education, I came as a woman called of God into full-time Christian ministry. I also came naively, ignorant of the fact that the role of women in ministry was an "issue." Having been nurtured, supported, and encouraged by a Southern Baptist church in my pilgrimage toward finding God's will for my life, I was unaware that other believers and churches would not similarly embrace my call or gifts. This personal background explains why the topic of the dissertation which led to this book was chosen. I desire my ministry to be guided by biblical principles. 1 Tim. 2:9-15 offers such principles which apply for a woman in Christian ministry today.

It is impossible to thank all those who have enabled me to accomplish this writing project. I owe a debt of gratitude to many significant women who have shaped and continue to shape my life, especially Bobbie D. Hodgin, Fay C. Dameron, Dana H. Woodcock, Pat C. Apple, Gale C. Golden, and Sharon M. Beougher. Gratitude is also expressed to all those fellow-colleagues who have challenged and encouraged me, especially Ruth Ann Foster and Martha S. Bergen. I would like to give special appreciation and gratitude to the late Professor Virtus E. Gideon, who supervised the dissertation from which this book was derived. Professors Lorin L. Cranford, James A. Brooks, John P. Newport, and E. Earle Ellis have all encouraged and helped me along the way in the academic world of teaching and scholarship.

I am also indebted to Phillip Copeland, Director of Public Relations Services at Southwestern Seminary, and his assistants, David Keerins and Rick Willis, for preparing the camera-ready copy of the manuscript for the publisher.

Without the support of my husband and best friend, Paul L. Gritz, I would never have undertaken this task. Paul has both challenged and sharpened my thinking on the biblical passages relevant to the role of women in the church. He has offered encouragement, acceptance, constructive criticism, and suggestions. He was always ready to hear about my work including both complaints and accomplishments. I thank him for all his help and all that he continues to do in enabling me to fulfill God's call to ministry. I am also thankful that our daughter, Lydia Ruth, took the naps necessary for her mother to finish the editing of this project.

Above all, I offer thanksgiving and glory to God. The Lord's grace, strength, guidance, and adequacy enabled me to start and finish this task.

Sharon Hodgin Gritz

INTRODUCTION

"But I do not allow a woman to teach or exercise authority over a man, but to remain quiet" (1 Tim. 2:12). This declaration apparently reflects one of the New Testament's clearest statements on a hotly debated issue among Christians in recent decades. Ministers, laypersons, and scholars from one end of the theological spectrum to the other have struggled with the questions surrounding the roles of women in the church as well as in the home. Many of those who desire an understanding of the place of Christian women have sought for answers in the biblical materials. The verse quoted above lies at the heart of one of these relevant passages, 1 Tim. 2:9-15. It seems to offer a clear and direct word on the subject. Do these words mean what they seem to say? Do they mean for contemporary believers what they meant for the early believers?

1 Tim. 2:9-15 has generated a variety of interpretations. Of these verses one scholar exclaimed, "One feels somehow that something is not expressed here to make it all clear."[1] The difficulty in interpretation develops from the fact that this passage appears to contradict other parts of the New Testament such as Jesus' relationship with women and their inclusion among his disciples, Paul's relationship with women coworkers, and affirmations of the exercise of spiritual gifts by women in worship assemblies (1 Cor. 11:5).

Several possible solutions exist to this apparent contradiction. The first explanation, which accepts Pauline authorship of the Pastoral Epistles,[2] tries to place the blame on Paul: "It cannot be admitted that Paul was inspired by infinite wisdom in this utterance. This was evidently the unilluminated utterance of Paul, the man, biassed by prejudice."[3] This approach has an inadequate view of the inspiration of Scripture.[4]

A second view, which rejects Pauline authorship of the Pastorals, sees no conflict. This solution merely acknowledges that the "Pastor's" teaching differs from that of Paul.[5] This explanation does not resolve the apparent contradiction in the biblical materials.

A third solution relegates the meaning and application of 1 Tim. 2:9-15 to the temporary situation of the first-century Ephesian church.[6] The Pastorals do contain some time-bound imperatives, such as "pick up Mark and bring him with you" or "bring the cloak which I left at Troas" (2 Tim. 4:11, 13).

The fourth explanation takes the words of this passage at their face value, believing that women always and in every place are explicitly prohibited from teaching and other offices in the church.[7] Quoting the Bible, however, does not in itself guarantee the correctness of a position. The literal interpretation involves the study of the plain meaning of a text using hermeneutical principles.[8]

Of these four approaches to the apparent contradiction which 1 Tim. 2:9-15 presents, the third and fourth deserve careful attention. Which, if either, of these approaches accurately interprets the text?

This discussion seeks to confront the problems raised by this passage and discover the meaning of these injunctions regarding women. The thesis of this book proposes that the prohibition of women in regards to teaching and exercising authority over men as expressed in 1 Tim. 2:9-15 resulted from the particular situation in the primitive Ephesian church, a situation complicated by pagan influences from the beliefs and practices of the cult of the Mother Goddess Artemis in Ephesus which had infiltrated the church through false teachers.[9] Although a specific situation occasioned this passage, it does contain principles relevant and applicable for Christians today.

Several presuppositions guide the following study. The authority of the Bible is accepted. This means that the Scriptures serve as the final word for the doctrine and behavior of Christians. Although the Bible is not a rule book, it offers principles and guidelines which speak to the issues of the twentieth century such as the role of women in the church. The teachings it offers on this subject must be studied seriously and accepted by Christians, women and men alike. Therefore, the message of 1 Tim. 2:9-15 requires adherence. The following discussion also affirms that Scripture does not contradict Scripture. Consequently, 1 Tim. 2:9-15 only stands in an *apparent* conflict with other biblical materials. This study will try to uncover the reasons for such a conflict.

The major critical problem of the Pastoral Epistles involves their authorship. More scholars have questioned their incorporation into the Pauline corpus than any other of the Apostle's writings.[10] Though cognizant of the many difficulties that Pauline authorship entails, this discussion has been written from that perspective. It accepts that Paul wrote these three epistles in the mid 60s of the first century A.D. It also recognizes the possibility that Paul might have utilized traditional materials in these writings, including the passage under discussion.[11] Even if Paul did not pen the Pastorals, however, they do form a part of the New Testament canon. If a later writer did have responsibility for these epistles, their inclusion in the canon still makes their message authoritative. One must accept the teachings of 1 Tim. 2:9-15 as valid despite the problem of authorship.[12]

The six chapters which follow represent applied hermeneutics. Indeed, the real issue involved in a study of 1 Tim. 2:9-15 centers in biblical interpretation. In order to understand the passage, this research figuratively pictures these verses at the center of a series of concentric circles. Each circle represents a different context. The task of interpretation necessitates an examination of each of these contexts and their relationship to the passage itself. Although the major emphasis for the thesis centers on the religious context, all must be considered. The study begins with the largest context—the historical setting. This embraces both the cultural context (chapter 1) and the religious context (chapter 2). The examination then narrows to the literary or interpretative contexts: the Old Testament context (chapter 3), the New Testament context (chapter 4), and the Pastoral Epistles' context (chapter 5). At the center of these various contexts lies the passage itself. Chapter 6 offers an exegesis of these debated verses.

In addition to the hermeneutical methodology outlined above, other interpretative principles underlie the discussion to follow.[13] As already implied, the historical context of a passage illumines the function and meaning a text had in its own day. Chapters 1 and 2 attempt to clarify this background. One should consider the entire biblical witness on a given subject. For instance, plain texts provide insight into obscure texts. Chapters 3 and 4 will purpose to do this. One must understand the literary form of a passage. The intention, methodology, theology, and practices of the author can provide interpretative clues. Chapters 5 and 6 will employ these principles. Biblical interpretation benefits from keeping the missionary factor central. The discussion in chapter 5 on the purpose of the Pastoral Epistles will reflect this principle. The interpreter should examine the immediate context of a passage. Grammatical, lexical, and linguistic tools should be utilized. Chapters 3 through 6 try to observe these guidelines. Interpreters of Scripture should seek the help of the past and present Christian community for the sharing of insights and the overcoming of biases of cultural and theological traditions. The use of secondary sources will facilitate this.[14]

The utilization of interpretative concepts such as those above enables the interpreter some degree of objectivity. One must recognize that her or his own ideological biases might govern the hermeneutical effort. It is hoped that the methodology established for this study will contribute to a distancing of the interpreter's personal value perspectives. The ultimate goal is to allow the text to speak for itself without imposing on it a predetermined interpretation.

Notwithstanding the attempt at objectivity, this discussion admits to being written from a feminine perspective simply because the writer is a woman. This study accepts as another interpretative principle that some translations and studies related to 1 Tim. 2:9-15 might have elements of sexual bias. The "feminist hermeneutical"[15] approach adopted in this study focuses on the reexamination of biblical texts in an effort to discover the teaching of the Scripture as opposed to the traditions of male interpreters. In this effort, this deliberation will utilize the writings of those from the feminist approach in addition to those from traditional perspectives.

Finally, the aim of this study is the affirmation that "the God who spoke in the past and whose word was recorded in the Bible continues to speak to all mankind in Scripture."[16] The interpretative task strives to transform believers within their own particular situations.[17] What, then, is God's transforming word from 1 Tim. 2:9-15?

NOTES

1. Archibald Thomas Robertson, *Word Pictures in the New Testament*, 6 vols. (Nashville: Broadman Press, 1931), 4: 570.

2. See the discussion on 5 n. 10 for the authorship of 1 Timothy, 2 Timothy, and Titus.

3. Elizabeth Cady Stanton et al., *The Woman's Bible* (New York: European Publishing Co., 1898), 163. This view is shared by contemporary feminists such as Virginia Ramey Mollenkott, *Women, Men and the Bible* (Nashville: Abingdon Press, 1977), 103-6.

4. See H. Wayne House, "Paul, Women and Contemporary Evangelical Feminism," *Bibliotheca Sacra* 136 (January-March 1979): 45-46.

5. Anthony Tyrell Hanson, *The Pastoral Letters: Commentary on the First and Second Letters to Timothy and the Letter to Titus*, in *The Cambridge Bible Commentary*, gen. ed. P. R. Ackroyd, A. R. C. Leaney, and J. W. Packer (Cambridge: University Press, 1966), 38.

6. David M. Scholer, "Exegesis: 1 Timothy 2:8-15," *Daughters of Sarah* 1 (May 1975): 7-8 and Don Williams, *The Apostle Paul and Women in the Church* (Glendale, Calif.: Regal Press, 1977), 144.

7. Georg Gunter Blum, "The Office of Women in the New Testament," *The Churchman* 85 (1971): 184-85 and Douglas J. Moo, "1 Timothy 2:11-15: Meaning and Significance," *Trinity Journal* 1 (Spring 1980): 71.

8. Willard Swartley, *Slavery, Sabbath, War and Women: Case Issues in Biblical Interpretation* (Scottdale, Pa.: Herald Press, 1983), 229.

9. Gordon Fee wrote of this passage, "Whether any of this is also related to the predominance of women in the local Artemis cult . . . is a moot point, but it is certainly possible." *1 and 2 Timothy, Titus: A Good News Commentary* (San Francisco: Harper and Row, Publishers, 1984), 34. This book attempts to shed light on that possibility.

10. There are four hypotheses for the authorship of the Pastoral Epistles: (1) the traditional view, which accepts Paul as author (representatives of this view include J. N. D. Kelly, Donald Guthrie, E. K. Simpson, Ceslaus Spicq, and Wilhelm Michaelis); (2) the modified traditional view, which accepts the genuineness of all the material and suggests a less controlled amanuensis or editor (Joachim Jeremias); (3) the fragmentary view, which proposes a second-century author who utilized genuine Pauline materials (P. N. Harrison, E. F. Scott, Burton Scott Easton, and Robert Falconer); and, (4) the pseudonymous view (Martin Dibelius, Hans Conzelmann, Werner G. Kümmel, C. F. D. Moule, and C. K. Barrett). The four approaches derive from different interpretations of the external and internal evidence. Externally, the majority of the Patristic and manuscript evidence points to the inclusion of the Pastorals in the Pauline corpus, even though Marcion and p^{46} omit them. The internal evidence presents greater difficulties. Linguistically, the vocabulary of the Pastoral Epistles differs from the other letters of Paul marked by the absence of key Pauline terminology. Yet, there is no reason why Paul could not have known this vocabulary. Historically, the data of the three epistles do not fit the Acts chronology. One can explain these inconsistencies by positing the release of Paul from Roman imprisonment at the end of Acts after which he traveled to Crete, Ephesus, and Macedonia. He penned 1 Timothy and Titus in Macedonia before being arrested and imprisoned in Rome again. During this second imprisonment Paul wrote 2 Timothy. Doctrinally, the identity of the heresies attacked in the Pastorals poses a problem. However, the descriptions of these heresies do not necessarily apply to second-century Gnosticism. (See chapter 5 of this book.) Finally, the ecclesiology of the Pastorals seems to be more advanced than that of other letters. Yet, Paul had concern about church organization from the very beginning (Acts 14). Despite the difficulties of the traditional view, its reconstruction of the data best fits the facts of the historical situation. The personal allusions and autobiographical passages are better attributed to Paul than to anyone else. The fragmentary and pseudonymous views cannot answer the question "Why were three letters written?" Also, the early church rejected pseudepigraphic writings. The non-traditional views restrict the abilities and flexibilities of the Apostle Paul. For works arguing against Pauline authorship, see P. N. Harrison, *The Problem of the Pastoral Epistles* (Oxford: University Press, 1921); idem, "Important Hypotheses Reconsidered: III. The Authorship of the Pastoral Epistles," *The Expository Times* 67 (1955): 77-81; idem, "The Pastoral Epistles and Duncan's Ephesian Theory," *New Testament Studies* 2 (May 1956): 250-61; K. Grayston and G. Herdan, "The

Authorship of the Pastorals in the Light of Statistical Linguistics," *New Testament Studies* 6 (October 1959): 1-15; and C. F. D. Moule, "The Problem of the Pastoral Epistles: A Reappraisal," *Bulletin of the John Rylands Library* 47 (March 1965): 430-52. For a defense of the traditional view, see Donald Guthrie, *The Pastoral Epistles and the Mind of Paul* (London: The Tyndale Press, 1956); E. E. Ellis, "The Authorship of the Pastorals: A Resume and Assessment of Current Trends," *Evangelical Quarterly* 32 (1960): 151-61; Bruce M. Metzger, "A Reconsideration of Certain Arguments against the Pauline Authorship of the Pastoral Epistles," *The Expository Times* 70 (1958): 91-94; J. W. Roberts, "The Genuineness of the Pastorals: Some Recent Aspects of the Question," *Restoration Quarterly* 8 (1965): 104-10; and Edmund K. Simpson, "The Authenticity and Authorship of the Pastoral Epistles," *Evangelical Quarterly* 12 (October 1940): 289-311.

11. See E. Earle Ellis, "Traditions in the Pastoral Epistles," 148-53, in *Early Jewish and Christian Exegesis: Studies in Memory of William Hugh Brownlee*, ed. C. A. Evans (Decatur, Ga.: Scholars Press, 1987).

12. Mark D. Roberts, "Woman Shall Be Saved: A Closer Look at 1 Timothy 2:15," *TSF Bulletin* (November-December 1981): 4.

13. The following works have supplied insight in hermeneutical procedures for the present study: Gordon D. Fee, *New Testament Exegesis: A Handbook for Students and Pastors* (Philadelphia: The Westminster Press, 1983); A. Berkeley Mickelsen, *Interpreting the Bible* (Grand Rapids: William B. Eerdmans Publishing Co., 1963), 99-176; and Bernard Ramm, *Protestant Biblical Interpretation: A Textbook of Hermeneutics*, 3rd rev. ed. (Grand Rapids: Baker Book House, 1970), 93-161.

14. For these and other principles see, Swartley, *Slavery, Sabbath, War and Women*, 229-34, and Robert K. Johnston, *Evangelicals at an Impasse: Biblical Authority in Practice* (Atlanta: John Knox Press, 1979), 69-75.

15. Feminist hermeneutics is a relatively recent development in the area of biblical interpretation. It is not deviant, subjective, and to be contrasted with "hermeneutics" in general, since no value-neutral position exists. Basically, feminist hermeneutics has developed to counteract the fact that male interpreters in male-oriented societies have dominated biblical and theological studies for centuries. There are four responses to the Bible by feminists. The first views the Bible as sexist and, consequently, rejects it. Proponents of this approach include: Mary Daly, *Beyond God the Father: Toward a Philosophy of Women's Liberation* (Boston: Beacon Press, 1973) and Naomi R. Goldenberg, *Changing of the Gods: Feminism and the End of Traditional Religions* (Boston: Beacon Press, 1979). The second response sees a prophetic-liberating vision within the Bible, even though the Bible still contains elements of sexism. Rosemary Ruether represents this position. "Feminism and Patriarchal Religion: Principles of Ideological Critique of the Bible," *Journal for the Study of the Old Testament* 22 (February 1982): 54-66. The third response closely relates to the second. Some scholars would group the two together. This view encourages historical reconstruction of biblical history because a greater role for women existed than the codified writings suggest. The developer of this approach is Elisabeth Schüssler Fiorenza. Her writings include "Interpreting Patriarchal Traditions," in *The Liberating Word: A Guide to Nonsexist Interpretation of the Bible*, ed. Letty Russell (Philadelphia: The Westminster Press, 1976), 39-61; "Toward a Feminist Biblical Hermeneutic: Biblical Interpretation and Liberation Theology," in *The Challenge of Liberation Theology*, ed. Brian Mahan and Dale L. Richesin (Maryknoll, N.Y.: Orbis Books, 1981), 91-112; "Feminist Theology and New Testament Interpretation," *Journal for the Study of the Old Testament* 22 (February 1982): 32-46; and *In Memory of Her: A*

Feminist Theological Reconstruction of Christian Origins (New York: Crossroad Publishing Co., 1983). The fourth view believes that the Bible is nonsexist if properly interpreted. The biblical tradition contains counter-cultural impulses of a remnant (that is, woman's) standpoint. Representative of this view is Phyllis Trible, *God and the Rhetoric of Sexuality* (Philadelphia: Fortress Press, 1978). For further analysis of feminist hermeneutics, see Mary Ann Tolbert, "Defining the Problem: The Bible and the Feminist Hermeneutics," *Semeia* 28 (1983): 113-26 and Phyllis Trible, "Feminist Hermeneutics and Biblical Studies," *Christian Century*, February 1982, 116-18. For discussions which compare the hermeneutics of the traditional/hierarchical and egalitarian/liberationist approaches to the role of women, see Johnston, *Evangelicals at an Impasse*, 51-68, and Swartley, *Slavery, Sabbath, War and Women*, 50-90. See also Krister Stendahl, *The Bible and the Role of Women: A Case Study in Hermeneutics*, trans. Emilie Sander (Philadelphia: Fortress Press, 1966).

16. C. René Padilla, "The Interpreted Word: Reflections on Contextual Hermeneutics," *Themelios* 7 (1981): 20.

17. Ibid., 22.

PART ONE

HISTORICAL STUDY OF 1 TIMOTHY 2:9-15

CHAPTER I

THE CULTURAL CONTEXT
OF EPHESUS

The broadest context for the understanding of 1 Tim. 2:9-15 involves the culture of the people to whom Paul wrote. He was writing to Christians in Ephesus in the first century A.D. What kind of city was Ephesus? What aspects of that city influenced the believing community? Since the passage deals with women, one would have to look with interest at the women of Ephesus. From what backgrounds did they come? What roles did they perform in society? How did they live? In order to understand 1 Tim. 2:9-15 the interpreter needs an answer to the questions raised above. This chapter attempts to provide insights and understandings into the cultural context of Ephesus and the women who lived there.

The City of Ephesus

Josephus (A.D. 37-ca. 95) identified Ephesus as "the metropolis of Asia."[1] Writing somewhat earlier than this first-century Jewish historian, Strabo (ca. 63 B.C.-ca. A.D. 21) stated that the city "because of its advantageous situation . . . grows daily, and is the largest emporium in Asia Minor this side of Taurus."[2] As these two remarks would suggest, Ephesus represented a "pivot of civilization" in the first century A.D. It served as a meeting place of the East and West standing as the main line of communication between Rome and the Orient. The city ranked with Antioch in Syria and Alexandria in Egypt as one of the three great cities of the eastern Mediterranean.[3]

Historically,[4] a city had existed at the Ephesus site several centuries before the Athenian Androclus settled there in 1044 B.C. Androclus increased the importance of the city and extended the worship of the Mother Goddess.[5] From this time Ephesus experienced a series of rulers and government changes. The Persians subjected the city from 548-325 B.C. During this period the Greek arts excelled, and the temple of Artemis was built and rebuilt three times on the same site. Alexander the Great (356-323 B.C.) freed Ephesus from Persian rule.[6] After his conquest of Ephesus and Asia, the Greek spirit began to increase in strength throughout the region.[7] Alexander's general Lysimachus (ca. 355-281 B.C.) enlarged and fortified Ephesus.[8] The next one hundred years saw frequent shifts in the government until Antiochus the Great (d. 187 B.C.) assumed control from 223-187 B.C. With his rule Ephesus again gained in significance until it became the chief mart of Asia Minor. The Romans under Antony (ca. 83-30 B.C.) eventually subdued the Ephesians in 41 B.C.[9] Ephesus became the capital of the Roman province of Asia and served as such during the first century of the Christian era. The Roman governor resided there.[10] The municipality, however, remained a free city—having home rule with a Greek constitution.[11]

Due to its harbor and linking of the East to the West Ephesus held a strategic position which made it a busy center of shipping and land traffic. As the chief commercial route by sea between Italy and the East, Ephesus offered two options for travel and trade further east: by sea along the south of Asia Minor to Syria and by land on a road from the city to the Cilician Gates. This situation created constant traffic between Ephesus and Corinth.[12] One noted with interest the close relationship between these two cities. The New Testament correspondence to both Corinth and Ephesus contains prohibitions for women in worship. The commercial interests of the metropolis increased under Roman rule. As the "greatest trading city"[13] of the province of Asia, Ephesus became a rich and populous center. Literary records and inscriptional evidence documented the wealth of the metropolis which derived not only from the maritime and land commerce but also from the large territory owned by the city.[14]

The Ephesian population of the first century A.D. comprised a melting pot of Anatolians, Greeks, Jews, Romans, and other peoples.[15] Evidently a large colony of Jews had settled there since the Romans allotted a quarter of the city to them.[16] The Jews enjoyed a somewhat privileged position.[17]

Ephesus did not exist only as a commercial center. Another part of the city grew up around the temple dedicated to Artemis, the Artemision, one of the seven wonders of the ancient world.[18]

A religious community had already been established when Greek colonists arrived in Asia Minor. The sanctuary of Artemis served as the center to which the whole valley looked long before the Greek city was built.[19] The earliest beginnings of the Artemision probably centered around the end of the eighth century B.C. Prior to this, primitive structures such as altars and platforms functioned as the worship center.[20] The worship of Artemis signalled the "most distinctive source of prestige and revenue" for Ephesus.[21] The Artemision and its land area served as a sanctuary offering legal refuge and right of asylum.[22] The consideration of the temple as sacred and inviolable led many foreign kings and other individuals to deposit money there for safekeeping. The temple itself used this money for loans making it the largest bank in Asia. This fact, as well as gifts made to the temple and its Mother Goddess, constituted another source of the city's wealth.[23] The Artemision not only stood apart geographically from the municipality proper, it often opposed the city politically. Throughout the history of Ephesus, influences from the marketplace clashed with those from the temple.[24]

Despite the prominence of the Artemis cult, the movement of peoples through the trading center brought other religions to Ephesus. Apart from some monotheistic Judaism, polytheism prevailed. In the Apostle Paul's time at least one temple dedicated to Rome and Caesar existed in Ephesus. Later two more temples were added. The municipality acquired the title "temple keeper" or "temple guardian" of the imperial cult.[25] The provincial capital also achieved fame as a center of magical practices and superstitions. Acts 19:13-14 referred to some Jewish itinerant exorcists in the city.

Many who practiced magic did become believers through the ministry of Paul and burned their books of magic as a sign of their repentance (Acts 19:19). Ancient Greek and Roman writers identified books of incantations and magical formulas as "Ephesian writings" because of their prevalent use there.[26]

Ephesus was the most important city visited by Paul next to Rome itself. This commercial metropolis served as a hub or pivotal point from which Paul's teachings would spread, especially to the inland towns of the Asian province.[27] The power and willingness to accept and effect change characteristic of cities[28] made Ephesus an ideal place to introduce and establish the Christian faith.

Paul first visited Ephesus on his second missionary journey. Although he stayed there only briefly, the Apostle did reason with the Jews before leaving for Caesarea. At this time, he left Priscilla and Aquila in Ephesus (Acts 18:19-21). On his third missionary trip Paul remained in Ephesus for three years speaking out boldly and reasoning about the kingdom of God (Acts 19:1-41). As a result of his efforts, "all who lived in Asia heard the word of the Lord, both Jews and Greeks" (Acts 19:10). When the Apostle finally departed from Ephesus, he continued his tour through Macedonia and Greece. On his return to Jerusalem, he met with the elders of the Ephesian church at Miletus (Acts 20:17-38). During this meeting he warned these church leaders against false teachers.

> "I know that after my departure savage wolves will come in among you, not sparing the flock; and from among your own selves men will arise, speaking perverse things, to draw away the disciples after them. Therefore be on the alert" (Acts 20:29-31a).

Paul himself had already experienced hostilities at Ephesus. His teachings caused a riot by those profiting from trade related to the worship of Artemis.[29] He told the Corinthian believers that he had "fought with wild beasts at Ephesus"[30] and that there were many adversaries (1 Cor. 16:9). In later correspondence to Corinth Paul mentioned deliverance from the peril of death in Asia (2 Cor. 1:8-10). The Apostle left Timothy at Ephesus to deal with "strange doctrines" which certain ones were teaching (1 Tim. 1:3-4). According to these biblical references, Ephesus proved to be both a fruitful and difficult area for Christian ministry and expansion.

The members of the Ephesian congregation to whom Paul directed his injunctions in 1 Tim. 2:9-15 lived out their Christian faith in a cosmopolitan environment. Thus, the city of Ephesus formed one context for understanding the passage under examination. This context revealed a steady stream of commercial, philosophical, and religious influences from East and West descending upon the city. As a cultural and religious center, Ephesus and its environment welcomed all contemporary secular and religious currents of opinion and developments.[31] To Christianity's advantage, one more new religion would not appear as a threat to authorities who already tolerated quite a diversity of religious thought. The danger for the recently introduced Christian faith, however, centered in its possible corruption by the cultic beliefs and practices already well established in the metropolis. New converts did not immediately forget or set aside their former cultic ideas and rituals. Syncretism had to be avoided; the purity of true apostolic doctrine had to be maintained. In light of such a background, Paul's warnings to the Ephesian elders were to be expected.

The "melting pot" nature of Ephesus reflected itself in the church membership.   Converts from various backgrounds joined with other believers to form the church at Ephesus. Christian women of the congregation came from different experiences. There were both Gentile and Jewish women believers. What perspectives did these women bring with them into the Christian faith? Did their distinctive environments have some relationship to Paul's injunctions in 1 Tim. 2:9-15?

The Status and Roles of Gentile
Women in Ephesus

In the centuries preceding the New Testament era a variety of concepts concerning the position of women either coexisted with or followed one another. Different periods and different geographical areas produced divergent views. Certainly the Ephesians knew of more than one of these customs and attitudes toward women and marriage which ranged from the traditional to the revolutionary.[32] As a general rule, greater freedom existed for women the further west one traveled though variations still existed.[33] Other variants besides time and geography complicated even more the study of women in the Hellenistic culture of Ephesus. Such factors included distinctions between urban and rural customs, upper and lower classes, and theory as opposed to practice.[34] One must exercise caution in making statements about the place of women in general since scholars derived most of their evidence from the wealthier classes. Also, one must take into account that a rapid rate of change characterized the Hellenistic period.[35]

Generally speaking, in the three to four centuries preceding Christ a gradual liberation of women occurred in the Greco-Roman world. This liberation probably had more strength in theory than in practice.[36] During the Hellenistic period forces did work to reduce the sharp differentiation between women and men.[37] For example, men did accord a rising esteem for women. Also, the definition of women's civil rights improved pronouncedly.[38] The Hellenistic culture itself brought certain emancipation and enlightenment due to the value placed on personal relationships.[39] The rhetoric of the period aroused egalitarian hopes as well.[40]

The women of first-century Ephesus, in particular pagan or Gentile women, would reflect the general trends mentioned above. The female members of the Ephesian population received influences from both the Greeks and Romans who ruled the city and brought with them their own unique cultures.

Women in General and the Domestic Context

The ancient Greeks thought very little of women.[41] They basically treated them as chattel. Women essentially existed on the same level with slaves. Wives always lived under the authority, control, and protection of their husbands.[42]   Women, especially wives, led lives of seclusion.[43]   Men confined their spouses to the household in order to make certain the legitimacy of their children as suggested by the following fourth-century B.C. Athenian statement quoted by Demosthenes: "We have harlots for our pleasure, concubines (παλλακάς) for daily physical use, wives to bring up legitimate children and to be faithful stewards in household matters."[44] None of these three classifications reflected a high view of women. Their roles seemed utilitarian in nature.[45]

The Greek attitude toward women, however, did alter. This was due in part to challenges, despite some ambiguity, from the great philosophers of classical Greece (fourth century B.C.). For instance, Plato (ca. 427-348 B.C.) treated women favorably in some of his writings. He affirmed that they should have equal opportunities in education and public office.[46] Although Plato argued for the equality of women, he also wanted to curtail the development of too much freedom for women by legally limiting their lifestyles.[47]   Aristotle (384-322 B.C.) indicated the desirability of women in democracy but at the same time argued that too much freedom for women served as a political evil.[48]   The Stoics did the most to promote the improved status of women. They stressed the worth of individual women and espoused a strict monogamy. The Stoic ideas spread widely on a grass-roots level and permeated all classes of society.[49]

During the Hellenistic period the status of women in marriage advanced. Both spouses committed themselves to monogamy and marital fidelity. Both possessed an equal right to initiate divorce.[50] Divorce was not uncommon. It occurred by common consent or by the unilateral action of the wife or husband after sending an official notice.[51] Wives now held extensive economic rights including the right over their own dowry. They could inherit personal patrimony, as well as buy, own, and sell goods and property. The law also allowed them to will these to others.[52]   Greek women finally moved beyond the constant confinement of their home.

Greek women, however, never reached the pinnacle of liberty achieved by Roman women. A more egalitarian attitude prevailed in Rome.[53] Evidence for this view did not exist as frequently in early Roman society. All Roman women still lived under the custody of males. An important feature of the earlier Roman culture resided in the *patria potestas* or the *paterfamilias*.[54] This represented a power without parallel in Greek law. A father had absolute power over his family members, even to the determination of their life and death. This male jurisdiction, however, gradually faded out.[55]

The traditional expectation of well-to-do Roman women involved marriage and motherhood.[56] Although women lived under the authority of fathers and husbands, they owned a strong role within the family. Wives were the mistresses of the household—*materfamilias domina*.[57] Women could not dissolve their marriages, but the law made it difficult for men to divorce their wives. Romans expected loyalty to spouses in marriage, but this did not necessarily mean sexual loyalty for men.

By the third century B.C. Rome moved to improve the status of women. For instance, women obtained property rights. Later in the Republic women could marry and divorce on their own initiative. In fact, some women chose their own husbands. The status of women improved even more dramatically in the Empire.[58] This period saw a progressive advancement in the lot of women. Women obtained increased emancipation. Romans perceived the position of housewife as a high one. Houses no longer contained special chambers for the seclusion of women. Monogamous marriage was encouraged.[59] Family affairs evidenced a new equality. Women had no obligation to obey their husbands. Husbands legally had no right of power over their wives.[60] The women of the poorer classes, however, might not have felt these egalitarian effects. Women's degree of freedom and opportunity depended on their rank in society.[61]

Since divorce became easier to obtain, marriages disintegrated. The standards of morality markedly declined. Moral corruption began to characterize the Roman Empire.[62] Immorality increased since the double standard of sexual morality had broken down.[63] One must remember, nevertheless, that more records came from the lives of the upper-class members of society which not only experienced emancipation to a greater degree but which also often abused wealth and leisure. Female freedom did not cause the family life and moral deterioration of the Roman Empire. Men still dissolved family ties as much, if not more so, than women. Also, family stability and high morals did not disappear.[64] The domestic realm represented the central context for the Gentile women of Ephesus. For some, it was their only context. What could and did these women do outside the home?

Women and the Public Context

In early Greek society women rarely left the confines of their homes. They had little contact with other women and almost none with men.[65] The Greeks considered it improper for husbands to take their wives out in public.[66] Consequently, married men turned to the heterae for female companionship outside the home. The heterae represented a well-educated class of foreign women, often Ionians. Men looked to these artistic, cultured, and intellectual companions for interesting conversation, entertainment, and social and sexual intercourse. The heterae entered into the male society with freedom to do as they pleased. Men admired these foreign women for their accomplishments. Yet, due to their courtesan status, the heterae could not marry Greek citizens. They lived on the margin of society with no family responsibilities.[67]

The secluded position of married Greek women did finally end. By Hellenistic times wives began to appear at social gatherings. They made long journeys. Some women moved into roles beyond that of housewife becoming professional athletes, musicians, and even physicians.[68] Capable Greek women, especially in Hellenistic Asia Minor where Ephesus was located but also in Greece itself, could and did possess independent and significant roles even in public life.[69]

Roman women had much more freedom outside the home than did Greek women.[70] Nevertheless, they still spent a great deal of time indoors though not sequestered. Wealthy women could come and go as they pleased. They attended public social events and visited friends.[71] Many women joined in all-female gatherings for religious purposes. The cultivation of upper-class women enabled them to participate in the intellectual life of their male associates. Roman women could make choices about the direction of their lives since society tolerated more than the one traditional role of housewife. Women became involved in business affairs, such as controlling their own dowry.[72] With ameliorated economic rights, women now could receive an inheritance. They held independent legal rights and could bear legal witness. Women could also attain Roman citizenship.[73] Basically, women now became involved in every aspect of their culture.

Most of the discussion above applied to Roman women of the well-to-do classes. The lower class women predominated numerically but had less notoriety. These women acquired no training beyond traditional household skills. Their daily household duties carried them outside the home. Their economic status did not allow them the luxury of confinement.

The Roman practices of exposing baby girls and selling daughters relegated many women to slavery and prostitution. Society viewed female slaves as always employable for sexual purposes. Slavery disqualified women and men from formal Roman marriage. There also existed a class of freewomen or working-class women who served as shopkeepers and artisans. Some of these did accumulate wealth.[74] Thus, Roman women did have some roles in public life.

Women and Education

Few ancient Greek women had access to education. The culture limited education to the heterae and members of the upper class.[75] The Hellenistic period brought the widespread practice of education for younger girls. The key to women's advanced status centered in their education. Plato encouraged the intellectual training of women as did the later Plutarch.[76] The Stoics especially stressed the need to educate women.[77] The Greek view of teachers, however, prevented respectable women from occupying that role. Greek education centered around a master who achieved a deep, personal, extended relationship with pupils. The Greek teacher represented an authority figure. Due to this authority inherent in the Greek conception of the teaching role, people saw women teachers as unacceptably domineering.[78] Rome did educate its daughters.[79] Women, again especially the rich women, probably were not as ignorant as some writers have portrayed them.[80]

The Gentile women of first-century Ephesus had achieved more freedom than any of their "sisters" of previous generations. No longer confined to the home, women moved relatively freely about the city. Some women chose roles other than or in addition to the traditional mother-wife. The period possessed a heightened awareness of the differentiation of male and female.[81] Although many persons probably still saw women as inferior, their education and growing legal rights brought them esteem and respect from others.

The Status and Roles of Jewish
Women in Ephesus

In discussing the status and roles of Jewish women in Ephesus, one had to take into account several factors. The first factor concerned the location of these women—outside of Palestine in the Diaspora. Did the Jews, including the Jewish women, believe and behave differently outside of Palestine? One could not make a sharp distinction between Palestinian Judaism and that of the Diaspora.   Even Palestinian Judaism received influences from the Greco-Roman culture. The Palestinian Jews probably reacted more strongly against assimilation.   So the materials on women in Palestine probably applied also to some extent to those of the Diaspora and vice versa.[82]

A second factor distinguished between "Hebrew" or Israelite women and "Jewish" women. There appeared to be a difference in the status of Hebrew, pre-exilic women as opposed to Jewish, postexilic women, although obviously a strong relationship existed between the two groups. Actually, these did not represent two groups as such, but the same group viewed from different periods of time. The primary sources for the study of Hebrew women centered in the Old Testament, while sources for understanding Jewish women of the first century consisted of intertestamental writings, rabbinical sayings, and comments by others who wrote during or about that time, such as Josephus.   Therefore, the examination of Hebrew women would be considered more appropriately in the discussion of the Old Testament context.[83]

Women in General and the Domestic Context

First-century Judaism presented women "as being subordinate and inferior to men in every sphere, with no real place outside the home, though within the home their role was recognized as important."[84]   The Jews had made the lower status of women explicit. This signalled a change in the Jewish perspective toward women. "Until the exile in Babylon, Yahwism, Prophetism and Wisdom point to a theological view of womanhood which was in no way demeaning or overbearing."[85]   Now, however, Jewish culture debased women in general. Writings and teachings usually linked women with children and slaves.[86]

Although women's legal status in Judaism gradually improved during the Hellenistic era, the number of negative or contradictory general remarks steadily increased.[87] Jesus ben Sirach reflected such contradition in his collection of proverbs written early in the second century B.C. Negatively he wrote:

Do not look upon any one for beauty, and do not sit in the midst of women; for from garments comes the moth, and from a woman comes woman's wickedness. Better is the wickedness of a man than a woman who does good, and it is a woman who brings shame and disgrace.[88]

Yet, positively this same author penned, "He who acquires a wife gets his best possession, a helper fit for him and a pillar of support,"[89] and "A good wife is a great blessing; she will be granted among the blessings of the man who fears the Lord."[90]

Philo, a contemporary of Jesus, exemplified real misogynism in his writings. He associated women with many pejorative expressions: weak, easily deceived, cause of sin, lifeless, diseased, enslaved, unmanly, nerveless, mean, slavish, and sluggish.[91] Josephus also stated that women were in all things inferior to their husbands.[92]

The rabbis did not present a homogeneous attitude toward women. Yet, despite some positive evaluations, the negative views outweighed these both quantitatively and qualitatively.[93] One rabbi contended, "Though a woman be as a pitcher full of filth and her mouth be full of blood, yet all speed after her."[94] A daily prayer for men which occurred in three of the most ancient rabbinic collections further revealed the negative status of women: "Praised be God that he has not created me a gentile; praised be God that he has not created me a woman; praised be God that he has not created me an ignorant man."[95] One commentator pointed out that this prayer's context did not indicate the confession of intrinsic male superiority but an expression of gratitude to God for the privilege of observing a greater portion of the Law.[96]

Nonetheless, even that observation does not lessen the inferior status of women which the prayer voiced. Also, the context of the prayer would not measure the attitudes and emotions of the man who prayed these words daily.

Why did the status of women in postexilic Judaism decline? The Jews felt the need to stress their identity and unity as a people. This caused them to reject the customs of the alien societies around them. They thought it important to ward off these outside influences, such as the expanding Hellenism with its increasing freedom for women.[97]

It is not difficult to understand why a pattern of restrictiveness against women developed in Judaism. Their felt need to develop in-group/out-group defenses in the early centuries after the exile, in view of the return of such a relatively small group of Jews to a land surrounded by peoples of different cultures and religions, particularly Goddess worship, is psychologically understandable. . . . The Hellenistic culture proved increasingly attractive and pervasive, and those Jews who saw it as a threat to Jewish identity felt that they had to insulate the Jewish community from its enervating influences. By increasing restrictions, half the population—the female half—was thereby more surely removed from Hellenism's baleful blandishments; . . . Such an ap-proach was also doubtless reinforced by the knowledge that a significant element in the to-be-rejected Hellenistic culture was the relatively much higher status women held in religion and society and the Goddess worship connected with it.[98]

Consequently, parts of Judaism viewed women as temptresses and political traitors to the security of the Jewish people.[99]

There did exist one area in which women received high esteem—their roles as wives and mothers. Children had to honor their mothers equally with their fathers. Wives could hold property in their own right.[100] Some women wrote their own bills of divorce.[101] The husband had the obligation to provide for his wife.[102] Women's presence and role in the home even had a certain spiritual significance. One rabbi remarked, "He who has no wife dwells without good, without help, without joy, without blessing, and without atonement."[103] This denoted a positive view of women and marriage. However, most positive statements, including this one, did not pertain to women as such but women as related to men. Husbands appreciated good wives, but often that appreciation expressed itself in terms of what the wives did for them. Thus, the Jewish women's world centered in their families and domestic responsibilities.

Women and the Public Context

The seclusion of Jewish women characterized mainly the wealthier families where female-male contact did not occur customarily.[104] In the rural areas women moved about more freely as necessity dictated, such as working in the fields.[105] Even in the cities some women helped their husbands by managing shops and stores.[106] Unmarried women represented the most secluded group.[107] On Jewish feast days, nevertheless, even orthodox women emerged from their houses.[108] In public, men did not normally speak to women, not even to their own wives or other relatives. Even in private men minimized their conversations with their wives. According to the prevalent opinion, this prevented the seduction of the man by the woman.[109]

Jewish women did not possess the legal rights of their Greco-Roman sisters. For instance, their testimony in court had no validity "on account

of the levity and boldness of their sex."[110]   There was, however, no
unified opinion among the rabbis on this matter.[111]   In practice, a woman's
word was probably accepted in some cases.[112]

Women and Education

First-century Judaism limited the education of women primarily to domestic
arts. They had no other formal education.[113]

Conclusion

The Gentile and Jewish women who embraced the Christian faith and joined
the Ephesian believers came from very different backgrounds. The "broad
stream of women's emancipation running through the Hellenistic world"
touched Gentile and Jewish women and men who united with the Christians
at Ephesus.[114] The legal and social status of women in the Greco-Roman
world seemed higher than that of Jewish women.

On the other hand, Judaism affirmed the places of wives and mothers
as significant and spoke of the obligations of husbands to wives. Paul
certainly had an awareness of these different attitudes. He had been trained
as a Pharisee, a strict Hebrew of the Hebrews, but he had lived in the
Diaspora, experiencing personally the impact of Hellenism. He also knew
the Ephesian church and the background of its women members.

Since Paul wrote to the Ephesian congregation cognizant of the
cultural context of the city of Ephesus and its women, the interpreter of
1 Tim. 2:9-15 must approach this passage with a similar understanding.
Attention will now focus on another aspect of the Ephesian culture—its
religious environment, particularly the worship of the Goddess Artemis. As
indicated earlier, the participation of women in the Goddess worship
prompted many of the postexilic restrictions on Jewish women. Could a
similar view have prompted Paul's injunctions in 1 Tim. 2:9-15?

NOTES

1. Flavius Josephus *Antiquities of the Jews* 14.10.11, in *The Works of Flavius Josephus*,
4 vols., trans. William Whiston (Dublin: n.p., 1738-1741; reprint ed., Nashville: Broadman
Press, 1974), 3:310. Hereafter all references to Josephus cite this edition.

2. Strabo *Geography* 14.1.24, in *The Loeb Classical Library*, 6:231. Hereafter this collection is abbreviated *LCL*.

3. Percy Gardner, *The Ephesian Gospel* (New York: G. P. Putnam's Sons, 1915), 1. Jack Finegan, *Light from the Ancient Past* (Princeton, N.J.: Princeton University Press, 1946), 265. Ephesus was situated on the Cayster River on the western coast of Asia Minor. This river valley descended to the Aegean Sea. Of the four cities located on rivers which emptied into this sea (Pergamum on the Caicus River, Smyrna on the Hermus, and Miletus on the Maeander), Ephesus held the most favorable location. Not only did the metropolis possess a good harbor, it also had access to the larger valleys of both the Hermus and Maeander Rivers. John Turtle Wood, *Modern Discoveries on the Site of Ancient Ephesus* (Oxford: The Religious Tract Society, 1890), 13; *The Interpreter's Dictionary of the Bible*, s.v. "Ephesus," by Jack Finegan, 2:ll4-l5. Hereafter this dictionary is abbreviated *IDB*.

4. For a summary history of Ephesus, see Merrill M. Parvis, "Archaeology and St. Paul's Journeys in Greek Lands. Part IV—Ephesus," *Biblical Archeologist* 8 (September 1945): 63-67.

5. See chapter 2.

6. Wood, *Modern Discoveries*, 13-15.

7. William M. Ramsay, *Letters to the Seven Churches of Asia and Their Place in the Plan of the Apocalypse* (London: Hodder and Stoughton, 1904), 221.

8. Gardner, *Ephesian Gospel*, 3.

9. Wood, *Modern Discoveries*, 16-17.

10. Charles F. Pfeiffer and Howard F. Vos, *Wycliffe Historical Geography of Bible Lands* (Chicago: Moody Press, l967), 357.

11. Wayne A. Meeks, *The First Urban Christians: The Social World of the Apostle Paul* (New Haven: Yale University Press, 1983), 44.

12. Floyd V. Filson, "Ephesus and the New Testament," *The Biblical Archaeologist* 8 (September l945): 74; A. E. Hillard, *The Pastoral Epistles of Paul* (London: Rivington, 1919), xvii.

13. Ramsay, *Letters to the Seven Churches*, 228.

14. Filson, "Ephesus and the New Testament," 74; Meeks, *First Urban Christians*, 44.

15. Reuben H. Falwell, Jr., "The Place of Ephesus in the Propagation of Christianity in New Testament Times" (Ph.D. dissertation, Southern Baptist Theological Seminary, 1948), 20.

16. Wood, *Modern Discoveries*, 18.

17. Josephus stated that Jews in Ephesus who were Roman citizens did not have to enter the army because of their religious beliefs and could assemble together for religious purposes. *Antiquities of the Jews* 14.l0.12-13, 25.

18. Pliny (A.D. 23-79) described the Artemision as a temple, "the building of which occupied all Asia Minor for 120 years." The structure was 425 feet long and 225 feet wide. It had 127 columns. Pliny *Natural History* 10.36.21, in *LCL*, 10:75.

19. Gardner, *Ephesian Gospel*, 3; William Ramsay, *The Historical Geography of Asia Minor* (London: John Murray, 1890), 84, 110.

20. Finegan, *Light from the Ancient Past*, 267.

21. Filson, "Ephesus and the New Testament," 75; see also Finegan, *Light from the Ancient Past*, 266.

22. Robert E. A. Palmer, *Roman Religion and Roman Empire: Five Essays* (Philadelphia: University of Pennsylvania Press, 1974), 72; Gardner, *Ephesian Gospel*, 5.

23. Filson, "Ephesus and the New Testament," 76.

24. Ramsay, *Historical Geography of Asia Minor*, 84; Gardner, *Ephesian Gospel*, 7.

25. Filson, "Ephesus and the New Testament," 77; Ramsay, *Letters to the Seven Churches*, 231.

26. Filson, "Ephesus and the New Testament," 78.

27. Hillard, *Pastoral Epistles*, xvii; J. McKee Adams, *Biblical Backgrounds*, rev. Joseph A. Callaway (Nashville: Broadman Press, 1965), 197; Josiah Blake Tidwell, *Bible Lands and Places with Their Biblical Connections* (Waco: Baylor University Press, 1939), 112.

28. Meeks, *First Urban Christians*, 15-16.

29. See Sherman E. Johnson, "The Apostle Paul and the Riot of Ephesus," *Lexington Theological Quarterly* 14 (October 1979): 79-88. Johnson developed the causes of the riot by tracing the history of the Artemis cult and the city of Ephesus.

30. 1 Cor. 15:32. This phrase should not be taken literally. See F. F. Bruce, *Paul: Apostle of the Heart Set Free* (Grand Rapids: William B. Eerdmans Publishing Co., 1977), 295. For a treatment of the evidence for both a literal and metaphorical interpretation of the "wild beasts" see Robert E. Osbourne, "Paul and the Wild Beasts," *Journal of Biblical Literature* 85 (June 1966): 225-30. Osbourne concluded that the beasts were legalists or Judaizers.

31. Marcus Barth, *Ephesians*, 2 vols., in *The Anchor Bible*, ed. William F. Albright and David N. Freedman (New York: Doubleday and Company, Inc., 1974), 2:661.

32. Barth, *Ephesians*, 2:658-59.

33. *Theological Dictionary of the New Testament*, ed. Gerhard Kittel and Gerhard Friedrich, trans. Geoffrey W. Bromiley, 10 vols. (Grand Rapids: William B. Eerdmans Publishing Co., 1964-76), s.v. "γυνή," by Albrecht Oepke, 1 (1964): 777. Hereafter this work is abbreviated *TDNT*.

34. Erhard S. Gerstenberger and Wolfgang Schrage, *Woman and Man*, trans. Douglas W. Stott (Nashville: Abingdon Press, 1981), 132-33.

35. James B. Hurley, *Man and Woman in Biblical Perspective* (Grand Rapids: Zondervan Publishing House, 1981), 74-75.

36. Jouette M. Bassler, "The Widow's Tale: A Fresh Look at 1 Tim. 5:3-16," *Journal of Biblical Literature* 103 (March 1984): 25. Leonard Swidler contended that this increasingly high status of women in the Hellenistic-Roman culture was actually higher than that which women generally held after the triumph of Christianity. He thus modified the claim that

Christianity raised the status of women. Instead, many restrictions appeared on women in the Christian world. The source of this inferior status derived not from Greek or Roman cultures or from Jesus' teachings but from Christianity as it developed. "Greco-Roman Feminism and the Reception of the Gospel," in *Traditio-Krisis-Renovatio*, ed. Bernd Jaspert and Rudolf Mohr (Marburg: N. G. Elwert Verlag, 1976), 41, 54-55. Swidler's thesis seemed to lack validity by comparing the status of women in the twentieth century to that of the first century. Christianity has improved the status of women despite misinterpretations of the Bible and inadequate applications of scriptural principles.

37. Wayne A. Meeks, "The Image of the Androgyne: Some Uses of Symbol in Earliest Christianity," *History of Religions* 13 (1974): 168.

38. William Houghton Leslie, "The Concept of Woman in the Pauline Corpus in Light of the Social and Religious Environment of the First Century" (Ph.D. dissertation, Northwestern University, 1976), 448.

39. Gerstenberger and Schrage, *Woman and Man*, 133.

40. Bassler, "Widow's Tale," 28.

41. For example, see Hesiod *Theogony* ll. 602-12, *LCL*, 123.

42. Aristotle *Politics* 1.5.1-2, *LCL*, 57-59.

43. See Aristophanes *Thesmophoriazusae* ll. 414-16, *LCL*, 3:167; ll. 790-94, *LCL*, 3:201; Plato *Laws* 781C-D, *LCL*, 1:489; Plutarch *Herod* 5.18, *LCL*, 3:19.

44. *TDNT*, s.v. "γυνή," Oepke, 1:778.

45. The women of Sparta provided an exception to this picture of women in ancient Greece. They exercised greater freedom outside the home. See Leonard Swidler, *Women in Judaism: The Status of Women in Formative Judaism* (Metuchen, N.J.: The Scarecrow Press, Inc., 1976), 8; Swidler, "Greco-Roman Feminism," 42. Also, the women of Macedonia never experienced either the seclusion or lower status of those in Achaia. Leslie, "Concept of Woman," 398. See also Alton Whitman Greenlaw, "Some Factors Contributing to the Distinctiveness of the Philippian Church" (Th.D. dissertation, Southern Baptist Theological Seminary, 1944), 27- 28. Greenlaw noted that Macedonian women were held in higher esteem than those in other places. They often acquired great prestige, influence, and in some cases great political power.

46. Plato *Republic* 456A, *LCL*, 1:449.

47. Plato *Laws* 805C-806C, *LCL*, 2:59-61.

48. Aristotle *Politics* 2.6.5-10, *LCL*, 135-37.

49. See Swidler, "Greco-Roman Feminism," 50-51.

50. Elephantine-Papyrus 2, text in *The Brooklyn Museum Aramaic Papyri: New Documents of the Fifth Century B.C. from the Jewish Colony at Elephantine*, ed. Emil G. Kraeling (New Haven: Yale University Press, 1953), 143.

51. *TDNT*, s.v. "γυνή," Oepke, 1:778.

52. Swidler, "Greco-Roman Feminism," 47-49.

53. Leslie, "Concept of Woman," 388, 449. For an extensive treatment of Roman women, see J. P. V. D. Balsdon, *Roman Women: Their History and Habits* (London: Bodley Head, 1962).

54. Justinian *Institutes* 1.9, 1.11 pr. 10; *Codex* 9.10.1; *Digest* 23.2.36.

55. Sarah B. Pomeroy, *Goddesses, Whores, Wives and Slaves: Women in Classical Antiquity* (New York: Schocken Books, 1975), 150-51; Leslie, "Concept of Woman," 415.

56. Pomeroy, *Goddesses*, 164.

57. Balsdon, *Roman Women*, 45.

58. Swidler, "Greco-Roman Feminism," 53.

59. *TDNT*, s.v. "γυνή," Oepke, 1:779-80.

60. Swidler, *Women in Judaism*, 24.

61. Hurley, *Man and Woman*, 76; Leslie, "Concept of Woman," 399.

62. Leslie, "Concept of Woman," 453; *TDNT*, s.v. "γυνή," Oepke, 1:780.

63. Some Roman women had become promiscuous according to Horace. *Odes* 3.6.17-32, *LCL*, 201-3.

64. Seneca (ca. 4 B.C.-A.D. 65) thought marital fidelity important. See *Epist.* 104.2-5, *LCL*, 3:191-93.

65. See Aristophanes *Thesmophoriazusae* ll. 414-16, *LCL*, 3:167; ll. 790-94, *LCL*, 3:201; Plato *Laws* 781C-D, *LCL*, 1:489.

66. Plutarch *Herod* 5.18, *LCL*, 3:19.

67. H. D. F. Kitto, *The Greeks* (Baltimore, Md.: Penguin Books, 1951), 220; Swidler, "Greco-Roman Feminism," 42; Leslie, "Concept of Woman," 395-96.

68. See Mary L. Lefkowitz and Maureen B. Fant, *Women's Life in Greece and Rome* (Baltimore: Johns Hopkins University Press, 1982), 27-31. These authors listed inscriptions found on gravestones and other ancient records indicating the professions of women.

69. *TDNT*, s.v. "γυνή," Oepke, 1:778.

70. Cornelius Nepos (ca. 99-24 B.C.) *Lives* "Preface," *LCL*, 369-70.

71. Suetonius *Galba* 5.1, *LCL*, 2:199.

72. Gellius *Attic Nights* 17.6.4-10, *LCL*, 3:223-25.

73. Pomeroy, *Goddesses*, 170, 176, 188-89; Hurley, *Man and Woman*, 76.

74. Pomeroy, *Goddesses*, 190-99.

75. Leslie, "Concept of Woman," 404.

76. Plato *Laws* 805C-D, *LCL*, 2:61; Plutarch *Moralia* 145C-E, *LCL*, 2:339-41.

77. Leslie, "Concept of Woman," 407.

78. James G. Sigountos and Myron Shank, "Public Roles for Women in the Pauline Church: A Reappraisal of the Evidence [1 Cor. 11:2-16; 1 Cor. 14:33-36; 1 Tim. 2:15]," *Journal of the Evangelical Theological Society* 26 (Spring 1983): 289.

79. *TDNT*, s.v. "γυνή," Oepke, 1:780.

80. Sigountos and Shank, "Public Roles," 286.

81. Meeks, "Image of the Androgyne," 179.

82. Eduard Lohse, *The New Testament Environment*, trans. John E. Steely (Nashville: Abingdon Press, 1976), 120-28; Leslie, "Concept of Woman," 336-40, 452.

83. See chapter 3.

84. Mary J. Evans, *Woman in the Bible: An Overview of the Crucial Passages on Women's Roles* (Downers Grove, Ill.: InterVarsity Press, 1983), 131. See also Joachim Jeremias, *Jerusalem in the Time of Jesus: An Investigation into Economic and Social Conditions during the New Testament Period* (Philadelphia: Fortress Press, 1969), 275.

85. Samuel Terrien, "Toward a Biblical Theology of Womanhood," *Religion in Life 42 (1973): 330.*

86. See bBer. 20a.

87. Leslie, "Concept of Woman," 339; Gerstenberger and Schrage, *Woman and Man*, 130.

88. Sirach 42:12-14 RSV; see also 25:24

89. Sirach 36:24 RSV.

90. Sirach 26:3 RSV.

91. Meeks, "Image of the Androgyne," 176. For references to these expressions in Philo, see Richard A. Bauer, Jr., *Philo's Use of the Categories Male and Female* (Leiden: E. J. Brill, 1970), 42.

92. Josephus *Against Apion* 2.25.

93. Swidler, *Women in Judaism*, 72, 82.

94. bShab. 152a.

95. Tos. Ber. 7.18.

96. Leslie, "Concept of Woman," 342.

97. Swidler, "Greco-Roman Feminism," 54.

98. Swidler, *Biblical Affirmations,* 158-59. Although Swidler was speaking of the Jews who returned to Palestine, his remarks would apply also to those of the Diaspora.

99. Margaret Sittler Ermarth, *Adam's Fractured Rib: Observations on Women in the Church* (Philadelphia: Fortress Press, 1970), 14.

100. See M.Ket. 6.4, 8.1, 5.

101. M.Git. 2.5

102. M.Git. 1.6.

103. Genesis Rabbah 2:18, Parashah 17.2.

104. See Philo *The Special Laws* 3.169-71, *LCL*, 7:581-83.

105. M.Ket. 1.10.

106. Tobit 2:11-14.

107. See 2 Mac. 3:19-20; 3 Mac. 1:18-19; Jeremias, *Jerusalem*, 360.

108. M.Taan 4.8; Tossukk. 4.1.

109. bNed. 20a; bBer. 43b; bKid. 70a-b; M.Aboth 1.5.

110. Josephus *Antiquities* 4.8.15.

111. See Ben Witherington, III, *Women in the Ministry of Jesus: A Study of Jesus' Attitudes to Women and Their Roles as Reflected in His Earthly Life* (New York: Cambridge University Press, 1984), 9.

112. M.Ket. 1.8; see also M.Kid. 4.3.

113. Jeremias, *Jerusalem*, 363; Swidler, *Women in Judaism*, 114.

114. Barth, *Ephesians,* 2:660.

CHAPTER II

THE RELIGIOUS CONTEXT
OF EPHESUS

Religious interests permeated Ephesus and its greater metropolitan area. Indeed, part of the city's reputation derived from the great temple to the goddess Artemis and the cult associated with her. The Christian community at Ephesus found themselves in the midst of people whose lives possessed a religious orientation. Their primary deity, the Great Mother Goddess, seemed concerned about every area of their lives. As one of the mystery religions, her cult attempted to satisfy all of the needs of her followers. What was a mystery religion? How did the mystery cult at Ephesus express itself? The church at Ephesus no doubt numbered former Artemis worshippers among its converts. Therefore, an understanding of the dynamics of that church requires some knowledge of the previous religious views of all its members. This has to include also a study of the Jewish element in Ephesus. Since 1 Tim. 2:9-15 relates specifically to women in the Ephesian church, an examination of the religious context needs to focus especially on the roles of women in the mystery religions and in Judaism.

The Mystery Religions

In the Hellenistic and early Christian eras a variety of Greek and Oriental religions spread throughout the Roman world. These religions, called "mysteries" due to the injunction to silence imposed on their followers,[1] satisfied people's needs for a personal, spiritual, redemptive, and universal religion. The mysteries provided an answer to and escape from the anxieties

31

and complexities of life. This made them attractive and popular, especially since membership embraced all persons without regard to their distinctive social positions—women and men, free and slaves, Greeks and foreigners. The mystery religions had diverse origins and worship practices peculiar to each, yet all possessed certain characteristics in common.[2]   Since the worship of Artemis at Ephesus numbered among the mysteries, the examination of the religious context of that metropolis needs to focus briefly on the nature of the mystery religions in general.

A Description of the Mystery Cults

The mysteries were "cultic rites" which portrayed the destinies of a god "by sacred actions before a circle of devotees in such a way as to give them a part in the fate of the god."[3]   Thus, worship centered in a drama which reenacted the life of the deity whom the believers confessed.[4]   In order to participate in this sacred drama, one had to undergo prescribed ritual initiation rites. Through the initiatory process, a person achieved salvation and immortality. These goals represented the key attraction of the mystery cults.[5]   One could not attain the spiritual, other-worldly salvation as a result of her or his unaided efforts. It came as a result of the deity dwelling inside and controlling the devotee's life.[6]   As in other sacramental religions, the initiation ceremonies of the mysteries consisted of magical processes which had an essential efficacy of their own. The worshipper achieved redemption and triumph over death by the actual mechanics of the ritual.[7]   The mystery cults denied access to the sacred actions and knowledge of them by the uninitiated. Only the initiated could know the sacred formulas and symbolic signs.[8]   Consequently, historical data on the mysteries deal with the public, outward rites.[9]

A basic element of the mystery religions portrayed by the sacred drama centered in myths about a hero-deity. This deity either returned to life after death or else triumphed over his enemies. Since the various deities of the mysteries experienced the fate of suffering and dying yet still obtained ultimate victory, the initiates had the certainty of similar triumph over the evils of human suffering.[10]   The cyclical death and rebirth of the deities found its basis in the annual vegetation cycle. Deities passed through the metamorphosis of living and dying just as nature's vegetation grew and flourished in the spring but died in the autumn.[11]

Doctrine or correct belief did not characterize the mystery cults. These religions found their bases in emotional yearning and experience as opposed to thought and rational content.[12] They "made their appeal not to the intellect, but through eye, ear, and imagination to the emotions."[13] The theological vagueness of the mysteries made them adaptable "to the most varied tastes by an elasticity of interpretation which could make them mean anything to the participant. . . ."[14]

With the emphasis on feeling rather than thought, these cults utilized many different means to affect the emotions and imaginations of their followers: drama, acts of purification, processions, fasting, and esoteric liturgies. If knowledge did have a place in the cult, it was a secret or esoteric knowledge. While several mysteries stressed the role of γνῶσις in achieving redemption, this term referred more to a "higher knowledge" associated with their secret ceremonies rather than to the cognizance of a set of truths.[15]

The mystery cults did not demand exclusive religious loyalty.[16] Whenever these various religions encountered each other, the tendency existed to equate or identify the deities revered in each. Such syncretism promoted polytheism. At best, the mysteries signified henotheism—having a supreme god in a particular religion itself but not excluding the possibility of valid gods in other religions.[17]

The mysteries did not consider ethical interests a primary concern. In fact, these cults possessed offensive features. Yet, had they been as intrinsically bad as some scholars assert, one would have difficulty in accounting for their success as missionary religions.[18]

Two features of the mystery religions contrasted greatly with each other—asceticism and sensuality. The mysteries made ascetic preparations of all kinds and degrees—fasts, absolute continence, bodily mutilations, uncomfortable pilgrimages to holy places, and public confession.[19] Initiates commonly had to abstain from certain foods. The holy season required sexual abstinence even for wives and husbands.[20] On the other hand, extreme sensuality, especially sexual, characterized many of the mysteries. The appeal to the emotions and senses accentuated this tendency. Many mysteries had a religious or sacred marriage ceremony as part of their worship.[21] This symbolized the most intimate union known to religious experience. Basically, "phallic associations never became quite extinct in the Mysteries."[22]

In summary, the mysteries represented

a curious blend of higher and lower elements, sensuousness and spirituality, sensuality and asceticism, magic and prayer, remnants of naturalism and symbolic mysticism, deafening music and silent contemplation, brilliant lights and deepest darkness.[23]

One other feature typified most of the mystery religions—a female deity.

The Prominence of the Mother Goddess

One salient feature of the mystery religions centered in the primary role given to the female deity.[24] Most of these cults, with the exception of Mithraism,[25] focused on the goddess to a degree that subordinated her male consort. Known as the Great Mother Goddess, this deity personified the feminine principle in its various attributes and symbols. The Mother Goddess represented a universal, syncretistic figure. Wherever her cult diffused itself, she would absorb one divinity after another.[26] Consequently, devotees of the mysteries worshipped the Great Mother Goddess under a number of different names and guises depending on their localities. These names included Rhea in Crete and Greece, Artemis or Diana in Ephesus, Aphrodite in Cyprus and Greece, Demeter in Greece, and Isis in Egypt.[27] Even some more ancient names, such as Nammu in Sumer, Ishtar in Babylon, and Astarte or Asherah in Canaan, represented variants of the Mother Goddess. "Cybele" figured as the most familiar name of the Asiatic Mother in the Roman world.[28]

The Mother Goddess represented the great parent of all nature. She had responsibility for the health and well-being of both humans and animals. She protected her people in times of war. As the Earth Goddess, her divine authority rested in her ability to create new beings continually. Other deities were the daughters and sons of the all-creating Earth Mother. It followed naturally that the *Magna Mater* also served as the goddess of fertility and all reproduction in nature.[29] As a mighty and popular deity, the Mother Goddess held the power over life and death. In mythology and later in cult practice, she often associated with a young lover-turned-devotee, the god of vegetation. This male consort held a subordinate position.[30]

When did the Mother Goddess cult first appear in Asia Minor?[31] One cannot answer with certainty as to the religion's inception. When the Phrygian[32] race invaded Asia Minor in ca. 900 B.C., they found there a matriarchal people. The Cybele cult belonged to this native population, but the Phrygian invaders modified the deity.[33] Doubtless the worship of the Great Goddess predominated in Asia Minor by the sixth[34] or fourth[35] century B.C. By the end of the third century B.C. the Goddess began to be regarded especially as Phrygian. The cult had its strongest center in

Pessinus in Galatia, a city beyond the borders of Phrygia.[36]

The mystery religions elevated the status of women. How did this affect their religious roles?

The Role of Women in the Mystery Cults

Most mystery religions except Mithraism initiated women on a par with men. They accepted anybody regardless of distinctions of origin, family, class, or servitude.[37] Many of these cults stressed the importance of women and allowed them a key role.[38] These Oriental religions provided an outlet for women whose lives society circumscribed in other ways.[39]

It seemed natural to the Greek and Roman minds that priestesses should serve goddesses.[40] Therefore, women received appointments to the priesthood. Women took part in the cultic meals and processions. Attendance at the mysteries' rituals provided one of the few occasions they had permission to leave the confines of the home.[41] Indeed, with some of the mysteries, women actually gathered for worship without the presence of men.[42] One ancient manuscript referring to the Mother Goddess (Isis) exclaimed, "Thou . . . gavest to women the same power as men."[43] The mysteries, consequently, claimed the loyalty of many women. "The devotion of . . . women to these mystery religions demonstrated their appreciation for this area of freedom and this opportunity for expression of feeling."[44]

What functions did the priestesses to the Mother Goddess fulfill? Probably the status of priestesses, like that of priests, varied.[45] A brief historical survey may aid in some understanding at this point. In many parts of the Ancient Near East priestesses and female devotees of the Great Goddess (Ishtar, Cybele, Asherah, Aphrodite, Astarte, or whatever name used) lived in and around the temples dedicated to this deity. Scholars have sometimes described these women as "harlots" or "ritual prostitutes." People in their own times and places called them "holy women." These women engaged in sacred rites that often included a free and active sexual life. Cult followers perceived the Goddess as a source of fertility and abundance. Therefore, these priestesses had a high status. Although they took part in sacred sexual rites involving intercourse with men outside of marriage, the cults viewed this activity as sacred. "Sacred ones," "pure ones," and "holy ones" designated such priestesses. The sexual rites practiced by both priestesses and lay votaries possessed a widely acknowledged sanctity. The holiness of sexual acts performed in and near the temples gave way to profane prostitution. Male counterparts to these "holy women" also practiced the sacred sexual rites of the great goddesses. By the mid-Assyrian period and up to Greco-Roman rule, the temples of the Near East employed thousands of hierodules or slaves of both sexes for this purpose.[46]

Did all the cults of the Mother Goddess, however, utilize sacred prostitution? This question has to be answered "apparently not."[47] For instance, the pervasive Isis cult popularly worshipped at the beginning of the Christian era did not promote sexual excesses or promiscuity. It had a reputation for its rules of chastity. Sexual freedom did not necessarily characterize this specific manifestation of the Great Goddess.[48] Yet, cultic asceticism frequently mingled ironically with eroticism. Social pleasure and sensual gratification rewarded the devotees. Often temple locations near marketplaces and brothels made them ideal meeting places for profane prostitutes.[49] Worship of the goddesses of fertility by ascetic practices does seem contradictory. What practices characterized the worship of the Mother Goddess in Ephesus?

The Cult of Artemis at Ephesus

The Phrygian Cybele became identified with the Greek goddess Artemis in Ephesus.[50] Wherever devotees worshipped her and under whatever name, she was the same Goddess, the All-Mother.[51] The worship of Artemis at Ephesus modelled a "conspicuous instance of the fusion of Eastern and Western religious ideas."[52] This mystery religion represented the most important of all the hybrid cults since it became known in every Greek city. Artemis worship spread to the western-most parts of the Mediterranean.[53] The cultus honoring the Ephesian Goddess achieved wide-spread popularity in the early Roman age. Many people regarded Artemis as the greatest of all the deities. Numerous cities constructed temples for her worship.[54] What then were the characteristic features of the cult of the Ephesian Artemis?

A Description of Artemis and Her Cult

When Greek colonists arrived in Asia Minor in the eleventh century B.C.,[55] they discovered that Cybele was already established as the *Magna Mater* of that subcontinent. The excesses of this Oriental cult probably shocked the

Greeks. The ideas and practices of the Phrygian Mother Goddess sharply contrasted with their customs and beliefs.[56]

The cult of Cybele was violent, orgiastic, and ecstatic. Barbaric music and frenzied dances characterized the cultus like those of Dionysius.[57] Self-mutilation by the lacerating of one's arms and body occurred in the celebrations of the Goddess.[58] The music and dance would provoke the devotees to a fever pitch of excitement that rendered them insensitive to pain. By wounding themselves they sought to imitate Cybele in her grief for her dead consort, Attis, and call him back to life. These followers believed such actions united them to the deity. The self-mutilation reached its height when some votaries sacrificed their virility by castrating themselves.[59] In the myths of the Great Mother other attendants called corybantes accompanied her. The name meant noisy and orgiastic or to be in a state of divine madness. This term sometimes referred to the followers or priests of the cult of Cybele.[60] Evidently, "promiscuous sexual indulgence" or "ceremonial licentiousness" formed a part of the temple rites for this Mother Goddess.[61]

The standard icon of Cybele pictured a woman enthroned upon a chariot yoked by lions. She often wore a crown of towers on her head and carried a variety of regalia in her hand such as a typanum, key, scepter, or a bunch of ripened wheat. The riches of the earth would cover her cloak: flowers, fruits, or precious gems. The Phrygian boy, Attis, frequently stood with her holding cymbals and his shepherd's staff.[62] As the goddess of fertility, her images often depicted physical fullness with the organs of conception and reproduction emphasized.[63]

How did the Greek Artemis compare with the wild Cybele? The poems of Homer presented Artemis as a chaste huntress who was the most beautiful of the nymphs and the sister of Apollo. Testimonies earlier than Homer did not portray her as a goddess of chastity and the sister of Apollo but as an independent divinity connected with waters and wild vegetation. Greek poetry more usually described Artemis as a huntress and destroyer, while the older religion showed her as the protector and patroness of wild animals. Artemis had a special concern with the loss of virginity and with childbearing. Maidens of marriageable age did certain honors to Artemis. Women in travail called on her for aid. The worship of Artemis developed from a savage earth-goddess associated with wild life in early Greece to a more settled and civilized goddess later connected with agriculture and the breeding of domestic animals. In the imaginations of poets and artists the character of Artemis acquired a higher spiritual value which her cult did not generally display.[64]

Despite the differences between Cybele and Artemis, the Greek settlers adopted and continued the already-established cult of Cybele by identifying their own Artemis with the *Magna Mater*.[65] The Ephesian Artemis became the deity of the reproductive powers of nature and the source of overflowing life. She possessed the powers of the life-giving earth. The Ephesian Artemis reinforced those traits that both the Phrygian Goddess and the Greek Artemis had shared in common—their attachment to nature, animals, the moon, and childbirth.[66] The Oriental influence tinged the Greek Goddess with ideas proper to a primitive, orgiastic nature-worship.[67]

The image of the Artemis of Ephesus featured a human head, hands, and many breasts. These multiplied signs of her motherhood symbolized her fertility yet made her look grotesque.[68] This form supposedly based itself on the "image from heaven." This image appeared to have been a meteorite roughly shaped into mummy form in which viewers discerned some semblance of a many-breasted female figure. Reliefs of Artemis showed lions, rams, and bulls wrought upon her shoulders denoting her as the goddess who fostered the life of the wilds and fields. Often a bee was engraved just above her feet. The coins of Ephesus frequently featured this same bee. The turret crown worn on the head of the Goddess marked her affinity to the city. The crown stood as the badge of the City-Goddess.[69]

As indicated above, the Ephesian Artemis did not maintain the chaste, virgin image of the Greek Goddess. It appeared strange that her maidenly character could not prevent her association with the Oriental Cybele of generation and her notoriously impure rites.[70] Although devotees might have called Artemis παρθένος, the word did not always have the meaning of virgin as in never having had sexual intercourse. παρθένος also meant unmarried.[71] One scholar stated,

> The multiplicity of content is not clarified when the term παρθένος is used in the religious sphere. To some degree it cannot really be said which of the various nuances is really predominant here. This is, of course, connected with the fact that female deities had to take over the manifold characteristics of the goddesses whom they replaced. In the last resort the epithet παρθένος could not be ascribed to them unless it carried a varied meaning.[72]

The Ephesian Artemis might have enjoyed many consorts, yet people still considered her a virgin because she had never submitted to a monogamous marriage. Persons misinterpreted her failure to marry as virginity because they associated loss of virginity with conventional marriage. No bonds tied Artemis to any male she would have to acknowledge as master. She retained her independence due to her lack of a permanent connection to a male figure in a monogamous relationship.[73]

The Ephesian Artemis "united virginity, motherhood and queenship in one person."[74] Isis further enriched her functions by making her the symbol of women's liberation. This liberation illustrated itself in her character. She exemplified the fulfillment of womanhood by motherhood without male assistance.[75]

How could the Greeks identify their Artemis with the hideous Ephesian Artemis even to the point of veneration and acceptance of religious customs and institutions full of primitive barbarism? The Greek religion itself did not possess any proselytising power. It did not satisfy the deep needs of the human heart as did the mysteries. The Ephesian mystery cult of Cybele-Artemis offered indwelling spiritual power and immortality. It dealt with one's sense of sin and the desire for purity through its initiatory rites. The Greek Artemis had no place in the central elements of human life with the exception of childbirth. The hybrid cult of the Anatolian Great Goddess met these needs.[76]

In the Artemision in Ephesus, worshippers reverenced the Goddess as πρωτοθρονία, supreme in divine power and place. They honored her as the power of fertility in nature, the mother of life, and the nourisher of all creatures of the earth, air, and sea. She especially assisted females of all species to bring forth their young and helped women in the pains of childbirth.[77] According to Acts 19:27, Demetrius the silversmith proclaimed Artemis as "she whom Asia and the world worship." The immense and widespread influence of the Ephesian Artemis continually brought vast numbers of pilgrims from considerable distances to visit the shrine.[78]

"Vasta era l'organització del temple d'Efeso."[79] Hundreds, perhaps thousands, of cult functionaries served the Mother Goddess in connection with the temple ritual and special religious festivals. Since Artemis was supreme, her cult officials had precedence over those who had charge of the emperor cult.[80] The Megabyzus or chief priest stood at the head of the temple hierarchy. The Megabyzus as well as the other priests, the megabyzi, served the Great Mother as eunuchs. The cult considered these priests as drones who "died" in fertilizing the queen bee, Artemis herself. Some referred to the college of drones as Essenes.[81]

Multitudes of priestesses ministered in the religion of Artemis. The cult called these women melissae or bees. The bee, often featured in images of the Mother Goddess, symbolized the Ephesian priesthood. These women came to the temple as virgins, dedicated to the service of Artemis. They worked under the superintendance of the chief eunuch, the Megabyzus.[82]

Did these priestesses function as temple prostitutes or did they retain their virginity? Scholars appeared divided on this issue. Some contended that the cultic rites at the Artemision did not include sacred prostitution.[83] "Wahrend ihrer Priesterschaft mussten sie jungfraulich leben."[84]   The Ephesian religion, in spite of its orgiastic and sensuous elements, seemed to have possessed in some respects an austere character. For instance, the cult imposed rigid rules of chastity and purity on the Essenes, the priestly society attached to the temple.[85]   Others, however, asserted that ceremonial prostitution did exist at Ephesus.[86]

The perception of a fertility cult which did not utilize sacred prostitution remained a difficulty. Even the icon of Artemis herself belied sexual purity. "Between this bounteous form and the notion of virginity there seems to be little in common."[87]   The Mother Goddess did combine many contradictory attributes in her service, and that could have included extremes of sexual behavior. Even if the priestesses of Artemis were virgins, there existed elements of sexual impurity in her festivals.[88]   Also, one could question the ancient sources which gave evidence of the virginity of these priestesses. How did these view the concept of virginity? As the Mother Goddess herself, priestesses could serve in temple rites without preserving their chastity and still be considered "virgins" or "sacred" simply because they had not married.[89]   This argument found support in the fact that "einer verheirateten Frau bei Todesstrafe verboten war, den Tempel zu betreten."[90]   Contemporary writers would not have perceived temple harlotry as impure or immoral because it had an accepted sacred function. Some form of temple prostitution probably did exist in Ephesus even if with limitations.

Besides the priestesses and priests the temple sustained a large staff of vergers, cleaners, and attendants. Other officials included the theologi who transcribed, interpreted, and recited the sacred legends. These probably offered some explanation of the origin of the Ephesian Mother Goddess. Since music formed an important part of Artemis worship, the cult employed hymn-makers to compose music. A boys choir performed for cultic functions. Elders or presbyters of the temple handled the financial matters of the Artemision related to its function as a bank. In addition to all of these functionaries, hierodules or slaves assisted also.[91]

The worship of Artemis included a variety of methods. As previously mentioned, the cult featured music in its services. Ecstatic, orgiastic dances performed by priestesses also had prominence.[92]   Recitations and chants were expressed. "Great is Artemis of the Ephesians" represented a stock phrase in the religion.[93] Worshippers of the Great Goddess showered her with gifts—money as well as material items. Young women and girls especially favored Artemis with gifts of clothes as thanksgiving for a happy marriage or fortunate childbirth.[94] The cultus included wild orgies in which her votaries castrated themselves in dedication to her service.[95] Magical formulae known as the Ephesian sentences or letters had a close relationship to the temple worship.[96] Sympathetic magical rites, such as coitus with a sacred votary, insured fertility of crops, secured children with divine sanction, or assimilated one to the deity.[97]

The Artemis cult dedicated the month Artemision (March-April) especially to the Goddess. At this time tourists and devotees flooded the city. This spring festival, the Ephesia, depicted the greatest of all the religious events. In addition to the usual cultic rituals, worshippers participated in athletic, dramatic, and musical contests.[98] Part of the festival's activities included a processional between the city of Ephesus and the temple of Artemis with temple officials carrying gold and silver images of the Goddess.[99]

The above description gave some idea as to the nature of the Artemis cult in Ephesus. More specific details of the religion remained obscure. As with most of the mysteries, devotees carefully guarded the ritual practices.[100] Given its importance, what influence did this cult have upon the people in Ephesus?

The Attraction of the Cult of Artemis in Ephesus

The cult of Artemis greatly benefited the city of Ephesus. It contributed to the city's population, wealth, commerce, and prestigious reputation. The Artemision dominated the area with its legions of cult employees, power, riches, and city-wide celebrations. No resident of the metropolis remained untouched by the Great Mother cult.

Artemis of the Ephesians constantly attracted new votaries. Part of her appeal centered in the character of the Great Mother herself. Her followers perceived her as chaste, beautiful, and intelligent. She met the needs of her servants, especially women. Her ministers also led "pure" lives in her service. Her maternity role as the Mother of all the creatures in the world appealed to people. As the supreme Earth Goddess, her blessing brought good harvests. The religion of Artemis satisfied one's soul.

Devotees could unite with the divine because the Mother communicated with them spiritually. Secret rites acquainted the worshippers with a wisdom considered divine. Sacred dramas promised believers triumph over death and immortality. Even emasculation had an appeal. In this mystery religion one could have a consciousness of duty performed and deeds accredited.[101]

In short, the Mother Goddess represented a major factor in the religious context of Ephesus and a formidable challenge to Christianity. This mystery, however, did not represent the only religious interest in the city. A large Jewish population made their home in Ephesus.

The Role of Women in Judaism

Much of the role of women in the Jewish faith found its basis in the teachings of the Old Testament.[102] For instance, the Law obliged women to observe all ordinances except the positive time-bound ones. Their physical nature and its demands (menstruation, pregnancy, nursing) as well as their domestic duties excused them from these observances. According to some scholars, with the passage of time many of these non-obligations for women became outright restrictions.[103]

Another change occurred in postexilic Judaism relative to the religious participation of Jewish women. In Palestine the Temple structure segregated the women. They were restricted to the Court of the Gentiles and the Court of the Women. Barrier walls prevented their access to the inner Temple courts.[104] The Old Testament had not introduced a lower, separate court for women. This represented "an intertestamental and un-Biblical innovation that developed out of corrupted Judaism."[105] Restriction from the men's courts kept the women from the sacrifice area. Jewish strict monotheism and intolerance of syncreticism might have promoted this practice of separation.[106] The Jews after the exile wanted to distinguish themselves from the pagan cults which featured priestesses serving in the various cult temples.

Scholars differed as to whether or not the synagogues also segregated women.[107] Inscriptional evidence revealed some synagogue titles for women. Most scholars interpreted these titles as honorific. This view might be based on the presupposition that Jewish women could not serve in leadership positions. If some women did serve as head of synagogues, they functioned as exceptions to the norm. Women did participate in the synagogue worship services. Some actively supported the synagogues financially.[108]

Rabbis debated over whether or not to teach women the Torah even in the home. The responsibility of religious education rested with the girls' parents, particularly the father.[109] One rabbi, however, equated teaching one's daughter the Torah with teaching her lechery.[110] Exceptions did exist. Some capable women did study and become learned in both written and oral law and tradition.[111] Nevertheless, most of the religious privileges women possessed were those they participated in at home.[112]

Conclusion

Gentile or pagan women and Jewish women in Ephesus came from two extremely different religious orientations. The very existence of the cult of the Great Mother and the Artemision in Ephesus stamped this city more than others as "the bastion and bulwark of women's rights."[113] The lesser education of women as well as the social restrictions upon them encouraged them to embrace the mysteries which featured superstition, magic, and opportunities for religious expression.[114] This explained the popularity of the Artemis cult among pagan women. This religion allowed them greater freedom than anything experienced previously. By contrast, Jewish women found increasing restrictions in their worship of Yahweh. Religious leadership functions, especially public roles, did not exist for them. As with much of Judaism of the first century A.D., the dominance of legalism hindered a true understanding of God and spiritual growth.

The church of Ephesus had women converts from both of these religious backgrounds. Paul would naturally want to curtail or circumscribe any practices among these Christian women that might confuse them with the devotees of Artemis and their emotional excesses. He would want the pagan converts to comprehend that neither ascetic continence, sacred intercourse, nor any other cultic activity could provide them with salvation or eternal life. True salvation came from grace through faith not from works. Paul would want Jewish women to relax in the equality before God that faith in Jesus Christ offered. They too could study, learn, and serve in the Christian community.

The understandings gleaned from this study of the religious context of Ephesus will aid in interpreting 1 Tim. 2:9-15. Now that the broad historical context of this passage has been analyzed, the focus shifts to the interpretative aspect of the study. This necessitates a look at the various biblical contexts.

NOTES

1. For example, see Apuleius *Metamamorphoses* 11.23, *LCL*, 579.

2. Lohse, *New Testament Environment*, 233. The mysteries did not, however, possess a common theology. Frederick C. Grant, "Greek Religion in the Hellenistic-Roman Age," *Anglican Theological Review* 34 (January 1952): 16.

3. *TDNT*, s.v. "μυστήριον," by G. Bornkamm, 4 (1967): 803.

4. Lohse, *New Testament Environment*, 234.

5. Wayne H. House, "Tongues and the Mystery Religions of Corinth," *Bibliotheca Sacra* 140 (April-June 1983): 136.

6. Shirley Jackson Case, "Christianity and the Mystery Religions," *The Biblical World* 43 (January 1914): 9; Harold R. Willoughby, *Pagan Regeneration: A Study of Mystery Initiations in the Graeco-Roman World* (Chicago: University of Chicago Press, 1929), 30-31; Ronald H. Nash, *Christianity and the Hellenistic World* (Grand Rapids: Zondervan Publishing House 1984), 124.

7. Willoughby, *Pagan Regeneration*, 31.

8. *TDNT*, s.v. "μυστήριον," by Bornkamm, 4:804, 806; Nash, *Christianity*, 123.

9. House, "Tongues and the Mystery Religions," 139.

10. Lohse, *New Testament Environment*, 234-35; Willoughby, *Pagan Regeneration*, 31; Nash, *Christianity*, 123.

11. Nash, *Christianity*, 122; Lohse, *New Testament Environment*, 234. The mythical motif of a dying-rising savior god marked a major difference between the mystery religions and historically based Christianity. The cultic gods died by compulsion, not by choice. Pagan devotees mourned and lamented annually with their dead gods, while Christians rejoiced over Christ's triumphant once-for-all resurrection. Bruce M. Metzger, "Considerations of Methodology in the Study of the Mystery Religions and Early Christianity," *Harvard Theological Review* 48 (January 1955): 12, 16-17. For an analysis of the relationship between the mysteries and Christianity, see Metzger's article mentioned above, 1-20; Nash, *Christianity*, 149-81; John R. Hinnells, "Christianity and the Mystery Cults," *Theology* 71 (January 1968): 20-25; and J. Gresham Machen, *The Origin of Paul's Religion* (Grand Rapids: William B. Eerdmans Publishing Co., 1947), 237-51.

12. House, "Tongues and the Mystery Religions," 136.

13. Samuel Angus, *The Mystery-Religions and Christianity: A Study in the Religious Background of Early Christianity* (New York: Charles Scribner's Sons, 1925), 59.

14. Ibid., 263.

15. See Plato *Republic* 364E-365A; see also Nash, *Christianity*, 123-24; Angus, *Mystery-Religions*, 52-53.

16. Tatian (*Ad Graecos* 29) stated that he had taken part in "mysteries."

17. Willoughby, *Pagan Regeneration*, 31-32; Lohse, *New Testament Environment*, 233.

18. Angus, *Mystery-Religions*, 244-45.

19. For fasts, see Apuleius *Metamamorphoses* 11.23, *LCL*, 579; for pilgrimages and ablutions, see Juvenal *Satires* 6.521-30, *LCL*, 125-27.

20. See Demosthenes *Against Neaera* 78, *LCL*, 6:411.

21. See Josephus *Antiquities* 18.3.4, 4:11-13.

22. Angus, *Mystery-Religions*, 114. For a discussion of the sacred marriage in its earlier form and its relationship to the goddess of fertility, see Samuel Noah Kramer, *The Sacred Marriage Rite: Aspects of Faith, Myth, and Ritual in Ancient Sumer* (Bloomington, Ind.: Indiana University Press, 1969).

23. Angus, *Mystery-Religions*, 245.

24. The mysteries seemed to occur more frequently in connection with cults devoted to female deities. Joan Chamberlain Engelsman, *The Feminine Dimension of the Divine* (Philadelphia: The Westminster Press, 1979), 47.

25. Mithraism was a male religion. Maarten J. Vermaseren, *Mithras, the Secret God* (New York: Barnes and Noble, Inc., 1963), 163-64.

26. E. O. James, *The Cult of the Mother-Goddess* (New York: Frederick A. Praeger, Inc., 1959), 252.

27. Isis appealed to women as the promoter of their liberation and equality to men. Sharon Kelly Heyob, *The Cult of Isis among Women in the Graeco-Roman World* (Leiden: E. J. Brill, 1975), 52.

28. Richard Cavendish, *Mythology: An Illustrated Encyclopedia* (New York: Rizzoli International Publications, Inc., 1980), 152; Lewis Richard Farnell, *The Cults of the Greek States*, 5 vols. (New Rochelle, N.Y.: Caratzas Brothers, Publishers, 1977), 3:289; John Ferguson, *The Religions of the Roman Empire* (Ithaca, N.Y.: Cornell University Press, 1970), 16, 26; Grant Showerman, *The Great Mother of the Gods* (Chicago: Argonaut, Inc., Publishers, 1901; reprint ed., 1969), 12-13; Judith Ochshorn, *The Female Experience and the Nature of the Divine* (Bloomington, Ind.: Indiana University Press, 1981), 43-44. Livy (24.10-11, *LCL*, 8:245-47) provided an account of the Great Mother's entrance into Rome during the second century B.C.

29. Maarten J. Vermaseren, *Cybele and Attis: The Myth and the Cult*, trans. A. M. H. Lemmers (London: Thames and Hudson, Ltd., 1977), 9, 11, 13; Showerman, *Great Mother*, 14; James, *Cult of the Mother-Goddess*, 161.

30. Ochshorn, *Female Experience*, 31.

31. The Mother Goddess existed early in the history of mankind. Archaeological excavations in Old World areas (the Indus Valley, the Near East, Old Europe [that is, the Balkans, Asia Minor, and the Eastern Mediterranean islands], and Egypt) at the upper paleolithic levels have uncovered innumerable female statuettes. The discoveries from the neolithic period indicated that the worship of the Goddess had become even more vigorous and explicit. With the development of animal husbandry which made apparent the role of paternity, the total dominance of the Great Mother gradually shifted. The role of the male deity then advanced. Leonard Swidler, "Goddess Worship and Women Priests," in *Women Priests: A Catholic Commentary on the Vatican Declaration*, ed. Leonard Swidler and Arlene Swidler (New York: Paulist Press, 1977), 167-68; Vermaseren, *Cybele*, 13. Debate still continued over the precedence and dominance of female deities as opposed to male deities. Some contended that the divine was first worshipped as female. See Swidler, "Goddess Worship," 167. For an extreme and undocumented presentation of this view, see also Merlin Stone, *When God Was a Woman* (New York: Harcourt-Harvest Press, 1978). For a view which attacked the female

dominance, see M. I. Finley, "Archaeology and History," *Daedalus* 100 (1971): 168-86. Pomeroy, *Goddesses*, 13-14, summarized the two opposing views. What does have importance for the present discussion was the existence of the Mother Goddess and her worship in the first century A.D.

32. Phrygia was an ancient country in central Asia Minor.

33. Showerman, *Great Mother*, 11, 26.

34. Willoughby, *Pagan Regeneration*, 119.

35. James, *Cult of the Mother-Goddess*, 162.

36. Showerman, *Great Mother*, 11, 26. According to legend, Pessinus received its name from being the spot where the sacred stone fell (πεσεῖν) from heaven. This stone represented the Great Mother Goddess. Acts 19:35 refers to this "image which fell down from heaven" in reference to Artemis in Ephesus. A number of legends explained the origin of Cybele and her subordinate consort Attis. Depending on the particular myth Attis was her son, lover, victim, and/or devotee. He suffered an untimely, brutal death which brought barrenness to the earth. The gods resurrected Attis each spring in order to save the world. Attis' death and resurrection symbolized the vegetation cycle. Ovid (*Fasti* 4.221-46, *LCL*, 204-7) provided one account of the Attis legend. For further details of legend variations, see Gertrude Jobes, *Dictionary of Mythology, Folklore and Symbols* (New York: Scarecrow Press, 1962), 155, 400; Cavendish, *Mythology*, 152; Vermaseren, *Cybele*, 90-91, 99; Ferguson, *Religions*, 26; James, *Cult of the Mother-Goddess*, 155, 162; and, James George Frazier, *Adonis, Attis, and Osiris: Studies in the History of Oriental Religion*, 2nd ed. (London: Macmillan and Co., Ltd., 1907), 220-21.

37. Meeks, "Image of the Androgyne," 169-70.

38. House, "Tongues and the Mystery Religions," 141; Leslie, "Concept of Woman," 435.

39. Pomeroy, *Goddesses*, 205. Ross S. Kraemer believes that the Dionysiac mystery "afforded Greek women a means of expressing their hostility and frustration at the male-dominated society by temporarily abandoning their homes and household responsibilities and engaging them in somewhat outrageous activities." Women possessed by Dionysius could defy their normal roles and participate in activities usually reserved for men only. The religious framework did not permit serious sanctions against them. "Ecstasy and Possession: The Attraction of Women to the Cult of Dionysos," *Harvard Theological Review* 72 (January 1979): 80.

40. E. R. Hardy, "Priestesses in the Graeco-Roman World," *Churchman* 84 (1970): 266; Lewis R. Farnell, "Sociological Hypotheses concerning the Position of Women in Ancient Religion," *Archiv für Religionswissenschaft* 7 (1904): 78.

41. Leslie, "Concept of Woman," 436, 444; Gerstenberger and Schrage, *Woman and Man*, 134; Sigounts, "Public Roles," 288; Swidler, "Greco-Roman Feminism," 52.

42. Barth, *Ephesians*, 2:656.

43. Papyrus Ox. 1380, ll. 214-16, 200, in *The Oxyrhynchus Papyri*, Part 11, ed. and trans. Bernard P. Grenfell and Arthur S. Hunt (London: Egypt Exploration Fund, 1915).

44. Leslie, "Concept of Woman," 436.

45. Hardy, "Priestesses," 266.

46. Ochshorn, *Female Experience*, 127-29.

47. Hardy, "Priestesses," 267, contended that "ancient and modern writers have sometimes seen the institution [of sacred prostitution] on slight evidence; it is certainly frequently referred to as something practised far away or long ago."

48. Heyob, *Cult of Isis*, 125-26.

49. Pomeroy, *Goddesses*, 222.

50. Gardner, *Ephesian Gospel*, 13-14; Ferguson, *Religions*, 21; James, *Cult of the Mother-Goddess*, 161; Leslie, "Concept of Woman," 441; W. K. C. Guthrie, *The Greeks and Their Gods* (London: Methuen and Company, Ltd., 1950), 99; Farnell, *Cults of the Greek States*, 2:473.

51. Guthrie, *Greeks and Their Gods*, 101.

52. Farnell, *Cults of the Greek States*, 2:480.

53. Ibid. Many cities besides Ephesus stamped their coins with the figure of the Ephesian Goddess: Pergamon, Smyrna, Sardis, Adramytteum, Prusa, Cyzicus, and Astyra.

54. Gardner, *Ephesian Gospel*, 14.

55. See chapter 1, p. 12.

56. Guthrie, *Greeks and Their Gods*, 101.

57. See Horace *Odes* 1.16.5, *LCL*, 49.

58. Apuleius *Metamamorphoses* 8.27-28, *LCL*, 389-93.

59. Lucian *De Syria Dea* 51, *LCL*, 4:403-5; Ovid *Fasti* 4.221-46, *LCL*, 204-7.

60. Farnell, "Sociological Hypotheses," 86-87.

61. Guthrie, *Greeks and Their Gods*, 54; Showerman, *Great Mother*, 16.

62. Peter S. Hawkins, "From Mythology to Myth-Making: Spenser and the Magna Mater Cybele," *Sixteenth Century Journal* 12 (1981): 51-52. For plates depicting the archaeological finds relating to Cybele, see Maarten J. Vermaseren, *Corpus Cultus Cybelae Attisdisque* (Leiden: E. J. Brill, 1977).

63. Vermaseren, *Cybele*, 13.

64. Farnell, *Cults of the Greek States*, 2:427, 434, 444, 449, 456, 472.

65. Ibid., 2:482; Vermaseren, *Cybele*, 24.

66. Gardner, *Ephesian Gospel*, 13-14.

67. Farnell, *Cults of the Greek States*, 2:479-80.

68. Gérard Seiterle believed that the supposed breasts actually represent the testicles of animals and men offered to the Goddess. "Artemis—die grosse Göttin von Ephesos," *Antike Welt* 10 (1979): 9, 13. Based on Seirtle's "neue Deutung der Vielbrüstigkeit," Marcus Barth suggested that the figure of Artemis depicted woman's glory at the price of man's castration. "Traditions in Ephesians," *New Testament Studies* 30 (January 1984): 16.

69. Gardner, *Ephesian Gospel*, 5; Farnell, *Cults of the Greek States*, 2:481; Guthrie, *Greeks and Their Gods*, 101; Camden M. Cobern, *The New Archeological Discoveries*, 9th ed. (New York: Funk and Wagnalls Company, 1929), 468.

70. Farnell, *Cults of the Greek States*, 2:484, 486.

71. *TDNT*, s.v. "παρθένος," by Gerhard Delling, 5 (1967): 827; Guthrie, *Greeks and Their Gods*, 102. In fact, one lexicon gave this as a meaning of the word: "of unmarried women who are not virgins." Henry George Liddell and Robert Scott, *A Greek-English Lexicon*, 9th ed., rev. Henry Stuart Jones and Roderick McKenzie (Oxford: Clarendon Press, 1940), s.v. "παρθένος," 1339. Hereafter this work is abbreviated *LS*.

72. *TDNT*, s.v. "παρθένος," by Delling, 5:827-28.

73. Pomeroy, *Goddesses*, 6. παρθένος symbolized the personality which is independent, self-derived, and self-contained. *TDNT*, s.v. "παρθένος," by Delling, 5:829. She, like Cybele with whom she was identified, probably had a youthful lover-attendant but no husband.

74. Barth, "Traditions in Ephesians," 16.

75. Ibid.

76. Gardner, *Ephesian Gospel*, 6.

77. Farnell, *Cults of the Greek States*, 2:480; Ferguson, *Religions*, 21; James, *Cult of the Mother-Goddess*, 150; Cobern, *New Archeological Discoveries*, 468.

78. William M. Ramsay, *The Church in the Roman Empire Before A.D. 170* (New York: G. P. Putnam's Sons, 1893; reprint of 5th ed., 1897, Grand Rapids: Baker Book House, 1954), 128. Ramsay noted that the constant stream of pilgrims necessitated a vast number of workers in marble and terra-cotta to supply the demand for shrines (miniature temples or statuettes of the Goddess). Economic opposition roused against Paul when his evangelizing efforts affected the trades connected with the Artemis cult. See Acts 19.

79. Bartomeu Pascual, "El temple efesià d'Artemis i la primera carta a Timoteu," in *Analecta sacra Tarraconensia* (Barcelona: n.p., 1925), 80.

80. Cobern, *New Archeological Discoveries*, 464.

81. Robert Fleischer, "Artemis Ephesia und Aphrodite von Aphrodisias," in *Die Orientalischen Religionen im Römerreich*, ed. Maarten J. Vermaseren (Leiden: E. J. Brill, 1981), 299; Gardner, *Ephesian Gospel*, 4; Ferguson, *Religions*, 21. The eunuch-priest might have developed with the ascetic ideal as a reaction against the sexual excesses which arose from the fertility cults. William F. Albright, "Historical and Mythical Elements in the Story of Joseph," *Journal of Biblical Literature* 37 (September-December 1918): 123. Farnell noted with interest the predominance of the priest over the priestess. "Sociological Hypotheses," 91.

82. Cobern, *New Archeological Discoveries*, 465; Gardner, *Ephesian Gospel*, 4.

83. Farnell, *Cults of the Greek States*, 2:481; Ferguson, *Religions*, 21; James, *Cult of the Mother-Goddess*, 151; Gardner, *Ephesian Gospel*, 4.

84. Seiterle, "Artemis," 6.

85. Farnell, *Cults of the Greek States*, 2:481.

86. Pfeiffer and Vos, *Wycliffe Historical Geography*, 362; Cobern, *New Archeological Discoveries*, 465; Curtis Vaughan, *Acts: A Study Guide Commentary* (Grand Rapids: Zondervan Publishing House, 1977), 25.

87. Gardner, *Ephesian Gospel*, 5. If Seiterle's view of the "breasts" as "testicles" was true, then the icon did portray virginity. See n. 68.

88. Ibid., 6.

89. Guthrie, *Greeks and Their Gods*, 102; Pomeroy, *Goddesses*, 6.

90. Seiterle, "Artemis," 6. See also Farnell, "Sociological Hypotheses," 92.

91. Ferguson, *Religions*, 21; Gardner, *Ephesian Gospel,* 4; Cobern, *New Archeological Discoveries*, 466.

92. James, *Cult of the Mother-Goddess*, 151; Gardner, *Ephesian Gospel*, 14.

93. Ramsay, *Church in the Roman Empire*, 135-56.

94. F. Sokolowski, "A New Testimony on the Cult of Artemis of Ephesus," *Harvard Theological Review* 58 (October 1965): 428.

95. James, *Cult of the Mother-Goddess*, 151.

96. Hillard, *Pastoral Epistles*, xvlii.

97. Beatrice A. Brooks, "Fertility Cult Functionaries in the Old Testament," *Journal of Biblical Literature* 60 (September 1941): 230.

98. Filson, "Ephesus and the New Testament," 76; Cobern, *New Archeological Discoveries*, 465; James, *Cult of the Mother-Goddess*, 151.

99. Xenophon of Ephesus, a second-century A.D. author, described this annual festival with its procession. *The Ephesian Story*, trans. Paul Turner (London: The Golden Cockerel Press, n.d.), 10.

100. If the spring festivals in honor of Artemis paralleled those of Cybele, there are more detailed descriptions of their public aspects. See Vermaseren, *Cybele*, 114-16, 124; Cumont, *Oriental Religions*, 47, 56-57; Ferguson, *Religions*, 28-29.

101. Showerman, *Great Mother*, 80-82; Willoughby, *Pagan Regeneration*, 129.

102. See chapter 3.

103. Swidler, *Women in Judaism*, 83-84, 88; Leslie, "Concept of Woman," 385.

104. Witherington, *Women*, 8; Swidler, *Women in Judaism*, 88.

105. J. Barton Payne, *The Theology of the Older Testament* (Grand Rapids: Zondervan Publishing House, 1961), 229.

106. Metzger, "Considerations of Methodology," 7.

107. Swidler, *Women in Judaism*, 88, and Witherington, *Women*, 8, stated that women were segregated. Bernadette J. Brooten contended that the vast majority of synagogues did not seem to have possessed a separate gallery for women. *Women Leaders in the Ancient Synagogue: Inscriptional Evidence and Background Issues* (Chico, Calif.: Scholars Press, 1982), 123.

108. For a thorough discussion of women as related to synagogues, see Brooten, *Women Leaders in the Ancient Synagogue.*

109. "A man ought to give his daughter a knowledge of the Law." M.Sotah 3.4.

110. Sotah 3.4.

111. See the discussion of Beruria in Swidler, *Women in Judaism*, 97-104.

112. Witherington, *Women*, 8; see also Meeks, "Image of the Androgyne," 175; Leslie, "Concept of Woman," 378-81.

113. Barth, *Ephesians*, 2:661.

114. Swidler, *Women in Judaism*, 21.

PART TWO

INTERPRETATIVE STUDY OF 1 TIMOTHY 2:9-15

CHAPTER III

THE OLD TESTAMENT CONTEXT

The Old Testament writings formed the "Scriptures" for the early church. In order to explain 1 Tim. 2:9-15 correctly, an interpreter needs to understand the Old Testament context which provided guidance both doctrinally and practically for the first Christians. The reference to the narratives of Genesis 1-3 in 1 Tim. 2:13-14 heightens the importance of this interpretative context. Knowing the status of women in the Old Testament will also aid in understanding 1 Tim. 2:9-15.

The Hebrew texts present a variety of pictures and teachings on women.[1] The views which emerge from these writings often appear to conflict. At one extreme, one observes the ultimate submission of a woman to man in Jephthah's sacrifice of his obedient daughter in Judg. 11:29-40.[2] In contrast, Deborah possesses authority over men—judging, leading, and carrying out her own decisions in Judg. 4:4-24. Israel's law codes often depict a negative view of women as legal non-persons, visibly dependent, usually inferior to men, and almost always subjected to some male authority.[3] Yet, one notices that the Wisdom literature frequently indicates a positive view of womanhood, such as the women in the Song of Songs:

> In this setting, there is no male dominance, no female subordination, and no stereotyping of either sex. Specifically, the portrayal of the woman defies the connotations of "second sex." She works, keeping vineyards and pasturing flocks. Throughout the Song she is independent, fully the equal of man.[4]

The prophets also portray the dignity of womanhood by using marriage as an analogy of God's covenant relationship with the people of Israel.[5] Thus, the Old Testament texts offer contrasting situations for women which includes both merit and apparent devaluation.[6]

Not only do the biblical materials suggest contrasts, but those who interpreted them gave opposite conclusions. According to one theologian, the "Old Testament insists on the subordination of the woman to the man," always assigning her an inferior role in the religious and social life.[7] Another scholar, however, contended that "no higher status could be given anyone than was given the woman in ancient Israel."[8] Again, some authors viewed the Old Testament Scriptures as "written for men by men," reflecting primarily male interests and experiences.[9] Yet, another theologian believed that

> in certain biblical texts faith embraces feminism, even as it receives meaning from women. . . . Some portrayals [of women] are truly extraordinary for a patriarchal culture and indicate that female subordination was not unquestioned in Israel.[10]

The above comments indicate that an examination of the Old Testament context invites difficulties. The discussion which follows presupposes that the Old Testament does indeed reveal a positive status for women. Such a presupposition centers in the recognition that women had a position of equality before God in Israel's theocracy.[11] They shared in the grace of God toward the covenant community. Equal standing with men in a relationship with Yahweh signified the worth of women,[12] though the patriarchal society of the Hebrew people obscured this value. In spite of the fact that women in the Old Testament mirrored the patriarchal society in which they lived, they also challenged that same androcentric world.[13]

Woman in Genesis 1-3

The Genesis narratives concerning the creation and fall of humankind are foundational for understanding the nature of woman, her relationship to God, and her relationship to others, particularly man. What do the first three chapters of Genesis teach that will illumine Paul's use of these narratives in 1 Tim. 2:9-15?

Woman in Creation: Genesis 1-2

Genesis 1 and 2 offer two complementary stories about creation, including the creation of humanity.[14] Gen. 1:26-28 describes the origin of woman as the direct, intentional creation of God. The Hebrew word for man used here, *'ādām,* signifies the generic term for man and thus includes woman.[15] God created *'ādām* both in the image of God[16] and as male and female. Woman and man both share equally in the *imago Dei.*[17] The biblical writer gives no reason to think that woman's participation in God's image differs in any way from that of man.[18]

The words for female and male in verse 27 refer to sexual, anatomical differentiation. God's creation of humanity included sexual distinction. The plural "them" in Gen. 1:27 contrasts with the singular "him" and prevents the assumption of the creation of an originally androgynous man.[19] Some scholars did see *'ādām* here as an androgynous being or an earth creature.[20] This view failed to deal with the plural pronouns. A bisexual humanity makes each partner the complement of the other.[21] God creates mankind as a unity which includes both male and female. Woman and man depend on each other. They need each other.[22] The concurrent or simultaneous creation of male and female indicates their equality with one another.[23]

Gen. 1:28 begins with God's blessing on *them.* This blessing bestows not only a gift but a function.[24] Both male and female receive the divine commands to subdue and rule the earth as indicated by the plural Hebrew verbs. They share this assignment within creation which means that woman too exercises dominion over other creatures. This infers equality in function. Man does not have dominion over woman, but woman and man together have dominion over the rest of creation.[25]

Gen. 1:26-28 affirms that both woman and man represent the crowning glory of God's creation. "She, like man, was created in the image of God. . . . She, like man, was blessed. She like man, was given dominion over the created world."[26] Only woman and man together could fulfill God's injunction to be fruitful and multiply. This passage asserts the spiritual equality of woman and man—both made in the image of God. It also recognizes that the two share the same responsibilities with regard to the created universe.[27] What does the expanded creation account of Genesis 2 indicate about woman?

The creation account of Gen. 2:18-25[28] reveals that *'ādām* as male alone is incomplete. As a social being he cannot do without his female counterpart. His female complement essentially perfects his being. God creates woman as a succor to the man's loneliness.[29]   The preceding concepts stem in part from the use of the Hebrew word '*ēzer*. This term with its modifier "suitable for him" (*kᵉnegdô*) suggests the meanings of "counterpart," "corresponding to," or "the idea of parity."[30] '*Ēzer* generally applies to God (at least fifteen of the twenty-one times used in the Old Testament)[31] as one who brings aid to the needy and desperate. "The Hebrew word translated 'helper' does not in itself denote positions within relationships."[32] Even if the term suggested superiority, the modifying "fit for him" would deny this possibility here. This modifier emphasizes correspondence or equality. Woman thus fulfills the function of creative complementariness. Man needs her for his completeness.[33]

The fact that Yahweh "builds" the woman from man reveals her superiority over the animals.[34] The Hebrew word denotes aesthetic intent and considerable labor. It conveys the idea of reliability and permanence.[35] God builds the woman from one of the man's ribs or sides.[36] "Bone of my bones and flesh of my flesh"[37] signifies the sameness of being. The two possess a blood relationship. "One flesh" points to the concepts of unity and parity. The man ('*îsh*) calls the new creation woman ('*ishshā*).[38] He does not employ the technical naming-formula here, for '*ishshā* is not a proper name.[39] Instead, this Hebrew pun recognizes sexual differentiation and not subordination. The similarity between the Hebrew words emphasizes the equality of woman and man. Thus, man acknowledges before Yahweh and in the woman's presence the equality of the partnership between the couple. Woman and man relate in like mutuality.[40]

The responsibility of the man toward the woman now takes precedence over other communal ties revealing her high esteem. *Dābaq* ("to cleave") means "clinging to someone in affection and loyalty."[41] This verse establishes a strong basis for marriage. Despite the patriarchal culture of Israel, Gen. 2:18-25 preserves the primacy of the wife-husband bond over the link of filiality.[42]

The Genesis 2 narrative has provoked two positions concerning the woman-man relationship. One purports that man's priority in the "order of creation" indicates his superiority and authority in a relational hierarchy.[43] Other arguments which support this subordination of woman to man are: God took the woman from the man; man named the woman; and, woman was created to be man's helper.[44] The second view points out that the creative order is a climatic progression from the imperfect to the perfect. Consequently, woman represents the "crown and completion" of creation.[45] The primacy of the man over woman signals only a primacy of age or temporal priority. It does not signify that man has a natural or ethical superiority over woman. The fact that God took woman from the man emphasizes their relatedness and unity. "Helper" does not entail subordination.

Actually, the passage does not support either of these arguments.

> The concepts of superiority or inferiority, even of equality seem to be absent from this biblical story (Gen 2:18-24). A "divine plan of creation" in which man would be the head of the woman is not apparent. . . . In the beginning this [woman-man relationship] was a very unique and harmonious relationship in which the two were really one.[46]

Gen. 2:18-24 stresses the interrelatedness and mutual dependence of the woman and the man.

The two creation narratives basically affirm the same teachings about woman. God purposefully created both the woman and the man. Both reflect the divine image. Both need the other. Together woman and man constitute humankind.[47] Do the events of Genesis 3 affect this relationship of mutuality?

Woman in the Fall: Genesis 3

Genesis 3 portrays the temptation, disobedience, and judgment of humanity as represented by Eve and Adam. Their sin results in the Fall of mankind. This Fall changes the social status of the woman. Before the Fall she possesses equality before God and with man. Though the former relationship remains the same as man's, the latter deteriorates.[48] The sin of disobedience spoils the mutuality of the woman-man relationship. Adam's attempt to blame Eve for his own participation (verse 12) indicates the beginning of the breakdown in relationship.

Both woman and man participate in the Fall. Eve listens to the serpent. She is deceived by the intentionally deceptive serpent as to the results of her act. The serpent doctrinally beguiles her "into hostility toward God and sensual desire for the unknown."[49] Some contemporary writers perceived Eve's conversation with the serpent as indicative of her theological acumen. She is "intelligent, informed, and perceptive. Theologian, ethicist, hermeneut, rabbi, she speaks with clarity and authority."[50] On the other hand, Adam "does not theologize; he does not contemplate; . . . Instead, his one act is belly-oriented, . . . the man is passive, brutish, and inept."[51] Somehow, these descriptions of Eve and Adam do not ring true to the biblical texts.   Such portraits represent an imaginative reading between the lines.   The danger of this feminist interpretation resides in its glamorization of Eve's sin as if to excuse her actions.   Both the woman and the man sin.   Eve does not tempt Adam, as centuries of theological literature have suggested.[52]   Adam is not forced to eat the fruit.   The Hebrew text makes it clear that the woman and man are standing together during this episode.[53]   Both Eve and Adam have responsibility before God for their actions.

The disobedience of the woman and the man brings God's judgment upon them.   Neither receives a greater judgment than the other.[54]   Although neither the woman nor the man receive God's curse as do the serpent and the ground, their punishment is severe.

> The woman's punishment struck at the deepest root of her being as wife and mother, the man's strikes at the innermost nerve of his life: his work, his activity, and provision for sustenance.[55]

Woman and man reap the consequences of their sin.

The woman's sentence in Gen. 3:16 involves three elements: pain in childbirth, desire for her husband, and the husband's rule over her. Childbirth, God's great blessing, will entail great suffering.   Pain thus touches a major area of significance for the woman.[56]

Interpreters have offered various views to explain the meaning of the woman's "desire."[57]   Following the traditional root for "desire," some equate this with sexual longing.   The woman will crave her husband so fiercely that "she will be ready to face all the pains and sorrows of childbearing."[58]   A second view sees the woman's desire as "the attraction that woman experiences for man which she cannot root from her nature."[59] A third view draws a linguistic parallel between Gen. 3:16 and 4:7 and suggests that "desire" relates to the desire of the woman to possess or control the man.[60]   The use of the word in Gen. 4:7, however, is figurative while in 3:16 it is literal.   Woman may desire to dominate man, but this characterizes all sin against God.   A final view suggests that Song of Solomon 7:10 provides the context for understanding "desire."   Both texts use "desire" literally and address relationships between the opposite sexes. In spite of the Fall, woman will long for closeness with the man involving more than sexual intimacy.   The wife will desire her husband's company.[61] This last view appears to fit the context of Gen. 3:16 best.   It offers an explanation of why women and men still marry despite the problems in marital harmony resulting from sin.

Although the wife still longs for intimacy with her husband, Gen. 3:16 further states that he will rule over her. The Hebrew word for rule here (*māshal*, "to rule, have dominion over, reign") is less harsh than a synonym (*rādâ*, "to have dominion, rule, dominate, chastise").[62] Man now rules over the woman. The mutual relationship between woman and man of Genesis 1 and 2 which encourages cooperation and complementariness has become one of conflict and competition as a result of the Fall. Man asserts his power and authority over the woman in Gen. 3:20 when he names her using the technical naming-formula. He reduces her status to that of the animals he previously named.[63] Yet, the name Adam gives to Eve is honorific, the mother of all the living. Genesis 4 relates Eve's fulfillment as a mother. Despite the Fall and its resultant punishment, the woman, as mother, continues to play a central role.[64]

Women and the Domestic and Societal Contexts

Women and the Domestic Context

The primary position of women in Israel focused within the structure of the family and home. As the basic unit of society, the family provided biological survival, economic security, and personal identity.[65] This involved for women two essential roles: wife and mother.

"Wife" represented the comprehensive category that described the destiny of almost all women in Israel.[66] It signified their most important relation in early society. The Old Testament identifies the wife as a member of the household in Exod. 20:17 and Deut. 5:21—a member of the family, not property.[67] Though the Decalogue includes a man's wife along with his possessions, she was not mere property. The bride price (Gen. 29:18) did not signify a transfer of property but the surrender of authority over a woman by one man to another.[68]

The family contracted marriages for the children. Though some women displayed initiative in arranging their own marriages, this rarely occurred (Num. 36:6; 1 Sam. 18:20). The Israelites did practice polygamy (for example, Jacob, David, and Solomon), but monogamy predominated.

Within the home women exercised considerable power, authority, and freedom. Children had to revere and obey their mothers as well as their fathers (Exod. 20:12; Lev. 19:3). Striking or cursing one's mother or father brought death (Exod. 21:15, 17). These laws made no distinction between mother and father. Both parents shared the position of authority and responsibility in the care of their children. Women also had control over their personal slaves (Sarah and Hagar, Genesis 16, 21).[69]

Legally, wives had fewer rights than husbands. Husbands could divorce their wives.[70] Wives had to uphold a stricter chastity than did husbands, probably to insure the legitimacy of children for inheritance reasons (Num. 5:11-31). Wives could not inherit except where there was no male heir (Num. 36:8). Husbands in some instances even permitted their wives or daughters to be mistreated or abused (Gen. 12:10-20; Judges 19). The Old Testament reports these incidents; it does not condone them. In examining the legal restrictions as illustrated above perhaps the idea of "clan right" or "strength of family" aids in explanation. Since the women in Israel had the sufficient backing of their families in the case of injustice, families took the place of legal measures.[71] For example, a father could declare his daughter's marriage void (Judg. 15:21; 1 Sam. 25:44).

Wives received more respect after the birth of their first child, especially a boy. This was the highest status women might achieve. Childbearing fulfilled their function in Old Testament society. It bound their husbands to them. This explains the desperation of Rachel's cry, "Give me children or I die" (Gen. 30:1-2). Barrenness became a shame and reproach, and was seen as divine punishment (Gen. 16:2). It brought the derision of other women (Gen. 16:4; 1 Sam. 1:6) and even threatened the wives' marital status.[72]

Women's status in the Old Testament within the home suggests only distinction and honor. Their roles centered in God's purposes for and favor toward them. Women, nonetheless, also possessed roles outside the home.

Women and the Societal Context

The Old Testament presents women as discharging various duties usually associated with men. For example, women engaged in economic functions. The wife in Prov. 31:10-31 engages in real estate transactions (verse 16) and the manufacture and sale of garments (verse 24). She acts on her own initiative. The writer points out these economic activities with approval. A few women participated as leaders in the society. Deborah led the Israelites both as a judge and as a military figure (Judges 4). Jezebel, unfortunately, proved to be a political force (1 Kings 21), as well as the wicked Athaliah who usurped the throne and ruled for six years (2 Kings 11:1-3). One wise woman's influence aided in suppressing Sheba's revolt against David (2 Sam. 20:14-22). Women appealed directly to the king or courts for justice: the wise woman from Tekoa (2 Sam. 14:1-24) and the two harlots with the one living child (1 Kings 3:16-28). Prophetesses also served in Israel. These roles evidence challenges to the male patriarchy. Normally these did not result as alternatives to the wife and mother functions but complemented or supplemented these activities. The biblical authors accepted women in these different leadership roles by not giving any special attention to them. These functions aided women's status in Israel.[73]

Women and Israel's Cultic Law

Regulations Requiring Sacrifices of Women

Hebrew women had to offer sacrifices for various reasons. Childbirth, which represented one of the uncleanness categories, required a sacrifice from mothers for their purification (Leviticus 12). Paradoxically, women's supreme function—childbearing—brought them uncleanness. The Hebrews recognized forces of good and evil as present at the mysterious time of childbirth: the power of God to give life and power of evil to take life away. For their own protection and that of their children mothers needed to thank God and make atonement through this sacrifice.[74]

The atonement offering indicated women's involvement in Israel's cult. Women individually brought the sacrifice to the door of the tent of the meeting (Lev. 12:6). They themselves had a way of immediate access to God. This requirement of the burnt offering signified that women did have a place and privilege in the covenant community. They could function autonomously and independently.[75]

An abnormal discharge also required a sacrifice (Lev. 15:25-30). This law for women paralleled that for men (Lev. 15:1-17). Women and men both presented the same sacrifice. Again, the women themselves could bring the offering to the sanctuary (Lev. 15:29-30). In the purification of women after leprosy (Lev. 14:1-32) which also necessitated a sacrifice, parity again existed between women and men. Both had equal requirements.

Though males led in Israel's theocratic life, women too maintained some functions. The above regulations which required a sacrifice from them illustrate this. Women could and did approach God through the offering of sacrifices.

Regulations Exclusively for Women

Some regulations related exclusively to women. For instance, Exod. 22:18 mentions death for the sorceress only with no mention of the sorcerer. Lev. 15:19-24 deals with the menstruant. Considered an uncleanness, menstruation made women cultically unfit to enter the sanctuary. This regulation shows that even the most intimate details of existence reminded Israel of the Lord's claim upon their lives.[76]

Num. 5:11-31 presents the "law of jealousy" or the ordeal of testing law which seems to elevate men over their wives by implying a double standard. Only men could charge infidelity. This regulation combines the cultic and social aspects of Israel's life. It affirms the social subordination of women which resulted from the Fall.[77]

All women could make vows (Numbers 30). Vows bound one in a promise to God. They revealed an individual's status in the cult because only those with standing before the Lord could make such a commitment. Thus, women did have status and standing in the cult before the Lord. They had freedom to initiate these promises to God. The Nazarite vow (Num. 6:1-21) did not discriminate between the sexes. This special vow consecrated one to the service of Yahweh. The stipulations and ceremonies the Nazarite observed resembled those of a priest. Women too obtained this high level of consecration. However, the validity of women's vows depended upon the approval of their fathers or husbands. This reflected the primacy of the male in Israel. God held women (wives with husbands' approval) accountable for their vows.[78]

A final regulation for women involved the death penalty for harlotry on the part of a priest's daughter (Lev. 21:9). Her privileged position of permission to eat holy things and identification with her father's vocation insisted upon her purity. There could be no confusion or mistaken identification of the daughters of the priests of Yahweh with the priestesses of the pagan religions.

After examination of these cultic regulations with their similarities for women and men, one can affirm that the Israelite women had an equal place with the men in the community. The laws continually designated men's function as leader and representative of others. That women did not have this explicit leadership role did not imply their inferiority. Their own unique function—childbearing—awarded a crucial intimacy with Yahweh according to the theological perspective of the Israelites.[79]

Women and Israel's Worship

The status of women in the Old Testament depends heavily upon their participation in the cult.[80] The biblical materials reveal that women did share in Israel's cultic life.

Women in Prescribed and Voluntary
Acts of Worship

Yahweh prescribed two specific acts of worship: circumcision and entering into the covenant. Only one reference cites a woman in relation to circumcision—Zipporah (Exod. 4:24-26). Although debate surrounds this passage as to the meaning of Zipporah's actions for her husband Moses, the text does indicate that she "officiated" in circumcising her son.[81] The covenant renewal given in Deut. 29:9-14 specifically mentions wives among those who may enter the covenant with the Lord. This precise identification of wives would not exclude unmarried women.

Women could participate voluntarily in worship in many ways. As earlier noted, they had the freedom to bring sacrifices to the door of the tent of the meeting. In 1 Sam. 1:4-5 Elkanah offered his wives portions of the sacrificial offerings. This same chapter of 1 Samuel depicts Hannah's independence in entering the shrine and even addressing Eli the priest. She showed no hesitancy in approaching Yahweh directly and even made a vow (verse 11). Eli gave Hannah his benediction. The entire episode illustrates the freedom and respect women exercised in the cult. Other women too inquired of the Lord, such as Rebekah (Gen. 25:22) and Jeroboam's wife (1 Kings 14:1-18).

Women participated in both singing and dancing as a part of worship (Exod. 15:1, 20; Judg. 5:1; 21:21). Exod. 38:8 and 1 Sam. 2:22 suggest some kind of ministry performed by women at the tent of the meeting. One author believed that these women "constituted a type of spiritual militia who kept watch."[82]

The theophany signified the most important cult event. Women too received these divine revelations, Hagar (Gen. 16:7-14; 21:16-19) and Manoah's wife (Judg. 13:2-25). These passages indicate that the biblical writers took for granted that women too could engage in such a significant cultic act.

Women as Religious Functionaries

Prophets belonged to the most intimate group of Yahweh's servants. The Old Testament identifies five women as prophetesses: Miriam (Exod. 15:20), Deborah (Judg. 4:4), Huldah (2 Kings 22:14; 2 Chron. 34:22), Isaiah's wife (Isa. 8:3), and Noadiah (Neh. 6:14). No evidence exists to suggest that these women were unusual in their role, though they surfaced infrequently. God bestowed this charismatic gift irrespective of sex. As these women proved, people sought out those with God's message. "Perhaps these prophetesses may have been more prominent in history than the tradition was allowed to present in an age characterized by man's dominance over women."[83]

The case of Deborah certifies that men did not reject a woman's leadership. She spoke for Yahweh. Furthermore, her leadership role did not preclude marriage. Huldah stands out as a remarkable figure during Josiah's reign. Though Jeremiah and Zephaniah prophesied actively during this time, the king's men sought out Huldah to interpret the words of the recently discovered book of the law. Why did they entrust so important a matter to a woman of whom so little is known? Obviously, they held no prejudice against the instruction of a woman. They accepted her judgment without question.[84]

The priestly class excluded women. Various practical and religious reasons explain this restriction. The nature of the priests' work made it difficult for women to be in this position (for example, the slaughter of animals). Since the women's most important tasks centered in the home and in mothering, they had no time to give to the profession of priesthood. Women's periodic uncleanness made it impractical. The most significant reason relates to the rival fertility cults which surrounded Israel and threatened her worship of Yahweh. These maintained priestesses, many of whom had a sexual function. Yahweh desired the elimination of any sexual motif which would undermine Israel's morality based on holiness.[85]

Thus, as active participants in Israel's worship, women had high standing in God's sight. As did men, they enjoyed a personal relationship to God. Though the female role in worship differed from the male in some respects, this did not intimate inferiority. Women could and did function in an official capacity. As indicated earlier, women's religious status changed after the exile.[86] Probably the Hebrews in earlier periods of history did not discriminate as much between women and men in regards to participation in religious practices. As the cult developed and as the Hebrews reflected upon their pre-exilic behaviors, women found themselves more excluded from cult participation.[87]

Israel and the Worship of Pagan Goddesses

Why did the Hebrews exclude women from the particular function of priest? Why did the postexilic Temple restrict women's access to the place of sacrifice? Did the prevalence of the Mother Goddess in the world of the Old Testament hold a clue to the answer to these questions?

In Israel's environment sexuality held a high significance. Sexual symbols, customs, and cultic prostitution dominated the Canaanite religion. The Canaanites believed that the deflowering of young girls in the sanctuary before marriage guaranteed the divine blessing of fertility.[88] The Hebrew-Jewish religion flourished for centuries surrounded by goddess cults. Unfortunately, the religion of Israel did not remain immune to these cults. The Hebrews did worship goddesses. In fact, some of the Hebrew people worshipped the goddess Asherah from the first days of settlement in Canaan.[89] Consequently, believers and spokesmen for Yahweh struggled for hundreds of years to suppress this Goddess worship.[90]

The Old Testament mentions several names for the goddess worshipped by the Hebrews: Anath, Asherah, Astarte, and the Queen of Heaven.[91] The amount of archaeological evidence, such as small clay figurines, uncovered in Palestine indicates the importance of Asherah as a household goddess. The images of male gods do not match the frequent occurrence of female figurines. Archaeologists concluded from this that all segments of Hebrew society must have worshipped this fertility goddess.[92]

As was true of other fertility cults of the Mother Goddess, sacred prostitution existed as a concomitant of the goddess cults in Palestine.[93] The contaminated Yahweh cult did not lack such sacred prostitution. 2 Kings 23:7 implies that sacred prostitutes practiced Asherah's rite even in the Temple in Jerusalem. Various campaigns or reform movements against this cultic activity arose from time to time in Israel.[94] After the exile, however, no public worship of goddesses manifested itself. The people had learned from the judgment of Yahweh.

The God of Israel desired his people to be holy—separate, distinct—even as he was holy (Lev. 19:2). The cult of Yahweh needed to reflect this holiness. Therefore, certain Hebrew legislation attempted to distinguish Yahwism from Baalism and the Mother Goddess cults. Deut. 9:1 excluded castrated males from marrying into the congregation of Israel. Lev. 21:21 prohibited members of the Aaronic priesthood who had physical defects from serving in the holiest precincts, specifically those with injury to testicles.[95] In other words, the Hebrew cult was not to have eunuch priests.[96]

In keeping with this legislation for men, it comes as no surprise that Israel excluded women from the priesthood. The priestesses in the rival fertility cults surrounding Israel had sexual functions. They were cultic prostitutes. Lev. 19:29 states explicitly: "Do not profane your daughter by making her a harlot, so that the land may not fall to harlotry, and the land become full of lewdness." Cultic prostitution was not an option for Hebrew women. To reinforce this, Lev. 21:7, 14-15 commands priests not to marry any "defiled" woman but virgins only. The daughters of priests who played the harlot (Lev. 21:9) received the death penalty.

> This extraordinarily strong penalty for prostitution is aimed specifically at women who lived near or in the Israelite sanctuary area, the daughters of priests. It indicates the danger of pagan cultic expression that existed when men and women were together in cultic contexts, a danger that to some extent necessitated the removal of one of the two sexes from cultic services.[97]

The religion of Yahweh had to remain distinct from pagan religious threats. Therefore, the sexual motif had to be removed. Rejection of pagan fertility deities meant the restriction of the priesthood to men and the exclusion of women.[98]

Conclusion

The Old Testament writings establish a positive, high status for women. The creation accounts indicate their equality with men in relationships of mutuality and shared responsibility. The Fall caused deterioration in the female-male relationship leading to conflict and competition. Despite the male domination of Israel's society, individual women did survive as people in their own right. Such exceptional women who emerged despite the patriarchal system included Puah, Shiphrah, Deborah, and Huldah. Women who were wives and mothers received high esteem because of their vital, essential role. Though some legislation appeared to treat women as inferior to men, it actually served to maintain the purity of Yahweh's holy covenant community against the defilement of paganism. Women had direct access to Yahweh through the personal, covenantal relation. They participated in many worship activities. Prophetesses functioned in an official capacity showing that women could speak and teach with authority. Only the priesthood excluded the service of women. The practical and religious reasons for this exclusion no longer seem applicable.[99] The status of Hebrew women in the Old Testament was generally less restricted and less subordinate than that of Jewish women in the first century.[100] By that time Judaism had developed into a legalism that exalted the letter of the law over its spirit and that placed more importance on the system rather than persons.

The Old Testament context points beyond itself in an eschatological view of womanhood that finds its fulfillment in the new covenant:

> "And it will come about after this
> That I will pour out My Spirit on all mankind;
> And your sons and daughters will prophesy,
> Your old men will dream dreams,
> Your young men will see visions.
> "And even on the male and female servants
> I will pour out My Spirit in those days . . ." (Joel 2:28-29).

The discussion now turns to the context of the new covenant for the role of women.

NOTES

1. Clarence J. Vos contended that the Old Testament laws represent the most important source for determining Israel's view of women since these are universal, timeless, and applicable to all women. *Women in Old Testament Worship* (Delft: Judels und Brinkman, 1968), 7-8. Calum M. Carmichael suggested that certain laws in the Deuteronomic legislation are about women in the Genesis narratives. The legislator identified the wrongs in the treatment of women in the Genesis stories and then attempted to counteract these wrongs by legislation. See *Women, Law, and the Genesis Traditions* (Edinburgh: University Press, 1979), 1-6.

2. For a discussion of this incident, as well as three other "tales of terror with women as victims" (Hagar, Tamar, and the unnamed concubine), see Phyllis Trible, *Texts of Terror: Literary-Feminist Readings of Biblical Narratives* (Philadelphia: Fortress Press, 1984).

3. Phyllis Bird, "Images of Women in the Old Testament," in *Religion and Sexism: Images of Woman in the Jewish and Christian Traditions*, ed. Rosemary Radford Ruether (New York: Simon and Schuster, 1974), 56-57, summarized this negative view as perceived in the laws.

4. Phyllis Trible, *God and the Rhetoric*, 161.

5. For example, see Hosea. Terrien, "Toward a Biblical Theology," gave these more positive views.

6. Swidler's organization of his discussion of women in the Hebrew-Jewish tradition revealed the variety of Old Testament teachings concerning women. He had chapters on positive elements, ambivalent elements, and negative images of and attitudes toward women in the Hebrew-Jewish writings. See *Biblical Affirmations*, 75-159.

7. Edmond Jacob, *Theology of the Old Testament*, trans. Arthur W. Heathcote and Philip J. Allcock (New York: Harper and Row Publishers, 1958), 172-73.

8. John Otwell, *And Sarah Laughed: The Status of Woman in the Old Testament* (Philadelphia: The Westminster Press, 1977), 66.

9. Gerstenberger and Schrage, *Woman and Man*, 23.

10. Phyllis Trible, "Biblical Theology as Women's Work," *Religion in Life* 44 (1975): 7.

11. Payne, *Theology of the Older Testament*, 229.

12. This opposed the statement of Ludwig Koehler that "Jahweh's covenant with Israel is a covenant with those competent to enter into such a thing; that is to say, with the men: they represent the people." *Old Testament Theology*, trans. A. S. Todd (London: Lutterworth Press, 1957), 69.

13. *IDB*, s.v. "Woman in the Old Testament," by Phyllis Trible, Suppl. vol. (1976): 963.

14. Katharine D. Sakenfeld, "The Bible and Women: Bane or Blessing?" *Theology Today* 32 (October 1975): 223. Some scholars have identified the Genesis 1 account of creation as the work of the Priestly writer (P, written during the fifth century B.C.) and the Genesis 2 account as that of a much older Yahwist writer (J, written during the tenth century B.C.). Swidler, *Biblical Affirmations*, 76-76. Although some would suggest that Genesis 1 and 2 present two different and contradictory conceptions of woman (see Thierry Maertens, *The Advancing Dignity of Woman in the Bible* [De Pere, Wis.: St. Norbert Abbey Press, 1969], 53-54), a basic unity does underlie the two narratives. "The whole text is perhaps more harmonious than has often been suggested." Walter Vogels, "It Is Not Good that the 'Mensch' Should Be Alone; I Will Make Him/Her a Helper Fit for Him/Her," *Église et Théologie* 9 (1978): 25-26.

15. G. Ernest Wright, "Women and Masculine Theological Vocabulary in the Old Testament," in *Grace upon Grace*, ed. James I. Cook (Grand Rapids: William B. Eerdmans Publishing Co., 1975), 66; Gerhard von Rad, *Genesis: A Commentary*, rev. ed., in *The Old Testament Library*, ed. G. Ernest Wright (Philadelphia: The Westminster Press, 1972), 57; *Theological Wordbook of the Old Testament*, 2 vols., ed. R. Laird Harris (Chicago: Moody Press, 1980), s.v. "'ādām," by Leonard J. Coppes 1:10. Hereafter this work is abbreviated *TWOT*. The use of 'ādām does not preclude the historical reality of the persons of Adam and Eve as portrayed particularly in Genesis 2 and 3.

16. The terms "image" and "likeness" of God are essentially synonymous. Michael F. Stitzinger, "Genesis 1-3 and the Male/Female Role Relationship," *Grace Theological Journal* 2 (Spring 1981): 26.

17. Scholars have suggested many possibilities for the meaning of the image of God. For a brief survey of various views, see *TWOT*, s.v. "'ādām," 1:10 and *Theological Dictionary of the Old Testament*, 5 vols., ed. G. Johanes Botterweck and Helmer Ringgren, trans. John T. Willis (Grand Rapids: William B. Eerdmans Publishing Co., 1974), s.v. "'ādhām," by Fritz Maass, 1:85. Hereafter this work is abbreviated *TDOT*. The image of God includes the will

or freedom of choice, self-consciousness, self-transcendence, rationality, self-determination, moral discernment for good and evil, righteousness, holiness, and worship. See Charles L. Feinberg, "The Image of God," *Bibliotheca Sacra* 129 (July-September 1972): 235-46, and Gordon H. Clark, "The Image of God in Man," *Journal of the Evangelical Theological Society* 12 (Fall 1969): 215-22. Paul Jewett, who followed Karl Barth's dynamic view of the image as being-in-fellowship, contended that human sexuality is grounded in the *imago Dei*. To be in the image of God is to be male and female. Paul K. Jewett, *Man as Male and Female: A Study in Sexual Relationships from a Theological Point of View* (Grand Rapids: William B. Eerdmans Publishing Co., 1975), 24, 33-40.

18. Vos, *Women in Old Testament Worship*, 15.

19. Von Rad, *Genesis*, 60; Theodorus Christiaan Vriezen, *An Outline of Old Testament Theology*, 2nd ed., trans. S. Neuijen (Newton, Mass.: Charles T. Branford Co., 1970), 411.

20. Trible, *God and the Rhetoric*, 80.

21. Derek Kidner, *Genesis*, in the *Tyndale Old Testament Commentaries*, ed. D. J. Wiseman (Downers Grove, Ill.: InterVarsity Press, 1967), 52.

22. Robert Davidson, *Genesis 1-11*, in *The Cambridge Bible Commentary*, ed. P. R. Ackroyd, A. R. C. Leaney, and J. W. Packer (Cambridge: University Press, 1973), 25-26.

23. Koehler, *Old Testament Theology*, 132.

24. Kidner, *Genesis*, 52.

25. Sakenfeld, "Bible and Women," 224; Vos, *Women in Old Testament Worship*, 13.

26. Nancy M. Tischler, *Legacy of Eve: Women of the Bible* (Atlanta: John Knox Press, 1977), 14.

27. Stitzinger contended that this passage does not indicate whether or not each was given equal status to exercise these obligations. These verses do not speak of the functional relationship between the sexes. A hierarchical relationship is not denied. "Genesis 1-3," 26-27.

28. For a summary of the history of the exegesis of Gen. 2:18-24 see Walter Vogels, "It Is Not Good," 9-35.

29. Terrien, "Toward a Biblical Theology," 324; see also Wright, "Women," 67, and Vriezen, *An Outline*, 411.

30. Sakenfeld, "Bible and Women," 224-25; Trible, *God and the Rhetoric*, 90.

31. For example, see Exod. 18:4; Deut. 33:7; Pss. 121:2, 124:8. For a listing of the references which contain '*ēzer* see Robert Young, *Analytical Concordance to the Bible*, 22nd ed. (New York: Funk and Wagnalls Company, 1936), s.v. "help," 475.

32. Trible, "Biblical Theology," 8. "As helper God is superior; as helpers the animals are inferior; as helper the woman is equal to man." Ibid.

33. Vos, *Women in Old Testament Worship*, 16; Sakenfeld, "Bible and Women," 224-25; Terrien, "Toward a Biblical Theology," 324. Jacob offered a contrasting view: "Man by himself is a complete being, the woman who is given to him adds nothing to his nature, whilst the woman drawn forth from the man owes all her existence to him. . . ." *Theology of the Old Testament*, 172-73.

34. Jewett, *Man as Male and Female*, 126.

35. Trible, "Biblical Theology," 8; Terrien, "Toward a Biblical Theology," 325.

36. The Hebrew word is usually translated "side" in the Old Testament. ". . . God took one of Adam's sides (or one part of Adam's being), out of which He 'builded' her." Katherine C. Bushnell, *God's Word to Women* (North Collins, N.Y.: n.p., 1978, reprint of 1923 ed.), sections 39, 43. For a discussion of the rib motif in Judeo-Christian tradition under the divisions of androcentric, gynocentric, and egalitarian interpretations, see William E. Phipps, "Adam's Rib: Bone of Contention," *Theology Today* 33 (October 1976): 263-73.

37. Walter Brueggeman developed the idea that these words represent "a convenantal formula which does not speak about derivation in a biological sense but means to speak about commonality of concern, loyalty, and responsibility." Gen. 2:18-24, therefore, deals with interpersonal relationships. "Of the Same Flesh and Bone," *The Catholic Biblical Quarterly* 32 (October 1970): 540.

38. Some scholars saw the creation of *'ādām* in Gen. 2:7 as that of an androgynous creature. Only in verses 22-23 does God create sexual differentiation. This view understood the creation of female and male as simultaneous, not sequential. The "earth creature" becomes female and male. "Sexuality originates in the one flesh of humanity." Trible, *God and the Rhetoric*, 97-99. Vogels also shared this view. "It Is Not Good," especially 25-35. These scholars pressed the *'ādām* as mankind distinction too far. *'Ādām* does not have to be translated "humanity" in every context. See Paul Ellingworth, "They Were Both Naked, the Mensch and His/Her Woman," *Église et Théologie* 9 (1978): 505-6.

39. The standard naming formula in the Old Testament employs the verb "to call" and the noun "name." In this verse (23) "name" does not occur. Both terms occur in verse 19 in the naming of the animals. Trible, *God and the Rhetoric*, 99-100.

40. *TDOT*, s.v. "'îsh, 'ishshāh," by N. P. Bratsoitis, 1:227; Vos, *Women in Old Testament Worship*, 18-19; Trible, *God and the Rhetoric*, 100.

41. *TWOT*, s.v. "*dābaq*," by Earl S. Kalland, 1:178.

42. Terrien, "Toward a Biblical Theology," 236.

43. This was the view of George W. Knight, III, in "Male and Female Related He Them," *Christianity Today*, 9 April 1976, 13-17, and Stitzinger, "Genesis 1-3," 30-33.

44. Vogels discussed these and other arguments. "It Is Not Good," 18-24.

45. Trible, "Biblical Theology," 3; Terrien, "Toward a Biblical Theology," 235; Vos, *Women in Old Testament Worship*, 17. The biblical writer describes man's creation in one verse. The woman's creation (verse 22) comes with man's response to it (verse 23) and as the climax of verses 18-23. "This is all the more extraordinary when one realizes that his is the only account of the creation of woman as such in ancient Near Eastern literature." John A. Bailey, "Initiation and the Primal Woman in Gilgamesh and Genesis 1-3," *Journal of Biblical Literature* 89 (June 1970): 143.

46. Vogels, "It Is Not Good," 35.

47. Bird, "Images of Women," 72.

48. *TDOT*, s.v. "'ishshāh," 1:229.

49. Stitzinger, "Genesis 1-3," 36. The temptation of Eve by the serpent does not have a sexual connotation. Consequently, the woman is not a sexual temptress who seduces the man. Bailey, "Initiation and the Primal Woman," 144-48.

50. Trible, *God and the Rhetoric*, 110; see also idem, "Biblical Theology," 8; Terrien, "Toward a Biblical Theology," 327.

51. Trible, *God and the Rhetoric*, 113; see also idem, "Biblical Theology," 8.

52. See Jean M. Higgins, "The Myth of Eve: The Temptress," *Journal of the American Academy of Religion* 44 (December 1976): 639-47. Mary Daly believed the "myth" of the Fall perpetuates the destructive image of women. See chapter 2, "Exorcising Evil from Eve: The Fall into Freedom," in *Beyond God the Father*, 44-68.

53. Sakenfeld noted the use of the plural verbs. "Bible and Women," 225. Higgins offered five reasons for thinking Adam was present during the serpent-Eve dialogue. "The Myth of Eve," 647-48.

54. Vos, *Women in Old Testament Worship*, 23.

55. Von Rad, *Genesis*, 93-94.

56. Bird, "Images of Women," 75.

57. For a discussion of the different views, see Stitzinger, "Genesis 1-3," 40-42; Susan T. Foh, "What Is the Woman's Desire?" *Westminster Theological Journal* 37 (1974): 376-77; Irvin A. Busenitz, "Woman's Desire for Man: Genesis 3:16 Reconsidered," *Grace Theological Journal* 7 (Fall 1986): 203-12.

58. David R. Mace, *Hebrew Marriage: A Sociological Study* (London: The Epworth Press, 1953), 196.

59. H. C. Leupold, *Exposition of Genesis*, 2 vols. (Grand Rapids: Baker Book House, 1942), 1:172. Leupold believed this yearning to be morbid.

60. Foh, "What Is the Woman's Desire?" 381-83.

61. Busenitz, "Woman's Desire for Man," 203, 208, 211.

62. *A Hebrew and English Lexicon of the Old Testament*, ed. Francis Brown, S. R. Driver, and Charles A. Briggs (Oxford: Clarendon Press, 1907; reprint ed., 1978), s.v. "*māshal*," 605 and "*rādâ*," 921.

63. Trible, *God and the Rhetoric*, 133; Sakenfeld, "Bible and Women," 226.

64. Bailey, "Initiation and the Primal Woman," 150.

65. Otwell, *And Sarah Laughed*, 31.

66. Bird, "Images of Women," 63.

67. Otwell, *And Sarah Laughed*, 76. Trible contended that these verses present women as the property of men. *IDB*, s.v. "Woman in the Old Testament," Suppl. Vol.:964.

68. *IDB*, s.v. "Woman," by O. J. Baab, 4:865.

69. See Otwell, *And Sarah Laughed*, 101-9.

70. The law protected women involved in divorce since husbands initiated the legal proceedings. Deut. 24:1 limited the caprice of husbands. They had to demonstrate a disgraceful or scandalous thing in their wives (Deut. 22:13-21; Num. 5:12-28). However, the prophet Malachi reminds Israel that God hates divorce (Mal. 2:13-16).

71. Walther Eichrodt, *Theology of the Old Testament*, 3 vols., trans. J. A. Baker (Philadelphia: The Westminster Press, 1961), 1:81.

72. Caroline M. Breyfolge, "The Social Status of Women in the Old Testament," *Biblical World* 35 (February 1910): 110; Roland de Vaux, *Ancient Israel: Its Life and Institutions*, trans. John McHugh (New York: McGraw-Hill Book Co., Inc., 1961), 39. Childbearing assumed such extreme importance because it concerned the survival of the nation. Women's biological

contribution was essential for population increase. Carol Meyers, "The Roots of Restriction: Women in Early Israel," *Biblical Archeologist* 41 (September 1978): 95, 98. Since the Hebrews attributed conception and barrenness to the action of Yahweh, it gained more significance, even a theological meaning. A new life pointed to God's continuing activity among the people, a proof of divine presence in their midst. This greatly increased women's distinction within a male-oriented culture. Otwell, *And Sarah Laughed*, 49-61.

73. Ibid., 135-49; Bird, "Images of Women," 67; Meyers, "Roots of Restriction," 102.

74. Ronald E. Clements, "Leviticus," in *The Broadman Bible Commentary*, 12 vols., ed. Clifton J. Allen (Nashville: Broadman Press, 1970), 2:35. A difficulty arises regarding this regulation for which no satisfactory or conclusive answer exists. It centers in the length of time of the mothers' uncleanness. The sex of the child determined that period of time. The law required twice the length of time for girls as for boys after which the mother presented the same offering. Does this indicate the inferiority of the female sex or more susceptibility to impurity? Some contended that since other nations already practiced this variation, in time, the Yahwistic cult conformed itself to their ideas. Vos, *Women in Old Testament Worship*, 65-70. Another interpretation suggested:

"The mother's uncleanness may have been the result of the afterbirth being regarded as a bodily emission, or the woman who had just given birth may have been 'unclean' because she had been too closely involved with the work of deity. She would need a period to be de-energized so to speak; and that period would need to be twice as long for the birth of a child which might become capable in its turn of bearing children as for a male child."

This view emphasized the working of Yahweh in the birth process, but even this interpretation represented conjecture. Otwell, *And Sarah Laughed*, 176-77.

75. Vos, *Women in Old Testament Worship*, 61-62, 71-73.

76. Ibid., 82-86, 110-15.

77. Ibid., 88-90. Vos believed this ordeal signified an attempt to restore domestic tranquility.

78. Otwell, *And Sarah Laughed*, 169-70.

79. There are other regulations that do not relate exclusively to women. For discussions on these, see Vos, *Women in Old Testament Worship*, 124-47. Women had to yield to the domestic duties which demanded their attention. They participated freely in cultic activities as responsibilities permitted. Caroline Breyfolge, "The Religious Status of Women in the Old Testament," *Biblical World* 35 (June 1910): 414.

80. Otwell, *And Sarah Laughed*, 152.

81. Vos, *Women in Old Testament Worship*, 133-43, thoroughly discussed this passage and its various interpretations.

82. Ibid., 164.

83. Breyfolge, "Religious Status," 414; see also Bird, "Images of Women," 68, and Terrien, "Toward a Biblical Theology," 329.

84. Vos, *Women in Old Testament Worship*, 174-86.

85. Ibid., 193-95; Bird, "Images of Women," 68.

86. See chapter 1, pp. 20-22.

87. Ismar J. Peritz, "Women in the Ancient Hebrew Cult," *Journal of Biblical Literature* 17 (1898): 114.

88. Gerstenberger and Schrage, *Woman and Man*, 106.

89. Raphael Patai, *The Hebrew Goddess* (New York: KTAV Publishing House, Inc., 1967), 18, 42.

90. Swidler, "Goddess Worship," 169. One author contended that the cult of Asherah lasted well into the Christian era. He based his argument on the similarities between the religions described in the Ugaritic texts and *The Syrian Goddess*. See R. A. Oden, Jr., "The Persistence of Canaanite Religion," *Biblical Archeologist* 39 (March 1976): 31-36. For a summary of the history of Asherah worship in Israel, see Patai, *Hebrew Goddess*, 42-51; Swidler, *Biblical Affirmations*, 25-29; Swidler, "Goddess Worship," 167-71; and James, *Cult of the Mother-Goddess*, 78-84.

91. Patai, *Hebrew Goddess*, 32. The word "Asherah" appears over forty times in the Old Testament. This named both a goddess and an upright wooden object. See William Reed, *The Asherah in the Old Testament* (Fort Worth: TCU Press, 1949).

92. Patai, *Hebrew Goddess*, 35.

93. James, *Cult of the Mother-Goddess*, 83.

94. Brooks, "Fertility Cult Functionaries," 246. See 1 Kings 15:12-15; 2 Kings 18:4; 23:6-7; Hos. 4:13-14; Amos 2:7; Isa. 17:8; 17:9; Jer. 17:2-3; 44:15-19; Ezek. 8:3, 14.

95. Brooks, "Fertility Cult Functionaries," 249, 252.

96. Chapter 2 of this study indicated that eunuch priests were cultic officials in some Mother Goddess religions. See p. 39.

97. Meyers, "Roots of Restriction," 100.

98. Vos, *Women in Old Testament Worship*, 194; Otwell, *And Sarah Laughed*, 158; Bird, "Images of Women," 68; Meyers "Roots of Restriction," 99. Meyers saw as another factor the Hebrew emphasis on childbirth and sexuality within the family. See pp. 99-100.

99. Vos, *Women in Old Testament Worship*, 209.

100. Sakenfeld, "Bible and Women," 226.

CHAPTER IV

THE NEW TESTAMENT CONTEXT

The New Testament forms an important context for the understanding of 1 Tim. 2:9-15 since the passage itself lies within its pages. What teachings on women can one derive from the New Testament? Does 1 Tim. 2:9-15 reflect a consistency with the other passages relating to women in the New Testament? In order to answer these questions, the interpreter must review several relevant issues in the New Testament. These include Jesus' and Paul's relationships with and teachings pertaining to women. Any passages on women in the General Epistles will also need examination.[1]

Jesus and Women

Women in the Ministry of Jesus

"The most striking thing about the role of women in the life and teaching of Jesus is the simple fact that they are there."[2] Indeed, the word "revolutionary" best summarizes Jesus' relation to women.[3] Jesus saw women as *persons* to whom and for whom he had come. He treated them as individuals of worth and dignity in contradistinction to Jewish society where people often viewed women as chattel.[4]

Examples abound which illustrate Jesus' treatment of women as responsible people. He talked with the Samaritan woman at the well in a conversation with profound theological implications (John 4).[5] He accepted the anointing of the repentant woman in the home of Simon the Pharisee and commended her for having an active faith (Luke 7:36-50). Jesus also respected and commended the faith of the Syrophoenician woman (Matt. 15:21-28; Mark 7:24-30).

Jesus rejected the rabbinic ideas of sin and sickness and the consequent preoccupation with ritual impurity and defilement for women. Consequently, he could relate to many women to whom others would have barred him access. For instance, Jesus called deliberate attention to the fact that the woman with the flow of blood had touched him (Mark 5:25-34). His action implicitly rejected the idea that blood flow in itself caused women both to be defiled and a source of defilement, thereby excluding them from synagogue worship or the periodic feasts as Judaism dictated.[6]

Unlike many of the rabbis of the first century, Jesus encouraged women to learn spiritual truths. He taught women publicly and privately. Mary sat at Jesus' feet in the posture of a student (Luke 10:38-42). Jesus' dialogue with Martha at the time of Lazarus' death showed his concern for instructing her faith (John 11:1-44). Martha's confession of faith (verse 27) equalled that of Peter's at Caesarea Philippi.[7] Prior to Martha's confession Jesus himself had made a major disclosure to her, a woman, by revealing himself as the resurrection and the life (verse 25).[8]

The area in which Jesus differed most from his contemporaries centered in his invitation to women to participate fully in the family of faith, including ministry. He ignored the traditional separations of women from men. Instead, a group of women traveled with the twelve disciples and others as fellow disciples and companions (Luke 8:1-3). Not only did these women and others travel with Jesus, but they contributed financially to his ministry. The presence of these female followers "reflect[s] an opening for women into the circle of Jesus' disciples that would have been anathema to the rabbinic custom of the day."[9] Jesus risked public scandal by including women among his closest followers. The presence of these women undoubtedly provoked speculation and misunderstanding as to their role in the group.[10] This did not prevent Jesus' acceptance and inclusion of women as disciples.

Did women disciples, however, serve in any "official" capacity, such as the twelve Apostles? Some contended that Jesus did not extend to women any official ministry function such as the apostles received. ". . . Jesus Himself differentiated between men and women in their spheres of activity."[11] He limited their activity by not choosing them for official work.[12] On the other side, some scholars questioned whether the male character was intrinsic to the function and mission of the Twelve and therefore to function in the church. This view suggested that the twelve Apostles did not have any successors. Instead, their function now resides in the church as a whole. The church does not have to maintain any historical-lineal connection with the Twelve and can therefore entrust apostolic ministry and power to whomever it chooses.[13] This position further stated that in the first century women did fulfill the criteria for apostleship as set forth by the New Testament: they were witnesses of Jesus' life, ministry, and resurrection.[14] The restriction of the Twelve to men did not indicate "male bias" on the part of Jesus. After all, neither did he include non-Jews.[15] Some would suggest Jesus carefully chose men as the twelve Apostles to match symbolically the twelve tribes of Israel.[16] Perhaps a better explanation rested in the cultural context of Jesus. Although Jesus distinguished himself from other first-century Jews in how he related to women, he acted carefully in order not "to upset the new development."[17] In other words, the Jewish world was not yet ready to accept the equality of women, much less their leadership. Even those male disciples closest to Jesus struggled to move from a Jewish to a Christian view of women.[18]

Jesus did commission some women witnesses to "go and tell my brothers" about the resurrection. He sent (ἀποστέλλειν) these women to the male disciples to bear witness to the resurrection despite the Jewish law's refusal to accept a woman's testimony (Matt. 28:10; Mark 16:7).[19]

> Jesus gave the best news of the gospel, the central, most important part—his resurrection—to women, and women were told to tell every-body. . . . Jesus sent women out to preach the good news.[20]

It should not surprise anyone that the male disciples refused to believe the testimony of these women (Mark 16:11; Luke 24:11).[21] In a sense, Jesus made these women "apostles."

Women in the Teaching of Jesus

Jesus referred directly to women in his parables. This made his parables notably different from those of the rabbis of his day since he enriched them "with materials drawn from the everyday world of a woman's cares and joys."[22]

Jesus' teaching on lust (Matt. 5:28) focused on the thoughts of men, not the presence of women. He viewed lust as a deliberate sin whose solution centered in disciplined thoughts and not in the avoiding of women. He refused to see women as sex objects. Jesus' attitude made social contact between the sexes possible. Women too could join the group of disciples on equal footing with men.[23]

The attitude of Jesus toward marriage was unpopular "because he presupposed that women had rights and responsibilities equal to men's."[24] Even his disciples wondered about his view: "If the relationship of the man with his wife is like this, it is better not to marry" (Matt. 19:10). Jesus appealed to God's original provision for marriage—one man and one woman in a lifelong monogamous relationship. His interpretation of Deut. 24:1 revealed that divorce did not fit with God's design. Divorce served as a regulatory measure to deal with the result of sin. Jesus' teachings on marriage consistently placed women and men on the same level (Matt. 5:31-32; 19:1-12; Mark 10:1-12; Luke 16:18). For instance, either the woman or the man could commit adultery against the other. Thus, marital unfaithfulness was the only valid ground for divorce. This strict view prompted the disciples' surprise as mentioned above.[25] Jesus affirmed "the unbreakable character of marriage in the original will of God."[26]

Another teaching of Jesus related to women came on an occasion when a woman exclaimed, "Blessed is the womb that bore You, and the breasts at which You nursed" (Luke 11:27). This exclamation reflected the Jewish view that a woman's worth depended on her role in procreation and nurturing. Children and motherhood represented the primary reasons for women's existence. Jesus' response, however, challenged this idea. He stated that women's highest calling centered in hearing and obeying the word of God. Childbearing had received undue focus. Jesus corrected this misplaced emphasis.[27] He insisted on "the personhood, the intellectual and moral faculties, being primary for all. . . ."[28]

Conclusion

In reviewing Jesus' relationship with women and his teachings about them, one sees how he differed from his Jewish contemporaries. Jesus treated women with a dignity that affirmed their equality with men. He accepted them fully as disciples and encouraged them in spiritual and intellectual matters. In many instances, Jesus affirmed women within the context of their traditional roles, such as preparing and serving food. He transformed these roles, giving them a new purpose—service for the Master.[29] Did Paul reflect the teachings and attitudes of Jesus toward women?

Paul and Women

The Apostle Paul often serves as a focal point for discussing the role of women in the church. His writings have proved to be controversial, and conflicting interpretations have arisen.[30] For example, some feminists believed that Paul's writings "are distorted by the human instrument [Paul], yet they are instructive in showing us an honest man in conflict with himself."[31] At the same time, however, others affirmed that Paul is "the only certain and consistent spokesman for the liberation and equality of women in the New Testament." For them, Paul inherited his perspective from the earliest days of the church.[32] This section now turns to Paul in order to continue establishing the context for 1 Tim. 2:9-15.

Paul and His Women Coworkers

Paul's reference to women coworkers leads one to the conclusion that women worked alongside of men in the Pauline churches. Nothing in the relevant texts gives any indication that the work of the women was of a subordinate character.[33] Paul uses the same verb, κοπιάω, not only to characterize his own ministry (1 Cor. 4:12; 15:10; Col. 1:29) but also that of women (Mary, Rom. 16:6; Tryphaena, Tryphosa, and Persis, Rom. 16:12). κοπιάω came to signify Christian work in and for the community. It meant "to work hard."[34] Paul tells the Corinthians to be in subjection to everyone (παντί) who so labors (κοπιῶντι) (1 Cor. 16:16). Would not this include women? The Apostle also identifies several women as his fellow workers (συνεργοί): Priscilla (Rom. 16:3), Euodia, and Syntyche (Phil. 4:2-3). He uses this same term to describe male fellow laborers such as Timothy (Rom. 16:21), Aristarchus, Mark, and Justus (Col. 4:11). Paul's choice of words appears to indicate that women worked with him on an equal basis. Euodia and Syntyche shared his struggle in the cause of the Gospel (ἐν τῷ εὐαγγελίῳ συνήθλησάν μοι, Phil. 4:3). συναθλέω derives from ἀθλέω which means to contend as the athlete who strains every muscle. In other words, these two women had contended with zeal for the Gospel's victory. Paul accepted their prominence and influential position.[35] In fact, he considered the authority of Euodia and Syntyche among the believers in Philippi so great that he feared their dissensions could harm the church.[36]

One feature of Paul's ministry was the conversion of women (Acts 16:13-15; 17:4, 12, 34). Luke often describes these Gentile women as "leading" or "prominent." The cooperation of these women with Paul in sharing in the missionary endeavor aided in the spread of Christianity.[37] Since many of the women converts possessed wealth and prominence, they played an important role in founding, sustaining, and promoting house churches (Apphia, Philem. 2; Nympha, Col. 4:15; Lydia, Acts 16:4; and Priscilla, 1 Cor. 16:19 and Rom. 16:5). Why should these women have been excluded from the leadership of these house churches or from presiding at worship?[38]

Lydia, Euodia, and Syntyche illustrate the freedom and acceptance with which women lived and worked in Asia Minor and Macedonia. Paul's first visit to Philippi showed the contrast between Judaism and Christianity. Judaism allowed Lydia and a group of women to meet to pray, yet deprived these women of the systematic teaching associated with a synagogue. Although the Jews would not allow these women to form a synagogue, Paul preached to them and from these female converts assembled the nucleus of the Philippian church. The church at Philippi provides a glimpse of the new status Christianity offered women.[39]

Of the twenty-six persons whom Paul addresses in Romans 16, ten are women: Phoebe (verses 1-2), Priscilla (verses 3-5), Mary (verse 6), Junia (verse 7), Tryphaena (verse 12), Tryphosa (verse 12), Persis (verse 12), the mother of Rufus (verse 13), Julia (verse 15), and the sister of Nereus (verse 15).[40] This fact arrests the reader of Romans 16 in a striking way when one considers the male-dominated culture of the first century.

One scholar described Phoebe as the "most controversial female figure in Paul's letters."[41] Many believed that the role of Phoebe in the first-century church remains an "open question." The issue concerns whether Phoebe held a fixed office or simply offered her services on behalf of the community.[42] The problematic nature of Phoebe's role exists because she was a woman. Phoebe stands as the "only person in the Pauline literature to receive an official letter of recommendation. . . ."[43] To her Paul entrusted the responsibility of delivering the epistle addressed to the Romans.[44]

Paul uses three terms to describe Phoebe. The first, ἀδελφή, indicates her membership in the Christian community. The second, διάκονος, has had various translations. "Whenever Paul uses the title διάκονος to refer to himself or another male leader, exegetes translate it 'minister,' 'missionary,' or 'servant.'" In the case of Phoebe they usually translate it "deaconess."[45]

A study of the references to this word indicates that the διάκονοι represented a special class of coworkers actively involved in preaching and teaching. In Paul's circle this included both itinerant workers as well as workers in local congregations.[46]   The most accurate translation of διάκονος in light of this is simply "minister."[47]   Thus, Phoebe was a servant, a minister, a teacher, a missionary of the whole church of Cenchrea —not just of the women.[48]

The third description of Phoebe, προστάτις, appears only once in the New Testament. Lexicographers have defined this word as "protectress, patroness, helper."[49] The word literally means "one standing before." One lexicon notes that the title applied to office-bearers in a heathen religious association.[50]   It represents the noun form of the verb προτστημι translated "rule" in 1 Thess. 5:12 and 1 Tim. 5:17. προτστημι characterizes persons with authority in the community.[51] The noun form also implies that Phoebe possessed social position, wealth, and independence.[52] The translation "helper"[53] probably does not convey the total scope of Phoebe's work within the church. προστάτις underscores her function as minister in the church at Cenchrea. She not only provided financial support and hospitality for fellow believers, but she may also have used her influence and connections as an individual of wealth for them.[54]   For Phoebe, προστάτις meant helper, patroness, and leader.

Thus, the evidence indicates that Phoebe served in a leadership capacity perhaps even to the point of some kind of "ruling authority" in the first-century church.[55]   The fact that she stands alone as the only woman in the position described by διάκονος and προστάτις does not mean that Paul used these words here in an unofficial sense.[56] It does not suffice to state that Phoebe "served in some very special and significant capacity of service in the church"[57] but then deny that her service had any "official" sense or capacity.

Paul counted Priscilla and her husband Aquila among his friends and fellow workers (συνεργοι). This couple played a significant role in the Apostle's ministry (Acts 18:2, 18; Rom. 16:3-5; 1 Cor. 16:19).   Paul commended them for their sacrificial service.   He left them in Ephesus where Priscilla and Aquila instructed Apollos (Acts 18:24-26).   Priscilla shared in this teaching ministry with her husband.   She taught a man in the very city where Paul commanded women not to teach.   This couple exemplified the cooperation of a wife and her husband in Christian service. Aquila did not overshadow or absorb his wife's personality.   Instead, Priscilla exercised the freedom to use and develop her own particular gifts for the benefit of the church.[58]   In fact, many scholars believed that Priscilla had prominence over her husband because her name precedes Aquila's in four of the six references listing the couple (Rom. 16:3; Acts

18:18, 26; 2 Tim. 4:19).[59]

One last woman coworker of Paul deserves mention: Junia (Rom. 16:7). Debate centers on the gender of 'Ιουνιᾶν because this person along with Andronicus εἰσιν ἐπίσημοι ἐν τοῖς ἀποστόλοις. If the word ἀπόστολος were not included, undoubtedly 'Ιουνιᾶν would be accepted as a woman. The earliest commentators who took Junia as female included Origen (third century), Jerome (fifth century), Theophylact (eleventh century), and Peter Abelard (twelfth century). Chrysostom stated: "Oh! how great is the devotion . . . of this woman, that she should be even counted worthy of the apellation of apostle!"[60] The first to consider the name as masculine was Aegidus of Rome (A.D. 1245-1316). Luther accepted the masculine form. The prevailing view of current scholarship viewed Junias as a shortened form of a masculine name, even though this is unattested in ancient literature. Consequently, most translators opted for the masculine Junias. Interestingly enough, the AV chose the feminine Junia as did the more recent Montgomery version. Some writers who conceded the possibility of Junia, translated εἰσιν ἐπίσημοι ἐν τοῖς ἀποστόλοις as "well-known to the apostles" instead of "outstanding among the apostles."[61] Rom. 16:7 introduces the possibility that the early church recognized a woman as an apostle—a missionary and church-planter.[62]

This survey of Paul and his women coworkers underscores his appreciation for and acceptance of women and their service in the cause of the Gospel. Paul's mention of them in his greetings does not indicate anything unusual or exceptional in their ministry. Their roles were important and necessary in the early propagation and expansion of Christianity. Now that Paul's relationship to women has been examined, what specific teachings did he provide on women? The key passages are Gal. 3:28, 1 Cor. 11:2-16, 14:34-36, and Eph. 5:21-33.

Galatians 3:28

Gal. 3:28 has received a variety of conflicting interpretations. On the one hand, some commentators claimed this verse as the "Magna Carta of Humanity," especially as this relates to emancipation for women. This view sees the verse as having social and practical implications.[63] On the other hand, some exegetes viewed this verse as having a soteriological meaning only. It relates to the Christian's relation to God (*Coram Deo*) and not to social relations.[64] Although the context of Gal. 3:28 emphasizes the

Coram Deo, consequences do exist for social relations. One cannot neglect the communal or social effects of religious distinctions.[65] Christianity transforms all relationships.

The context of Gal. 3:28 deals with the contrast between the law's bondage and faith's freedom. The Gospel belongs to all persons who accept Jesus Christ. Paul's thoughts on membership in the body of Christ lead him to think of the symbol of Christian initiation into that membership— baptism.[66] Gal. 3:28 might have concluded a traditional baptismal confession. This view draws support from the fact that the context actually deals only with the Jew-Gentile relation. The already strong relationship among the three pairs in a baptismal formula may have led Paul to include all three here.[67]

Scholars have suggested other interpretations of Gal. 3:28 in the light of the first-century ambience. Some believed this confession served as a rebuttal of the Jewish man's prayer thanking God for not being a Gentile, woman, or slave.[68] One position holds that Gal. 3:28 evokes the myth of androgyny. The affirmation of the verse restores "man's original divine, androgynous image."[69] Yet, the Genesis creation narratives, as previously indicated, do not point to an androgynous being.[70] Another approach sees Gal. 3:28, specifically "neither male and female" as refuting the Judaizers' claim of the necessity of marriage for women so that they could be full members of the community of faith.[71] One other perspective contends that the household code developed in Christian preaching to counteract those who appealed to Gal. 3:28 in an excessively enthusiastic manner.[72]

Gal. 3:28 does affirm that the deepest divisions which split the society of the ancient world find unity in Jesus Christ.[73] The new creation in him excludes racial, social, and sexual distinctions.[74] All individuals despite their race, status, or sex stand before God on an equal basis. Gal. 3:28 declares both the unity and equality of these three contrasting pairs. One cannot speak of oneness in Christ and at the same time exclude equality in him.[75]

What do the above truths mean especially for the female-male sphere of relationships?[76] First, Gal. 3:28 affirms, as do the Genesis narratives, the ontological equality of women and men.[77] Claims of superiority for one sex and inferiority for the other have no place in the life of faith. When one properly understands the "order of creation,"[78] there is no conflict with the new "order of redemption."[79] Both creation and redemption reveal the unity and equality of female and male.[80] The context emphasizes spiritual equality.

Gal. 3:28 also signifies that greater freedom and options now avail

84   PAUL, WOMEN TEACHERS, AND THE MOTHER GODDESS AT EPHESUS

themselves to women. This does not obliterate sexual distinctions.[81]
Being in Christ does not abolish sexuality but the antagonism and conflict
between the sexes.[82] Value judgments based on sexual differentiations are
now set aside.[83] Sexual distinctions "should be appreciated and used as
opportunities for service in ways that these distinctions naturally lend
themselves."[84]

1 Corinthians 11:2-16

Like 1 Tim. 2:9-15, two passages from Paul's correspondence to the church
at Corinth offer a direct word on women and their role in worship. Both of
these passages, 1 Cor. 11:2-16 and 14:34-36, occur in a lengthy discussion
of pneumatic worship, 1 Corinthians 11-14. The insights gained from these
texts should aid in understanding 1 Tim. 2:9-15. What does Paul[85] have
to say about women in worship in the first passage? One commentator
described 1 Cor. 11:2-16 as having obscure logic at best, contradictory at
worst, with a peculiar word choice and a peevish tone.[86] While this
description is an overstatement, difficulties do exist in the explanation of
this text. The interpretation hinges on the understanding of several key
words or concepts: κεφαλή, head coverings or hair, δόξα, ἐξουσία, and
mutual dependence.[87]

κεφαλή (verse 3)

Paul uses κεφαλή to describe not only the relationship of ἀνήρ to γυνή but
also of Christ to man and God to Christ. Is Paul speaking of wives and
husbands or of women and men in general? Taking the passage as a whole,
what the Apostle says has implications for women in general, for surely the
Corinthian congregation had single female members who participated in
worship by praying and prophesying. When one considers that marriage
was the most likely option for women, however, most of Paul's pronounce-
ments concerning the position of women could relate to marriage in
particular.[88]

κεφαλή has three possible meanings: (1) the literal, anatomical
meaning, "head"; (2) "first" in relation to time, beginning, or source; or (3)
"chief among," or "head over," connected with the idea of priority. The
LXX renders the Hebrew *rosh* in the literal sense as κεφαλή; the meaning
"first" or "beginning" as ἀρχή; and, "chief" or "ruler" as ἄρχων. κεφαλή

and ἀρχή tended to become interchangeable as renderings of *rosh*.[89] The 1 Corinthians 11 passage does use κεφαλή in the literal sense in verses 4-7 and 10. What does the word signify in verse 3? Here, the dominant sense approaches ἀρχή, "beginning" or "source," by pointing back to the Genesis 2 narrative. Eve derives her being from Adam.[90] The context here, however, would tend to indicate that κεφαλή is not confined to "source" alone. One must remember that Paul was writing to a Gentile community in the first century in a time in which marriage disintegration through divorce and infidelity was the norm. The church had to reflect a Christian view of family relationships even within the context of worship. For this reason, one must accept that κεφαλή in verse 3 also maintains overtones of submission. Had Paul wanted to emphasize "source" only,[91] he could have used ἀρχή. Had he desired to stress authority or a "chain of command,"[92] he could have used ἄρχων or κύριος. κεφαλή allows the expression of the unity of the wife-husband relationship while permitting the concept of submission as well.[93]

Head-coverings or hair? (verses 4-6, 13-15)

Traditionally exegetes have proposed that Paul refers in these verses to the custom of women wearing veils.[94] However, the only word approaching veil in meaning occurs in verse 15, περιβόλαιον, in the construction ἡ κόμη ἀντὶ περιβολαίου. This phrase maintains that women have their hair instead of or as a substitute for head-coverings. In the other verses (4, 5, 6, 13) where interpreters believed Paul refers to the veiling custom, other expressions are used: κατὰ κεφαλῆς ἔχων (literally "having down from the head" or "having the hair down"), ἀκατακάλυπτος, and καταλύπτω.

As recent interpreters have convincingly argued, the Corinthian women's error lay not in removing veils from their heads but in the manner in which they wore their hair.[95] Respectable fashion dictated that women wear their hair bound in some manner,[96] "la coiffure étant un signe d'honneur."[97] ἀκατακάλυπτος thus refers in the passage to unbound hair, as opposed to uncovered hair.[98] Paul's concern centered in the fact that Christian women should remain distinct from pagan women in their worship practices. Disheveled, unbound hair and wildly tossing heads characterized the worship of Isis, Cybele, and Dionysus.[99] Evidently some women converts from these pagan backgrounds still had an affinity for their former modes of worship and brought these to the Christian worship setting. This had to stop. Unbound hair to Paul was the equivalent of having a shaved head.   This had long signified for Jews either grief or a disgraceful punishment (for example, for conviction of adultery).[100]

Paul addresses these injunctions concerning hair also to men (verses 4, 7, 14). Evidently the problem in worship involved both sexes. Men should dress their hair in a manner consistent with their sex. One suggestion is that some men at Corinth dressed their hair in fashions generally associated with homosexuality.[101] Perhaps male converts from the pagan priesthood still wore their feminine garb including feminine hair styles.[102] Paul had not eliminated female-male distinctions. Yet, the Corinthians were blurring sexual differences by their unfeminine and effeminate hairdos. Accepted conventions rejected such behavior in the same way incest was rejected (which the Corinthian believers had approved, 1 Cor. 5:2).[103] Women and men were to observe the hair customs appropriate to their sex and distinctively nonpagan in the worship of the church.

δόξα (verses 7-9)

In verse 7 Paul does not deny that women too share in the image and glory of God. He purports to emphasize the proper distinctions between the sexes. To be the δόξα of someone means to reveal, represent, or manifest that person or to define that person in terms of the one revealed.[104]   When Adam saw Eve for the first time, he in essence exclaimed, "I see myself in her."[105]   Woman was created διὰ τὸν ἄνδα, that is, because of the man.[106] He needed one corresponding to him. In this sense, woman is the glory of man.[107]   In verses 7-9 Paul refers to the Genesis narratives to remind the Corinthian believers of the created differences between females and males. The new creation in Christ did not abrogate these sexual distinctions. Women should worship God as women and men as men.[108] Women's worship demeanor includes their own δόξα, their hair (verse 15).

ἐξουσία (verse 10)

Because women and men alike are to worship in a manner consistent with their sex, women should have ἐξουσία on their heads διὰ τοὺς ἀγγέλους. Most exegetes assumed that ἐξουσία signifies veil. The discussion above, however, concludes that the head-covering issue actually concerns hair style. How does this symbolize power or authority? Again, various interpretations abound concerning the symbolism of ἐξουσία:

magical powers that ward off the seduction of evil angels;[109] the honor
and dignity brought to the woman by the veil;[110] the authority to which
the woman is subject, that is, her husband;[111] and, the authority which
woman herself possesses.[112]   The last interpretation best represents the
active force of ἐξουσία. The New Testament does not use this word in a
passive sense.[113] The proper hair style marks a woman's authority, power,
or license to participate in the public worship of God.[114] It also identifies
her role in the creation of God, a place above all creation including those
angels present at worship as guardians of the natural order who desired
worship to be conducted in a fitting manner.[115] This verse gave Jewish
women converts a freedom in worship hitherto unexperienced. It reminded
their Gentile counterparts of the need for propriety in Christian worship.

Mutual dependence (verses 11-12)

Verses 11 and 12 form a theological climax for Paul's argument. Here he
affirms the equality and mutual dependence of woman and man. Though
man preceded woman in creation, he depends on her subsequently for birth.
The two sexes are interdependent. Paul gives this counterbalance to check
male abuse from a dominating headship and to reaffirm the unity of woman
and man despite their sexual differences.[116]

Summary

1 Cor. 11:2-16 deals with the demeanor of both women and men during
public worship. Women should worship as women; men should worship as
men. Equality in Christ does not obliterate the distinctions between women
and men determined at creation.[117] Nor does equality in Christ dissolve
the wife-husband relationship in the Christian congregation. The husband
remains the κεφαλή of the wife despite her participation and equal standing
in worship.[118] In keeping with Paul's argument on worship throughout 1
Corinthians 11-14, the emphasis in this passage resides in proper worship
—that done decently and in order (1 Cor. 14:40). Christian assembling
should not cause scandals. This main principle has relevance today as well
even though hair styles no longer receive focus as an issue in worship.[119]
      The entire discussion above has assumed what the passage itself
assumes, namely "that Paul here quite clearly allows women the right of
active participation in the gatherings of the local church."[120] Specifically,

Paul allows women to pray and prophesy.[121] In the context of 1 Corinthians 11-14 this prophesying relates to charismatic participation. Does this exclude any "official activity?"[122] Or, is the New Testament prophet "not simply someone inspired" but "someone who fills an office within the community?"[123] All Christians could on occasion prophesy, but there were prophets in the narrow sense who held recognized, authoritative positions in the community. Their prominent, continued use of their spiritual gift gave them the identity as a prophet (Eph. 4:11; 1 Cor. 12:28-29).[124] These prophets were Spirit-inspired preachers whose preaching offered guidance and instruction to believers.[125] One cannot draw a rigid line of distinction between the functions of prophet and teacher.[126] Exposition of Scriptures characterized the teacher's emphases. The prophet's task centered in mediating divine knowledge, bringing to bear on the lives of Christians the revelation of the word and will of God.[127] The prophet as such possessed greater authority of biblical interpretation than did the teacher.[128] The New Testament indicates that women too exercised this function of spiritual endowment as the daughters of Philip illustrate (Acts 21:9). Paul expresses the desire in 1 Cor. 11:2-16 that women and men who have the gift of prophecy exercise that gift decently and in order.

1 Corinthians 14:34-36

"Let the women keep silent in the churches" appears to conflict on the surface with 1 Cor. 11:2-16 where Paul permitted women to speak by praying and prophesying. One solution contends that 1 Cor. 14:34-36 represents a non-Pauline interpolation.[129] Or, Paul was inconsistent—he changed his mind.[130] 1 Cor. 11:2-16 does not give women permission to speak, so no conflict exists.[131] Chapter 11 refers to private services while chapter 14 refers to public services.[132] 1 Cor. 14:34-35 represents a quotation from the letter Paul is answering. It expresses the mind of the men Paul chides in verse 36 and not the opinion of the Apostle.[133] None of these options deals with the text and its context adequately.

The better efforts at resolving the apparent disagreement between the two passages attempt to determine the particular form of participation or speaking to which Paul refers since he has already permitted praying and prophesying. Again, several choices exist. Paul forbids women to speak in tongues.[134] Paul prohibits women teachers and their attempt to resolve problems in the church.[135] Those women who disturbed worship by their frequent questions and other interruptions should keep quiet.[136] Finally, Paul was counteracting the vocal, emotional aspect of the pagan mystery cults where women held important roles.[137]

In trying to interpret these three verses, one must pay attention to the context. 1 Cor. 14:26-36 gives rules for church worship. Verse 26 serves as an introduction and expresses the principle that all things should be done for edification. Verses 27-28 deal with regulations for tongues; verses 29-33, for prophets; verses 34-36, for wives.[138] Two clues in these verses point to the fact that Paul addresses wives here. The most obvious clue is the reference to the husbands of these women, τοὺς ἰδίους ἄνδρας. The second concerns ὑποτασσέσθωσαν. This voluntary submission characterizes the wife-husband relationship.

Why does Paul desire wives to be silent and to question their husbands at home? The Apostle implies by his directives here that the wives were asking their husbands questions in the worship setting. What made this undesirable? Again, one must consider the context. In the verses immediately preceding these injunctions for wives, Paul has given instructions for prophets and prophesying in worship. This part of worship included the evaluation and exploration of the prophets' messages. At this point wives should be silent.

> I Cor. 14:34-5 represents the application, in a particular cultural context, of an order of the present creation concerning the conduct of a wife *vis-a-vis* her husband. It reflects a situation in which the husband is participating in the prophetic ministries of a Christian meeting. In this context the coparticipation of his wife, which may involve her publicly "testing" (διακρίνειν, 14:29) her husband's message, is considered to be a disgraceful (αἰσχρόν) disregard of him, of accepted priorities, and of her own wifely role. For these reasons it is prohibited.[139]

The prohibition has nothing to do with ecclesiastical authority.[140] Paul's concern here centers in maintaining the wife-husband relationship even when both spouses participate together in worship. Wives should exercise their gifts in a way that does not involve the violation of their husbands' headship.[141] In the particular instance here, this means their silence while their husbands' prophecy was being discussed and tested. Consequently, σιγάτωσαν does not refer to complete silence on the part of wives or women in general but to the testing of the prophets. Other uses of σιγάω in this passage (verses 28, 30) also refer to specific situations and not silence in other ways of participating in worship.

Paul's appeal to the law may not have had a specific text in mind, although most commentators saw it as pointing to the Genesis narratives.[142] The Old Testament pattern affirmed the husband as the head of the family. The Apostle addresses the rhetorical questions of verse 36 to the entire congregation demanding that they recognize his instructions as words from the Lord.[143] Worship should be done properly and in an orderly manner (verse 40). It should not disrupt family relationships.

Ephesians 5:21-33[144]

Eph. 5:21-33 represents a central passage on the wife-husband relationship. Verse 21 establishes the context of the entire passage: mutual submission. This leads to an understanding of marriage in which no spouse has superiority over the other. Instead, both wife and husband are substantially equal. One should not confuse Christian submission with docile servility or subservience. After all, the same word applies to Christ's relationship to God.[145] Paul's use of ὑποτάσσω correlates the motivation of submission as love for Christ. In fact, ἀγάπη cannot exist apart from submission. The submissive spirit enables the renouncing of one's own will for the sake of others and the giving of precedence to others.[146]

Twice in this passage Paul exhorts wives to be subject to their husbands (verses 22, 24). They render this submission "as to the Lord," that is, as part of their obedience to Jesus Christ. The middle voice of both the elliptical ὑποτασσόμενοι and the stated ὑποτάσσεται leaves the initiation for submissive behavior with the wives themselves.

> Wives, in the autonomous responsibility for their own conduct under God, are expected to order their lives in voluntary adjustment to their husbands as rightful head of the family.[147]

One notes with interest that Paul does not use the word "obey" in reference to the wives' relation to their husbands.[148] The truths that wives' submission stems from their own voluntary initiative and grounds itself in their relationship to Christ elevates the submission concept and frees it from negative connotations which cause hostility and rejection on the part of some women. Although ὑποτάσσω is a military term describing the subordination of an inferior to a superior officer,[149] the context here, and especially Paul's exhortation to husbands, belies any "chain-of-command" theory.[150]

Although the passage exhorts women twice to be submissive, husbands are told three times to love their wives (verses 25, 28, 33). The main emphasis of the entire passage focuses on the husbands' obligation to love their wives.[151] Before Paul develops the nature of that love, he restates that the husband is the head of the wife. For this reason, the wife should submit herself to him. As previously discussed, κεφαλή means more than ἀρχή and less than ἄρχων or κύριος. The culture of that time already perceived the husband as head of the wife. "The Greek husband had nearly absolute power over his wife. . . . he erred in precisely this area—the misuse of superior power by degrading and misusing his wife."[152] Paul redefines headship for the husband in terms of ἀγάπη and uses the example of Christ himself for the husband's model. Christ expressed his headship by his total self-giving, cherishing, self-sacrificing, nourishing, and saving rather than through exercising authority, rule, and dominance.[153] Christ's relation to the church sets the ideal and standard for the wife and husband. The husband should treat his wife with the same kind of consideration he gives himself. Paul supports this view further by recalling the original ideal for marriage in Gen. 2:24. The love of a man for his wife must transcend that which he has for his parents, leading him to leave the latter and "be glued" to his wife. "One flesh" implies total life partnership and personal commitment.

Verses 32-33 show Paul "recognizing the difficulty of his standard and then reaffirming it with emphasis."[154] In Christian marriage both spouses have responsibilities to one another. The fact that Paul uses marriage as an illustration of the relationship between Christ and the church reflects the high value placed on marriage and, consequently, on the proper relationship between wife and husband. This positive emphasis on marriage may reflect a criticism of the Cybele-Artemis tradition. Paul's stress on self-giving, total love, and respect contradicts a merely sexual, mercantile, or utilitarian concept of marriage. Marriage does not center in fertility and childbearing. Thus, the Christian church protects and esteems women much more than did the Artemis cult.[155]

Conclusion

An examination of Paul's relationships with and teachings about women show him to be a consistent champion for the liberation and equality of women. He worked side by side with women fellow ministers and commended their work. He affirmed women's spiritual equality with men before God. He elevated the status of wives in the marital relationship. He did insist on the importance of maintaining the proper wife-husband relationship even in the context of the church and its worship. Paul should be cleared of the negative charges brought against him concerning the roles of women. He did not consider the place of women a problem. He did, however, deal with problems related to women as they learned to express their newly found freedom in Christ in a manner consistent with the Christian faith.

Women in the General Epistles

One passage in the General Epistles has significance for the current study, 1 Pet. 3:1-7. Basically, Peter affirms the same emphases as does Paul. Women should be submissive to their husbands even if these men are unbelievers. The principles of modesty and decency and of expression of inner conviction and character can possibly lead to the salvation of pagan husbands. Verse 7 teaches that though women are generally weaker physically and for the most part socially inferior to men, in the realm of grace equality prevails. Peter cautions husbands not to abuse their positions as heads of the family.[156]

Conclusion

What understanding does this New Testament context bring to 1 Tim. 2:9-15? The New Testament affirms the place of women in the life and ministry of the church and shows them in a variety of roles. Jesus accepted women as disciples equally with men. He gave them the significant responsibility of bearing witness to his resurrection. Paul also acknowledged women as ministers and coworkers in the work of the Gospel. He allowed women to exercise their gifts in the churches. In the worship context, Paul insisted that women do nothing in their participation that would negate or jeopardize their relationships with their husbands. This principle could probably be extended beyond the worship context. Married women in ministry should not deny nor ignore their responsibilities to their husbands. Although Priscilla may have been the dominant personality in her marriage as well as the more effective minister nowhere does the New Testament indicate that she embarrassed or criticized Aquila. Also in the worship setting, Paul required that female-male sexual distinctions be maintained. Those converts from the mystery religions had to abandon those behaviors and appearances that clouded their witness as believers in Jesus Christ.

With the examination of the broader historical and biblical contexts complete, it is now time to turn to the narrower, more specific contexts of 1 Tim. 2:9-15.

NOTES

1. This chapter purposes to provide a New Testament context for 1 Tim. 2:9-15. The reader is urged to consult endnote entries for more extensive materials.

2. Hurley, *Man and Woman*, 82.

3. Bertil Gärtner, "*Didaskolos*: The Office, Man, and Woman in the New Testament," *Concordia Journal* 8 (March 1982): 53. Leonard Swidler described Jesus as a "feminist" which he defined as a
"person who is in favour of, and who promotes the equality of women with men, a person who advocates and practices treating women primarily as human persons (as men are so treated) and willingly contravenes social customs in so acting."
"Jesus Was a Feminist," *South East Asia Journal of Theology* 13 (1971): 102. According to this definition, the portrait of Jesus painted by the Gospels does in fact depict him as a "feminist." For a refutation of this view see Ochshorn, *Female Experience*, 168-71, 224.

4. Alicia Craig Faxon, *Woman and Jesus* (Philadelphia: United Church Press, 1973), 11; Hurley, *Man and Woman*, 83; Jewett, *Man as Male and Female*, 94.

5. Swidler stated in *Biblical Affirmations*, 189,
". . . the woman's being a Samaritan more than doubled the shocking quality of Jesus' conversation with her, and especially his taking a drink from her, for she was considered certainly ritually unclean since customarily Jews considered Samaritan woman as menstruants (and hence unclean: Lev 15:19) from their cradle!"

6. Witherington, *Women in the Ministry*, 77-78; Swidler, "Jesus Was a Feminist," 107.

7. Matt. 16:13-16; Mark 8:27-29; Luke 9:18-20. John's Gospel does not include Peter's confession. See Raymond E. Brown, "Roles of Women in the Fourth Gospel," *Theological Studies* 36 (1975): 693.

8. For a discussion of Mary, Martha, and other women, see Elisabeth Moltmann-Wendel, *The Women around Jesus*, trans. John Bowden (New York: Crossword Publishing Co., 1982).

9. Eugene H. Maly, "Women and the Gospel of Luke," *Biblical Theology Bulletin* 10 (1980): 104.

10. Witherington, *Women in the Ministry*, 114, 116-17; Hurley, *Man and Woman*, 90-91.

11. Ryrie, *Role of Women*, 32.

12. Ibid., 38; Hurley, *Man and Woman*, 92; Stephen B. Clark, *Man and Woman in Christ: An Examination of the Roles of Men and Women in Light of Scripture and the Social Sciences* (Ann Arbor, Mich.: Servant Books, 1980), 247.

13. Elisabeth S. Fiorenza, "The Twelve," in *Women Priests: A Catholic Commentary on the Vatican Declaration*, ed. Leonard Swidler and Arlene Swidler (New York: Paulist Press, 1977), 120.

14. See Elisabeth S. Fiorenza, "The Apostleship of Women in Early Christianity," in *Women Priests*, ed. Swidler and Swidler, 136-39.

15. Stagg and Stagg, *Women in the World of Jesus*, 123-25. The Staggs seemed to indicate that the selection of the Twelve did indicate male bias: ". . . even in the example of Jesus there is not a complete overcoming of male bias." 123.

16. Cf. Luke 22:30; Swidler, *Biblical Affirmations*, 289; Stagg and Stagg, *Women in the World of Jesus*, 124.

17. J. Leipoldt, *Jesus und die Frauen*, (Leipzig, 1921), 26, quoted in Fritz Zerbst, *The Office of Woman in the Church: A Study in Practical Theology* (St. Louis: Concordia Publishing House, 1955), 20. See also Lee Anna Starr, *The Bible Status of Woman* (New York: Fleming H. Revell Co., 1926), 174.

18. For example, the disciples criticized Mary for anointing Jesus' feet (Mark 14:4-5). They expressed surprise at Jesus' conversing with the Samaritan woman (John 4:27). They did not believe the women's story about the resurrection (Luke 24:10-11).

19. See chapter 1, p. 23. "If Jesus commands that a woman's testimony be accepted, can we deny that women might be called to witness to the Gospel in the church?" Bruce D. Chilton, "The Gospel of Jesus and the Ministry of Women," *The Modern Churchman* 22 (1978-79): 20.

20. Mary C. Detrick, "Jesus and Women," *Brethren Life and Thought* 22 (Summer 1977): 160.

21. See Swidler, *Biblical Affirmations*, 198-204.

22. Jewett, *Man as Male and Female*, 102. These parables include the woman using leaven (Matt. 13:33), the ten maidens (Matt. 25:1-13), the woman who lost a coin (Luke 15:8-10), and the assertive widow (Luke 18:1-8). In the parable of the lost coin, the woman portrays God himself, an extraordinary implication for the first-century Jewish culture. Swidler, *Biblical Affirmations*, 170-72. Jesus also applied female imagery to himself. See Matt. 23:37, Luke 13:34, and the chapter "Jesus and the Mother Hen Image," in Rachel Conrad Wahlberg, *Jesus and the Freed Woman* (New York: Paulist Press, 1978), 89-103.

23. Hurley, *Man and Woman*, 109-10; Witherington, *Women in the Ministry*, 78; Swidler, "Jesus Was a Feminist," 106.

24. Swidler, *Biblical Affirmations*, 173-74.

25. Hurley, *Man and Woman*, 97-105.

26. Stagg and Stagg, *Women in the World of Jesus*, 135. See also Swidler, *Biblical Affirmations*, 173-76.

27. Detrick, *Jesus and Women*, 158.

28. Swidler, *Biblical Affirmations*, 193.

29. See Ben Witherington, III, "On the Road with Mary Magdalene, Joanna, Susanna, and Other Disciples—Luke 8:1-3," *Zeitschrift für die neutestamentliche Wissenschaft und die Kunde der alteren Kirche* 70 (1979): 247.

30. See Richard Boldrey and Joyce Boldrey, *Chauvinist or Feminist? Paul's View of Women* (Grand Rapids: Baker Book House, 1976). House identified three approaches to Paul's thinking about women: Paul as a misogynist, Paul as a philogynist, and Paul as a theological schizophrenic (that is, as both Jewish rabbi and Christian). "Paul, Women and Contemporary Evangelical Feminism," 40-44.

31. Mollenkott, *Women, Men and the Bible*, 104. Daly dismissed Paul altogether. *Beyond God the Father*, 5.

32. Robin Scroggs, "Paul and the Eschatological Woman," *Journal of the American Academy of Religion* 40 (September 1972): 283.

33. Elisabeth S. Fiorenza, "Women in the Pre-Pauline and Pauline Churches," *Union Seminary Quarterly Review* 33 (Spring-Summer 1978): 156; Scroggs, "Paul and the Eschatological Woman," 294.

34. *TDNT*, s.v. "κόπος, κοπιάω," by F. Hauck, 3 (1965): 827-30.

35. W. Derek Thomas, "The Place of Women in the Church at Philippi," *Expository Times* 83 (1972): 118-19; *TDNT*, s.v. "ἀθλέω," by E. Stauffer, 1:167-68.

36. Fiorenza, "Women in the Pre-Pauline and Pauline Churches," 156.

37. Jean Daniélou, *The Ministry of Women in the Early Church*, trans. Glyn Simon (Leighton Buzzard, England: The Faith Press, 1974), 7; T. B. Allworthy, *Women in the Apostolic Church: A Critical Study of the Evidence in the New Testament for the Prominence of Women in Early Christianity* (Cambridge: W. Heffer and Sons, Ltd., 1917), 54.

38. Elisabeth Schüssler Fiorenza, "Word, Spirit and Power: Women in Early Christian Communities," in *Women of Spirit: Female Leadership in the Jewish and Christian Traditions*, ed. Rosemary Ruether and Eleanor McLaughlin (New York: Simon and Schuster, 1979), 33.

39. Thomas, "Place of Women," 117-18, 120. Greenlaw gave the prominence of women as one of the six distinctive features of the Philippian church. "Some Factors Contributing to the Distinctiveness," 96.

40. Four of these women have been previously mentioned. See 79-80.

41. Hurley, *Man and Woman*, 122.

42. *TDNT*, s.v. "διακονέω, διακονία, διάκονος," by Hermann W. Beyer, 2 (1964): 93.

43. Fiorenza, *In Memory of Her*, 170. Edgar J. Goodspeed stated that Phoebe needed this introductory letter so that she, as a woman traveling alone, would have places to stay in Ephesus. "Phoebe's Letter of Introduction," *Harvard Theological Review* 44 (January 1951): 55-57.

44. Exegetes have ascribed both a Roman and Ephesian destination for Phoebe. See Bruce, *Paul: Apostle of the Heart Set Free*, 385-89.

45. Fiorenza, *In Memory of Her*, 170. Examples of commentators and translations which use "deaconess" included C. E. B. Cranfield, *A Critical and Exegetical Commentary on the Epistle to the Romans*, 2 vols., in the *International Critical Commentary*, ed. J. A. Emerton and C. E. B. Cranfield (Edinburgh: T. and T. Clark, Ltd., 1979), 2:781; C. K. Barrett, *A Commentary on the Epistle to the Romans*, in *Black's New Testament Commentaries*, ed. Henry Chadwick (London: Adam and Charles Black, 1957), 282; RSV; JB; Williams; Wuest; and Berkeley. More English translations, however, preferred the word "servant" or equivalents such as "worker" or "helper." See AV, NASB, NIV, NKJV, TEV, Dartmouth, Moulton, Beck

("worked"), and Goodspeed ("helper"). The only time the AV translates διάκονος as "servant" is in reference to Phoebe. See J. B. Smith, *Greek-English Concordance to the New Testament* (Scottdale, Pa.: Herald Press, 1955), 84, word 1249, "διάκονος." Several of the more recent translations such as the NASB and NIV adopted the word "servant" for many of the other appearances of διάκονος in addition to Rom. 16:1. The minority word choice for translating διάκονος among English versions has been "minister." These translations included Tyndale, Montgomery, NEB ("who holds office in the congregation"), and New World Translation. One modern paraphrase was unique in its rendering which bears little resemblance to the Greek text: "a dear Christian woman from the town of Cenchrae" (LB). English translations were not consistent in their rendering of the word διάκονος. Approximately seven references exist which link διάκονος to an individual's name: Phoebe (Rom. 16:1), Paul and Apollos (1 Cor. 3:5), Tychicus (Eph. 6:21; Col. 4:7), Epaphras (Col. 1:7), Paul (Col. 1:23), and Timothy (1 Tim. 4:6). The NASB identified only Tychicus (Eph. 6:21) and Paul (Col. 1:12) as "ministers." The NIV named only Tychicus (Col. 4:7) and Timothy (1 Tim. 4:6) as "ministers." The RSV described all as "ministers" except Phoebe ("deaconess") and Paul and Apollos when named together (1 Cor. 3:5). Why should there be such inconsistency since the contexts do not vary significantly?

46. E. Earle Ellis, "Paul and His Co-Workers," *New Testament Studies* 17 (July 1971): 442.

47. See Margaret E. Howe, *Women and Church Leadership* (Grand Rapids: Zondervan Publishing House, 1982), 30-32.

48. Fiorenza, *In Memory of Her*, 170-71. Ernst Käsemann observed,
"Insofar as Phoebe has a permanent and recognized ministry, as is emphasized by the participle [οὖσαν] and the place name [τῆς ἐκκλησίας τῆς ἐν Κεγχρεαῖς], one may at least see an early stage of what later became the ecclesiastical office. . . ." *Commentary on Romans*, trans. and ed. Geoffrey W. Bromiley (Grand Rapids: William B. Eerdmans Publishing Co., 1980), 411.

49. William F. Arndt, F. Wilbur Gingrich, and Frederick W. Danker, *A Greek-English Lexicon of the New Testament*, 2nd ed., trans. and adap. of Walter Bauer's *Griechisch-Deutsche Wörterbuch zu den Schriften des Neuen Testaments und der ubrigen urchristlichen Literatur* (Chicago: University of Chicago Press, 1979), s.v. "προστάτις," 718. Hereafter this work is abbreviated *BAGD*.

50. James Hope Moulton and George Milligan, *The Vocabulary of the Greek Testament Illustrated from the Papyri and Other Non-literary Sources*, reprint ed. (Grand Rapids: William B. Eerdmans Publishing Co., 1963), s.v. "προστάτις," 551. Hereafter this work is abbreviated *MM*.

51. Bushnell, *God's Word to Women*, sec. 367-68.

52. Cranfield, *Romans*, 2:783.

53. NASB. See also NIV ("great help") and AV ("succourer").

54. See Fiorenza, *In Memory of Her*, 181-82.

55. It was not exceptional for Greek women to hold office. No Greek would have doubted that Phoebe had some official position. See Gillian Clark, "The Women at Corinth," *Theology* 85 (July 1982): 259.

56. Contra Ryrie, *Role of Women*, 88.

57. George W. Knight, III, *The New Testament Teaching on the Role Relationship of Men and Women* (Grand Rapids: Baker Book House, 1977), 51.

58. Allworthy, *Women in the Apostolic Church*, 79.

59. Fiorenza, "Word, Spirit and Power," 34.

60. Chrysostom *Homily 31 on Romans*, in the *Nicene and Post-Nicene Fathers of the Christian Church*, first series, 12 vols., ed. Philip Schaff (New York: The Christian Literature Co., 1889), 11:555.

61. Examples of this view included Ryrie, *Role of Women*, 55-56, and Susan T. Foh, *Women and the Word of God: A Response to Biblical Feminism* (Grand Rapids: Baker Book House, 1979), 97 n. 16. Hurley said that if Junia was a missionary, she communicated the gospel only to women. *Man and Woman*, 122.

62. For a convincing argument, see Bernadette Brooten, "Junia . . . Outstanding Among the Apostles (Romans 16:7)," in *Women Priests*, ed. Swidler and Swidler, 141-44. See also Howe, *Women and Church Leadership*, 33-35, and Starr, *Bible Status of Woman*, 269-72.

63. Adherents of this view included G. B. Caird, "Paul and Women's Liberty," *Bulletin of the John Rylands Library* 54 (Spring 1972): 268-81; Elaine H. Pagels, "Paul and Women: A Response to Recent Discussion," *Journal of the American Academy of Religion* 42 (September 1974): 539-40; Meeks, "Image of the Androgyne," 185; Stendahl, *The Bible and the Role of Women*, 32; Herman N. Ridderbos, *The Epistle of Paul to the Churches of Galatia*, in *The New International Commentary on the New Testament*, trans. Henry Zylstra (Grand Rapids: William B. Eerdmans Publishing Co., 1953), 149; Jewett, *Man as Male and Female*, 144; and Gerstenberger and Schrage, *Man and Woman*, 150.

64. Proponents of this perspective included: John Jefferson Davis, "Some Reflections on Galatians 3:28, Sexual Roles and Biblical Hermeneutics," *Journal of the Evangelical Theological Society* 19 (Summer 1976): 202; Knight, "Male and Female," 13-17; House, "Paul, Women," 52; Ernest de Witt Burton, *A Critical and Exegetical Commentary on the Epistle to the Galatians*, in the *International Critical Commentary* (Edinburgh: T. and T. Clark, 1921; reprint 1975), 206; Hurley, *Man and Woman*, 126-28; Foh, *Women and the Word*, 140-41; Ryrie, *Role of Women*, 70.

65. See Clark, *Man and Woman in Christ*, 151. Madeleine Boucher contended that equality before God and inferiority in the social order are in harmony in the New Testament. The tension results from the modern person's inability to hold these two ideas together. "Some Unexplored Parallels to 1 Corinthians 11:11-12 and Galatians 3:28," *The Catholic Biblical Quarterly* 31 (January 1969): 50-58.

66. The difference between the initiatory rites of Judaism and Christianity illustrates the "superior Christian equality of spiritual privilege." Ryrie, *Role of Women*, 210. Circumcision was limited to males only. Women and men alike could participate in baptism.
> "This generated a fundamental change, not only in their [women's] standing before God but also in their ecclesial-social status and function, because in Judaism religious differences according to the law were also expressed in communal behavior and social practice."
Fiorenza, *In Memory of Her*, 210.

67. See Meeks, "Image of the Androgyne," 180-81; S. Scott Bartchy, "Power, Submission and Sexual Identity among the Early Christians," in *Essays on New Testament Christianity: A Festschrift in Honor of Dean E. Walker*, ed. C. Robert Wetzel (Cincinnati: Standard Publishing, 1978), 58.

68. Bartchy, "Power, Submission and Sexual Identity," 58; Leslie, "Concept of Woman," 32. Ben Witherington, III, noted that this saying was also known in a Gentile context. "Rite and Rights for Women—Galatians 3:28," *New Testament Studies* 27 (October 1981): 594.

69. Meeks, "Image of the Androgyne," 197.

70. See chapter 3, pp. 55, 70 n. 39.

71. See Witherington, "Rite and Rights," 599, 601.

72. J. E. Crouch, *The Origin and Intention of the Colossian Haustafel* (Göttingen: Vandenhoeck and Ruprecht, 1972), 144.

73. Caird, "Paul and Women's Liberty," 273.

74. Pagels, "Paul and Women," 539-40; Duncan, *Galatians*, 124.

75. See Foh, *Women and the Word*, 140.

76. Discussions of the Jew-Gentile and slave-free pairs are beyond the scope of this book. For such discussions, see Clark, *Man and Woman in Christ*, 149-60, and Jewett, *Man as Male and Female*, 144-46. One note needs to be made as to the implementation of the equality expressed in Gal. 3:28. Paul labored for the breaking down of the barriers between Jews and Gentiles. Why was he more cautious with the slave-free and women-men distinctions? Paul's reservations found their basis in his eschatological framework. He expected the eschaton immediately. The Apostle did not feel the pressure to change the present social situation of slaves and women in a world that was passing away. Also, from the perspective of the larger society the Jewish-Gentile division represented only a sectarian dispute. Social upheaval would have resulted had Paul proclaimed the abolition in Christ of the basic structures of the Hellenistic society. See Pagels, "Paul and Women," 545-46, and Sakenfeld, "Bible and Women," 230-31.

77. Witherington, "Rite and Rights," 600.

78. See chapter 3, pp. 56-57. The "order of creation" is discussed in relation to this verse because the words "neither male *and* female" breaks the pattern of the other two pairs, "neither-nor," and reflects the technical terms for female and male used in the LXX of Gen. 1:27. For further discussion of this aspect, see Leslie, "Concept of Woman," 34-36; Stendahl, *Bible and the Role*, 32; Fiorenza, *In Memory of Her*, 211; and Jewett, *Man as Male and Female*, 142.

79. Many maintained a distinction between the "order of creation" and the "order of redemption." See discussion in Fiorenza, *In Memory of Her*, 206.

80. Knight, *New Testament Teaching*, 20.

81. Stendahl erroneously claimed that Gal. 3:28 points to the overcoming of the division of creation between female and male. *Bible and Role of Women*, 32.

82. Jewett, *Man as Male and Female*, 143; Stagg and Stagg, *Woman in the World of Jesus*, 163.

83. Sakenfeld, "Bible and Women," 229.

84. Witherington, "Rite and Rights," 600.

85. This discussion accepts Pauline authorship of 1 Cor. 11:2-16 and rejects the theory that it represents a post-Pauline interpolation. No manuscript evidence indicates that this was an interpolation. For evidence from those advocating the passage's non-Pauline, interpolated character, see William O. Walker, "1 Corinthians 11:2-16 and Paul's Views Regarding

Women," *Journal of Biblical Literature* 94 (March 1975): 94-110; Lamar Cope, "1 Corinthians 11:2-16: One Step Further," *Journal of Biblical Literature* 97 (September 1978): 435-36; John P. Meier, "On the Veiling of Hermeneutics," *The Catholic Biblical Quarterly* 49 (April 1978): 212-26; and Garry W. Trompf, "On Attitudes toward Women in Paul and Paulinist Literature: 1 Cor. 11:3-16 and Its Context," *The Catholic Biblical Quarterly* 42 (April 1980): 196-215. For a refutation of this view, see Jerome O. Murphy-O'Connor, "The Non-Pauline Character of 1 Corinthians 11:2-16?" *Journal of Biblical Literature* 95 (December 1976): 615-21.

86. Scroggs, "Paul and the Eschatological Woman," 297.

87. For a history of the interpretation of this passage, see Linda Mercadante, *From Hierarchy to Equality: A Comparison of Past and Present Interpretations of 1 Corinthians 11:2-16 in Relation to the Changing Status of Women in Society* (Vancouver, B.C.: Regent College, 1978).

88. See Zerbst, *Office of Woman*, 33-35.

89. Stephen Bedale, "The Meaning of *Kephalē* in the Pauline Epistles," *Journal of Theological Studies* 5 (October 1954): 212-13.

90. Ibid., 214.

91. Those advocating this view included: Scroggs, "Paul and the Eschatological Woman," 300-301; Fred D. Layman, "Male Headship in Paul's Thought," *Wesleyan Theological Journal* 15 (Spring 1980): 56; Boldrey and Boldrey, *Chauvinist or Feminist?* 34.

92. Those espousing this view believed that the use of κεφαλή sets forth a hierarchical social structure in God's economy based on the order of creation. See Bruce K. Waltke, "1 Corinthians 11:2-16: An Interpretation," *Bibliotheca Sacra* 135 (January-March 1978): 48; Noel Weeks, "Of Silence and Head Covering," *Westminster Theological Journal* 35 (1972): 21-23; Hurley, *Man and Woman*, 167.

93. Leslie, "Concept of Woman," 97-100.

94. See F. W. Grosheide, *Commentary in the First Epistle to the Corinthians*, in *The New International Commentary on the New Testament*, ed. N. B. Stonehouse (Grand Rapids: William B. Eerdmans, 1953), 252-53; F. F. Bruce, *1 and 2 Corinthians*, in *The New Century Bible* (London: Oliphants, 1971), 104-5; Scroggs, "Paul and the Eschatological Woman," 301; Stagg and Stagg, *Women in the World of Jesus*, 175; Jewett, *Man as Male and Female*, 53-56; Andre Feuillet, "La dignité et le rôle de la femme d'après quelques textes pauliniens: comparaison avec l'ancien testament," *New Testament Studies* 21 (January 1975): 159-62.

95. Space hinders development of these arguments here, including the types of hair styles. See James B.Hurley, "Did Paul Require Veils or the Silence of Women? A Consideration of 1 Cor. 11:2-16 and 1 Cor. 14:33b-36," *Westminster Theological Journal* 35 (Winter 1973): 191-204; W. J. Martin, "1 Corinthians 11:2-16: An Interpretation," in *Apostolic History and the Gospel: Biblical and Historical Essays Presented to F. F. Bruce on His 60th Birthday*, ed. W. W. Gasque and R. P. Martin (Grand Rapids: William B. Eerdmans Publishing Co., 1970), 231-34; Jerome Murphy-O'Connor, "Sex and Logic in 1 Corinthians 11:2-16," *The Catholic Biblical Quarterly* 42 (October 1980): 482-500; and S. A. Reynolds, "On Head Coverings," *Westminster Theological Journal* 36 (1973): 90-91.

96. J. P. V. D. Balsdon described these coiffures. "Women in Imperial Rome," *History Today* 10 (1960): 24-31.

97. Annie Jaubert, "Le voile des femmes (1 Cor. XI:2- 16)," *New Testament Studies* 18 (July 1972): 425.

98. Murphy-O'Connor, "Sex and Logic," 489; Hurley, "Did Paul Require Veils?" 197-99.

99. Jaubert, "Le voile," 424; Richard Kroeger and Catherine Clark Kroeger, "An Inquiry into Evidence of Maenadism in the Corinthian Congregation," *Society of Biblical Literature Seminar Papers* 14 (1978): 2:332-34. The Kroegers identified Corinth as a major center of the Dionysiac cult. They noted that this cult featured pagan feasts where drunkenness prevailed and extramarital sex was considered sacramental. The Corinthians had problems in these areas. See also Fiorenza, "Women in the Pre-Pauline and Pauline Churches," 159, and Bruce, *1 and 2 Corinthians*, 104-5.

100. Charles Hodge, *An Exposition of the First Epistle to the Corinthians* (Grand Rapids: William B. Eerdmans Publishing Co., 1950), 209; Hurley, *Man and Woman*, 171.

101. J. Keir Howard, "Neither Male Nor Female: An Examination of the Status of Women in the New Testament," *Evangelical Quarterly* 55 (January 1983): 35; Layman, "Male Headship," 58.

102. For instance, the priests of Cybele adopted female attire and wore long hair. Willoughby, *Pagan Regeneration*, 127; James, *Cult of the Mother-Goddess*, 168.

103. See Murphy-O'Connor, "Sex and Logic," 490; Sigountos, "Public Roles for Women," 284; Robin J. Scroggs, "Paul and the Eschatological Woman Revisited," *Journal of the American Academy of Religion* 42 (September 1974): 536; Layman, "Male Headship," 56-59.

104. Leslie, "Concept of Woman," 107.

105. Gen. 2:23; see Leslie, "Concept of Woman," 106; Boldrey and Boldrey, *Chauvinist or Feminist?* 37.

106. The Kroegers maintained that Paul's use of διά here gives a positive, affirming emphasis and combats Greek ideas that women were made from inferior sources. Richard Kroeger and Catherine Clark Kroeger, "St. Paul's Treatment of Misogyny, Gynephobia, and Sex Segregation in 1 Cor. 11:2-16," *Society of Biblical Literature Seminar Papers* 17 (1979): 2:214-15.

107. Andre Feuillet saw "honor" as the best meaning for δόξα. Woman is the "honor" of man, that is, his glory and his pride. "L'homme 'glorie de Dieu' et la Femme 'glorie de l'homme,'" *Revue Biblique* 81 (April 1974): 161-82.

108. Hurley believed that man images God and woman does not in the sense that man has authority over his wife just as God has dominion over creation. *Man and Woman*, 173. Morna D. Hooker represented a common view of those following the "veil" interpretation. The veil which depicts "the effacement of man's glory in the presence of God" enables the woman also, with the glory of man hidden, to reflect the glory of God. "Authority on Her Head: An Examination of 1 Corinthians 11:10," *New Testament Studies* 10 (April 1964): 413-16. Women in worship should be covered to hide humanity's glory. See also Leslie, "Concept of Woman," 107-8.

109. Hans Lietzmann, *An die Korinther I, II*, 4th ed., compl. W. G. Kümmel (Tübingen: Mohr, 1949), 55.

110. William M. Ramsay, *The Cities of St. Paul, Their Influence on His Life and Thought* (1907; reprint ed., Grand Rapids: Baker Book House, 1960), 204.

111. Grosheide, *First Corinthians*, 253; Hodge, *First Corinthians*, 211. See also translations such as TEV, Moffatt, and Living Bible.

112. Hooker, "Authority on Her Head," 416; Boldrey and Boldrey, *Chauvinist or Feminist?* 39; Feuillet, "La dignité et le rôle," 160.

113. Leslie, "Concept of Woman," 110.

114. Caird, "Paul and Women's Liberty," 277.

115. See J. A. Fitzmyer, "A Feature of Qumran Angelology and the Angels of I Corinthians XI:10," *New Testament Studies* 4 (October 1957): 57; Hurley, *Man and Woman*, 177; Hooker, "Authority on Her Head," 413.

116. Scroggs, "Paul and the Eschatological Woman," 302; Hurley, *Man and Woman*, 178. Josef Kurzinger believed χωρίς of verse 11 should be translated as "different" or "distinct from." He translated verse 11 as, "However, neither is the woman different from the man nor the man different from the woman in the Lord." "Frau und Mann nach 1 Kor. 11, 11f," *Biblische Zeitschrift* 22 (1978): 270-275.

117. See Howard, "Neither Male Nor Female," 37, and Hurley, *Man and Woman*, 184.

118. Some writers, therefore, believed that even today women should wear head-coverings during worship. Waltke, "1 Cor. 11:2-16," 57.

119. Murphy-O'Connor suggested that the belief in the elimination of sexual distinctions resulted from an over-realized eschatology. "Sex and Logic," 490. Others thought gnostic beliefs which did eliminate sexual differences caused this attitude at Corinth. See Layman, "Male Headship," 59.

120. Howard, "Neither Male Nor Female," 33.

121. Ryrie stated this was probably limited to the Corinthian congregation. *Role of Women*, 77. Weeks contended that the passage actually teaches that women should not pray or prophesy. He believed verse 5 should read: "Every woman praying or prophesying, by means of the unveiling of the head, dishonors her head." "Of Silence and Head Covering," 26.

122. Blum, "Office of Woman," 178, would answer "yes." Waltke stated that this charismatic prophecy no longer exists. "1 Cor. 11:2-16," 57.

123. Daniélou, *Ministry of Women*, 9.

124. David Hill, "Christian Prophets as Teachers or Instructors in the Church," in *Prophetic Vocation in the New Testament and Today*, ed. J. Panagopoulos (Leiden: E. J. Brill, 1977), 110.

125. Ibid., 114, 128.

126. Ibid., 123; E. Earle Ellis, "Prophecy in the New Testament Church and Today," in *Prophetic Vocation*, ed. J. Panagopoulos, 51.

127. Hill, "Christian Prophets," 123, 128; *TDNT*, s.v. "προφήτης, etc.," by Gerhard Friedrick, 6 (1968): 854.

128. Ellis, "Prophecy in the New Testament Church," 51.

129. See Feuillet's review of these arguments, "La dignité et le rôle," 162-70. This discussion accepts Pauline authorship. E. Earle Ellis believed 1 Cor. 14:34-35 to be a marginal note by Paul himself. See "The Silenced Wives of Corinth (I Cor. 14:34-5)," in *New Testament Textual Criticism: Its Significance for Exegesis*, ed. by Eldon Jay Epp and Gordon D. Fee (Oxford: Clarendon Press, 1981), 213-20.

130. Thomas Charles Edwards, *The First Epistle to the Corinthians* (London: Hodder and Stoughton, 1885), 381.

131. Weeks, "Of Silence and Head Covering," 26.

132. Hodge, *First Corinthians*, 305; Grosheide, *First Corinthians*, 341-42.

133. Neal M. Flanagan, "Did Paul Put Down Women in 1 Cor. 14:34-36?" *Biblical Theology Bulletin* 11 (1981): 10-12. Note Montgomery's translation of verse 34: "In your congregation" [you write], "as in all the churches of the saints, let the women keep silence in the churches, for they are not permitted to speak. . . ." Montgomery included the bracketed words as indicated.

134. M. R. DeHaan, *Studies in 1 Corinthians* (Grand Rapids: Zondervan Publishing House, 1956), 121-23.

135. Feuillet, "La dignité et le rôle," 166-67; Jon Zens, "Aspects of Female Priesthood: A Focus on 1 Cor. 11:2-16 and 1 Cor. 14:34-35," *Baptist Reformation Review* 10 (1981): 9.

136. *TDNT*, s.v. "γυνή," by Oepke, 1:788; Howard, "Neither Male Nor Female," 38

137. House, "Tongues and the Mystery Religions of Corinth," 141; Kroeger and Kroeger, "Inquiry into Evidence of Maenadism," 334-35; Richard Kroeger and Catherine Clark Kroeger, "Pandemonium and Silence at Corinth," *The Reformed Journal* 28 (June 1978): 9-10. Consequently, the Kroegers interpreted ὑποτασσέσθωσαν as "let them control themselves." See 9.

138. See Fiorenza, *In Memory of Her*, 230; Hurley, *Man and Woman*, 189-90. Hurley saw verses 34-36 as applying to women in general.

139. Ellis, "Silenced Wives of Corinth," 218.

140. Contra Hurley's view. *Man and Woman*, 190-91.

141. Witherington, *Women in the Ministry*, 129; see also Sigountos, "Public Roles for Women," 284.

142. For example see, Bruce, *1 and 2 Corinthians*, 135-36.

143. Hurley, "Did Paul Require Veils?" 218.

144. Eph. 5:21-22 parallels Col. 2:18-21. Only the former passage will be discussed here.

145. Gerstenberger and Schrage, *Woman and Man*, 196-97.

146. Layman, "Male Headship," 55.

147. William Owen Carver, *The Glory of God in the Christian Calling* (Nashville: Broadman Press, 1949), 168. See also 166-67. David Fennema preferred "devotion" as a better translation than "subjection." This emphasizes the wife's giving herself completely to her husband. "Unity in Marriage: Ephesians 5:21-22," *Reformed Review* 25 (Autumn 1971): 65.

148. See Zerbst, *Office of Woman*, 77. ὑποκούετε is used for both children (Eph. 6:1) and slaves (6:5).

149. Ray Summers, *Ephesians: Pattern for Christian Living* (Nashville: Broadman Press, 1960), 120.

150. Bartchy observed that the chain-of-command theory of family relationships reinforces the pagan *patria postestas* model of power. "Power, Submission and Sexual Identity," 78. Fiorenza believed that Paul formulated his injunctions here for wives to be submissive to their

husbands as a political argument to show that the Christian community did not undermine the patriarchal-social Greco-Roman order.   See "The Biblical Roots for the Discipleship of Equals," *The Duke Divinity School Review* 45 (Spring 1980): 89.

151. Carver, *Glory of God*, 171; Leslie, "Concept of Woman," 233. Layman stated that this emphasis on husbands is radically new and innovative. "Male Headship," 55.

152. Patricia Gundry, *Heirs Together* (Grand Rapids: Zondervan Publishing House, 1980), 96.

153. Layman, "Male Headship," 54.

154. Carver, *Glory of God*, 173.

155. Barth, "Traditions in Ephesians," 16.

156. David L. Balch believed that the conduct expressed in 1 Pet. 3:1-7 as well as the other household codes represented the desired norm in Greco-Roman society. See *Let Wives Be Submissive: The Domestic Code in 1 Peter*, Society of Biblical Literature Monograph Series (Chico, Calif.: Scholars Press, 1981). The Domestic Code as expressed by Peter and Paul was motivated by one's relationship to Jesus Christ. It tried to correct the abuse of freedom by some converts to the Christian faith. See Stagg and Stagg, *Woman in the World of Jesus*, 187-89, 203-4.

CHAPTER V

THE PASTORAL EPISTLES' CONTEXT

The concentric circles of contexts for understanding 1 Tim. 2:9-15 have narrowed considerably. Now the discussion focuses on a more immediate context for the passage, the Pastoral Epistles themselves. The broader circles of cultural, religious, Old Testament, and New Testament contexts form only the background for interpreting these epistles. What do the epistles themselves have to say which will clarify the meaning of the passage?[1]

In order to understand this specific context, two questions need an answer. First, why were the Pastoral Epistles written? Paul may have included 1 Tim. 2:9-15 because of his overall purpose in writing these epistles. Since one purpose of the Pastorals relates to dealing with false teachers,[2] a second question involves the content of their false teachings. What was the nature of the heresy attacked in this correspondence?[3] Does a relationship exist between this heresy and the content of 1 Tim. 2:9-15?

The Purpose of the Pastorals

In determining the intent of these writings, the interpreter should consider their "*ad hoc*" nature. These epistles represent pieces "of correspondence occasioned by a set of specific historical circumstances, either from the recipient's or author's side—or both."[4] What was happening in the Ephesian congregation that prompted Paul to pen these epistles? A reading of these letters suggests several recurring concerns—the proper conduct of church members and the correct response to false teachings in the church. Most commentators accepted either one or both of these matters as relating to the purpose. Variations, however, do exist.

1 Timothy 3:14-15 reflects the key verses for those preferring encouragement of the proper conduct of church members as the motivation behind these letters.

> I am writing these things to you, hoping to come to you before long; but in case I am delayed, *I write* so that you may know how one ought to conduct himself in the household of God, which is the church of the living God, the pillar and support of the truth.[5]

The Apostle Paul directly relates the conduct of believers in the church to the perception of that conduct by unbelievers. Concern for the opinion of contemporary society permeates these three epistles.[6] For example, the ἐπίσκοπος "must have a good reputation with those outside *the church*" (1 Tim. 3:7). The Apostle wants the νεωτέρας to do those things which would "give the enemy no occasion for reproach" (1 Tim. 5:14). The δοῦλοι need to regard their own masters "as worthy of all honor so that the name of God and *our* doctrine may not be spoken against" (1 Tim. 6:1; Titus 2:10). Older women are to encourage the νέας to act such that "the word of God may not be dishonored" (Titus 2:5). Finally, Paul urges the νεωτέρους to behave in such a way that "the opponent may be put to shame, having nothing bad to say about us" (Titus 2:8). As these examples imply, the Pastoral Epistles offer guidance for the proper conduct of church members according to their various official positions or social stations in the church.[7] The Apostle desires his words to "build up a high standard of Christian character and intercourse in the Church as the family of God. . . ."[8]

A view which slightly modifies the above purpose of the Pastorals sees the epistles as providing a handbook for church leaders.[9] For example, Paul details instructions on the character and duties of the bishop/over-seer.[10] This approach perceives the Pastoral Epistles as "basically a church manual whose concern is to set the church in order."[11] This modification of purpose, however, still uses 1 Tim. 3:15 as its key verse. Also, the character qualities Paul enumerates for these leaders can serve as characteristics of Christians in general.

The second repeated concern in the Pastoral Epistles centers in the false teaching. Two interpreters observed that "approximately one-third" of the material in 1 Timothy alone deals with heresy.[12] Therefore, a primary purpose of the Pastorals focuses on stopping the false teachers.[13] The key verse for this position is 1 Tim. 1:3.

> As I urged you upon my departure for Macedonia, remain on at Ephesus, in order that you may instruct certain men not to teach strange doctrines, . . .[14]

The Ephesian church had a grave emergency at hand. Heresy seriously threatened the congregation. Paul writes in order to protect the faith and morals of the believers against the corrupting invasion of the false teaching.[15] The deep joys of Christian freedom "had turned sour" under the influence of these treacherous teachers.[16] As the main verse above denotes, the epistles authorize Timothy[17] to oppose the deceivers and their followers. As indicated previously, the city of Ephesus was important for missionary strategy. The church in this key center had to root out errors that could filter throughout the entire Asian province.[18]

Several exegetes discerned a different purpose in the Pastorals derived from the many references to heretical teaching and appeal to sound doctrine. This aim centers in asserting or maintaining the Pauline tradition.[19] This view accepts a later date for the writing of the Pastorals by a "Paulinist." This person responded to the threat of heresy by reaffirming the doctrines of the Apostle Paul. A curious variation of this view contends that the "author of the Pastoral Epistles wrote in Paul's name in order to counteract the image of Paul as given in stories told by women."[20] The "stories told by women" actually refer to the Acts of Paul.[21] According to this theory, celibate women in Asia Minor related the stories found in the Acts of Paul.[22] The Pastoral Epistles were composed to denounce Paul as depicted in these legendary traditions. The characteristics of this Paul matched those of the false teachers in the Pastorals. For instance in the Acts of Paul, the Apostle commissioned a woman to teach and told women that only the continent would obtain salvation. In contrast, the Paul of the Pastoral Epistles apparently forbade women to teach and stated that they would achieve salvation by bearing children.[23] The author of the Pastorals wanted to show that the socially radical Paul of the legends distorted the genuine Paul. This writer also wanted to silence these women who related these "old wives' tales."[24] Thus, this hypothesis also focuses the purpose of the three Pastoral Letters on maintaining Pauline traditions though for very distinctive reasons.

Actually, these two purposes—how Christians should conduct

themselves and the need to refute false teaching—do not necessarily exclude one another. They can be seen as two facets of the same goal. The opponents of sound doctrine caused social disruption in the church. Their teachings were confusing church members about how believers ought to behave. Paul handled this situation by outlining the true nature of Christian living and by equipping church leaders to promote the cause of ortho-doxy.[25] The question that now arises concerns the relation of 1 Tim. 2:9-15 to these two interrelated purposes. Were Christian women involved in misconduct that would promote outside criticism? Did women believers participate in some way with the heretics and their propaganda? Such questions demand an answer in order to interpret the passage. To respond to these questions, however, necessitates a closer look at the nature of the heresy attacked in the Pastorals and its adherents.

The Nature of the Heresy Attacked in the Pastorals

How would one describe the heresy attacked in the Pastoral Epistles? Basically, these three related letters do not fully describe nor refute false teachings as such. Paul's strictures on those who favored these deceptive instructions deals almost exclusively with their character and the methods they adopted and not with their beliefs. He directs his polemic against the general contentiousness and loose living promoted by these teachings and those who espoused them. Consequently, this makes it difficult to identify or label the heresy attacked in the Pastorals.[26] This does explain, however, the two-pronged purpose of Paul in writing to Timothy and Titus.

The heretical teaching confronted by the church at Ephesus produced moral behavior and attitudes incompatible with the godliness which should characterize Christians. Such behavior obviously did not contribute to spiritual health.[27] Several passages paint the character of those following the false teaching. For example, 2 Tim. 3:2-4 piles up a series of unfavor-able adjectives and nouns to describe these people:[28]

> For men will be lovers of self, lovers of money, boastful, arrogant, revilers, disobedient to parents, ungrateful, unholy, unloving, irreconcil-able, malicious gossips, without self-control, brutal, haters of good, treacherous, reckless, conceited, lovers of pleasure rather than lovers of God; . . .

φίλαυτοι of verse 3 stands in sharp contrast to φιλόθεοι of verse 4. Within this antithesis lay the root problem of the false teachers. They did not have the true center of life. "Self has taken the place of God, so all sense of the duty to others, whether man or God, disappears."[29] When self has replaced God as the nucleus of life, the vices listed in these verses naturally result.

A second passage further emphasizes the self-oriented nature of these teachers. Paul describes the one who advocates a different doctrine:

> he is conceited *and* understands nothing; but he has a morbid interest in controversial questions and disputes about words, out of which arise envy, strife, abusive language, evil suspicions, and constant friction between men of depraved mind and deprived of the truth, who suppose that godliness is a means of gain. . . . But those who want to get rich fall into temptation and a snare and many foolish and harmful desires which plunge men into ruin and destruction. For the love of money is a root of all sorts of evil, and some by longing for it have wandered away from the faith, and pierced themselves with many a pang (1 Tim. 6:4-5, 9-10).

τετύφωται (verse 4) reveals the selfish orientation of these heretics, an orientation that leads to other vices. The final indictment of the character of the false teachers centers in their greed. They had come to believe that religion was the way to become rich. They thought godliness was "a means of financial gain—just like the religious hucksters of the Artemis cult (Acts 19:23-41)."[30] Paul voices this same thought in Titus 1:11 where he portrays these rebellious persons as "teaching things they should not *teach*, for the sake of sordid gain."[31]

By way of contrast, in enumerating the qualifications of the ἐπίσκοπος and διάκονος the Apostle specifically notes that such leaders should be "free from the love of money" and not "fond of sordid gain" (1 Tim. 3:3, 8). In fact, all the instructions for church leaders stand in sharp contradistinction to what is said about the false teachers. Paul's lists do not specify the *duties* of these leaders but their *qualifications* in terms of outward, observable behavior. This evidences a concern for the reputation of the church as reflected by her leaders and their conduct. The actions of the false teachers do not measure up to the standards Paul has set forth. They brought the gospel into disrepute by their ungodly behavior.[32]

What behavior did these attitudes of the false teachers mentioned above produce? Primarily, their greed and self-centeredness caused them to stray from the faith. Paul repeats this theme throughout the Pastoral Epistles.[33] The heretics had missed the mark,[34] deviating from the gospel of Jesus Christ and the Apostle's sound teachings. They turned instead to Satan (1 Tim. 1:20; 5:15). Their self-exaltation displaced the Lord.

By turning away from the truth, these errant ones opened themselves to all kinds of distortions. They turned to non-Christian teachings to fill the void they had chosen to create. These teachings stemmed from deceitful spirits and doctrines of demons (1 Tim. 4:1). The heretics participated in teaching a different doctrine (ἑτεροδιδασκαλεῖν, 1 Tim. 1:3; 6:3). Speculations (ἐκζητήσεις) for them involved myths and endless genealogies (1 Tim. 1:4; Titus 1:14;3:9).[35] Paul links these genealogies with foolish controversies (μωρὰς ζητήσεις), strifes (ἔριν), and disputes about the Law (μάχας νομικὰς, Titus 3:9).[36] The adjectives alone used to describe their "discussions" tell of the futility of such activities. This kind of talk was unprofitable and worthless (ἀνωφελεῖς καὶ μάταιοι, Titus 3:9), useless (ἐπ' οὐδὲν χρήσιμον, 2 Tim. 2:14), caused quarrels (μάχας, 2 Tim. 2:23), and led to ruin (ἐπὶ καταστροφῇ, 2 Tim. 2:14). One concludes from this that the false teaching confronting the church held danger "more because of its irrelevance than because of its falseness."[37] However, its adherents had rejected the faith which made it a serious threat indeed. The conflicts they caused did little to promote Christian love, church unity, and the spread of the gospel.

What did these rebellious men and empty talkers (ἀνυπότακτοι, ματαιολόγοι, Titus 1:10) propose in their speculations? As previously mentioned, the Pastoral Epistles delineate very few details of the actual content of their false teachings. Some false teachers did forbid marriage and encouraged abstaining from certain foods (1 Tim. 4:3). Such advice upset whole families (Titus 1:11). What family would not be upset upon learning that marriage hindered spiritual perfection? Under such influence, some wives probably became proud, arrogant, and convinced that they should not live with their husbands.[38] This would explain why Paul encourages marriage in the Pastoral Epistles, such as for the younger widows (1 Tim. 5:14). He refutes this heretical nonsense by affirming the goodness of God's creation (1 Tim. 4:4-5). Some of the heretics also taught that the resurrection had already taken place (2 Tim. 2:18). Beyond these specific teachings, Paul's mention of the law (1 Tim. 1:7-10; Titus 1:14) perhaps indicates some preoccupation with the law and its interpretation.

Despite the unorthodox promotion of ascetic tendencies in the Ephesian congregation, there also appeared to be a more licentious element.[39] This libertarian trend included unlawful acts, the indecent dress by women, and the licentiousness (σπαταλῶσα), idleness, and gossip of widows (1 Tim. 1:8-10; 2:9-10; 5:6-15). Based on their prominence in these activities, women seemed to be at the forefront of the libertarian element.[40] Some of the heretical teachers evidently took advantage of women in the church. They found a fruitful field among some of them:[41]

> For among them are those who enter into households and captivate weak women weighted down with sins, led on by various impulses, always learning and never able to come to the knowledge of the truth (2 Tim. 3:6-7).

These two verses indicate that the heretical teachings had indeed influenced certain women at Ephesus. These women had become involved in learning and perhaps even disseminating false teaching.[42] Paul describes such women by employing the diminuitive of γυνή, γυναικάρια, which the NASB version cited above renders "weak women." The force of this pejorative connotes contempt or scorn.[43] These women were little, silly, or foolish. γυναικάρια is best translated by using these latter adjectives, "little, silly women," as opposed to "weak women."[44] This guards against reading into the passage the "myth of feminine evil" which views women as more prone to sin than men.[45] Some commentators, however, still insisted on this fallacy of viewing women as the most impressionable or impulsive.[46]

> La conversion au christianisme de . . . femmes devait demander beaucoup de précautions et de prudence, car leurs engouements pour le premier prophète venu, ou pour l'hypocrite qui cache bien son jeu, rendaient fragile leur perseverance.[47]

If the Ephesian female believers were not more inclined to sin than men, why did they accept the heretics and embrace their teachings? What made them targets or victims for these deceivers? Women, as well as men, possessed a religious hunger that charlatans would be quick to manipulate for their own advantage.[48] The active religious ambience of the city of Ephesus as well as the participation of non-Christian women in the pagan cults promoted or intensified the spiritual longings of all women dwelling in the metropolis. The less-than-satisfying social position of women in Greco-Roman society[49] also contributed to the feminine susceptibility. The seclusion of many women as well as their little if any education would foster credulity on the their part.[50] The heretics' tactics of entering households would suggest the particularly wealthy nature of these women —a not unlikely fact in the commercial center of Ephesus. Women of wealth had few duties to occupy their time and found themselves fairly restricted to their homes. They would be flattered and delighted by the attention of "spiritual leaders." The quacks' strategy involved beginning with the women in order to win entire households. Once a mistress was convinced to embrace new doctrines, she would influence other household members to do the same. Such women converts would also assist in the financial support of these charlatans who loved money.[51] This suscepti-bility on the part of women resulted not from any inherent weakness in their nature as females. Their cultural socialization and the fluid religious milieu of Ephesus led to their gullibility as "little, silly women."

Paul utilizes the word αἰχμαλωτίζοντες (2 Tim. 3:6) to describe what the false teachers did to women. αἰχμαλωτίζω represents a military term for imprisonment in war. The Apostle applies it here figuratively to the inner moral and religious struggle of the silly women.[52] The heretics took these women captive. The ones who did this were called οἱ ἐνδύ-νοντες. This does not present a positive image. They crept in by insinuating themselves into these homes.[53] They "wormed their way into" families.[54] The impure motives of these charlatans made them resort to cunning and underhanded means.[55] Paul's characterization of them as deceivers is well justified.[56]

The Apostle's description of the women who succumbed to these deceptions does not flatter. He depicts these women as σεσωρευμένα ἁμαρτίαις. This metaphor suggests the idea of being so covered with sin that they could not struggle out of it.[57] The sins of these women weighed them down. Perhaps they were conscience-stricken by the genuine guilt of a sinful past. The burdens they brought with them when they became Christians overwhelmed these women. Their lives possessed two current realities—the guilty memory of the past and the strong power of old habits. They were immature in the Christian faith. Consequently, they welcomed teachers who professed esoteric knowledge of ways to receive absolution. Unfortunately, the tutelage of the false teachers did not provide the help these women needed. Apart from the sound doctrines of Jesus Christ they would have only greater bondage.[58]

Paul further portrays the silly women as ἀγόμενα ἐπιθυμίαις ποικίλαις.[59] They were swayed by various impulses. This included sensual desires and the desire for novelties and the name of "learned women."[60] The new doctrines excited them. They enjoyed the reputation of being learned women and feeling themselves important. Their "learning" enabled them to patronize other believers, including teachers and perhaps their own husbands.[61]

The tragedy of this situation for these women is illustrated by the words of 2 Tim. 3:7, "always learning and never able to come to the knowledge of the truth." Though they heard the heretics sympathetically, they could not make up their minds about the rightness or wrongness of what they heard.[62] These women quested for sensational rather than serious information. One commentator stated that "their minds have become so fickle and warped that they have become incapable of attaining the knowledge of the truth."[63] This appears to be an overstatement despite the Apostle's use of μηδέποτε for emphasis. Paul uses ἐπίγνωσιν for knowledge, that is, "knowledge directed toward a particular object, perceiving, discerning, recognising."[64] The term refers to "full knowledge"[65] of the truth in Christ. The heretics had hypnotized these silly women who possessed no intellectual skills needed "to cut through the fog of words."[66] The Christian message, however, could transform its adherents, making them new creatures. Hope did exist for these women. "A change of heart might still enable them to know. . . ."[67]

The women of Ephesus whom the Apostle describes here had several problems. First, they possessed only rudimentary knowledge of the faith. Second, they had not thoroughly repented or reformed.[68] Perhaps they had not allowed the power of Christ-in-them to abolish their old patterns of life. Perhaps they needed more support and training in their new faith from maturer believers. In the freedom of the Christian community, most of these women, particularly those of Jewish backgrounds, had experienced their first opportunity to become serious students of religious matters. Paul does encourage women to learn (1 Tim. 2:11). 2 Tim. 3:6-7 in no way indicates that the error of these women resided in "craving" what God had forbidden them—"authority, publicity, and masculinity."[69] Despite the fact that this passage and the Pastoral Epistles in general project women as involved in the heretical teachings, the writings also suggest "evidence of the growing importance of women in the Church."[70] Otherwise, why would Paul have felt compelled to deal specifically with the subject of women and their participation in the life of the church?

Some of these women may have been involved in sexual immorality. Several phrases and verses in the Pastorals suggest the possibility of sexual liason,[71] which one would expect of a licentious trend. Paul speaks of a concern for the chastity of women (1 Tim. 2:9-10). He urges the overseer to be faithful to his own wife (1 Tim. 3:2). Timothy should treat younger women as sisters with all purity (1 Tim. 5:6, 11-15). The expressions "burdened with sins" and "various impulses" contain hints of sexual lapses as well as doctrinal error (2 Tim. 3:6).[72] Instructions for young wives urge them to be pure or chaste and husband-lovers (Titus 2:4-5). Certainly the prominence of the sex-oriented mystery cult of Artemis would prompt a social, though non-Christian, acceptability of sexual immorality. Paul, therefore, condemns such waywardness and encourages sexual purity and marital fidelity for the Ephesian believers.

One verse aptly summarizes the foregoing discussion on the character and methodology of the heretics: "They profess to know God, but by *their* deeds they deny *Him*, being detestable and disobedient, and worthless for any good deed" (Titus 1:16). Religion amounted to no more than an empty shell for these false teachers. In fact, they denied the force of true godliness, rejecting its effective power. They did not perceive of the Gospel as a regenerating force.[73] Their self-serving attitudes reflected their poor spiritual condition and unsuitability for service. "Thus lack of real spiritual substance in both the false teachers and their teaching was the foundation of the uselessness of what they promoted."[74] Paul affirms that these charlatans would have no success (2 Tim. 3:9).

After this examination of the heretics, can one now identify who these people were as well as label their heresies? The emergence of these false teachers should have surprised no one. Paul through the Holy Spirit had predicted earlier that "from among your own selves men will arise, speaking perverse things, to draw away the disciples after them" (Acts 20:30). The Pastoral Epistles do depict the realization of this prophecy. Some of the Ephesians' own elders were leading astray the church. The Apostle actually names and excommunicates two of the ringleaders (1 Tim. 1:19-20).[75] Also, that these false teachers had access to female believers in the congregation supports the fact that they were members of the church. When Timothy and other church leaders barred them from teaching openly in church assemblies, they visited the women in their homes.[76] Many house-churches composed the church in Ephesus. Each of these probably had one or more elders. This situation made it easy for various house-churches to go astray by following their errant elders.[77]

The identity of the Pastoral Epistles' opponents based on the nature of their heresies is much more difficult to determine. One scholar listed nineteen possible identifications.[78] An examination of the discussion above reveals two different tendencies dealt with in various parts of the Pastoral Epistles. These are a Jewish element and a Gnostic element.[79] Evidence for Jewish aspects of the false teachings include: professing to be teachers of the Law (1 Tim. 1:7); concern with myths and genealogies (1 Tim. 1:4), specifically Jewish myths (Titus 1:4);[80] reference to those of the circumcision (Titus 1:10); disputes about the Law (Titus 3:9); and speculative exegesis of the Old Testament leading to fanciful interpretations (1 Tim. 1:7-11). Some interpreters saw the teaching of abstinence from certain foods as related to Jewish influence.[81] This Jewish strain tends to indicate that the exponents of such teachings still remained within the church.[82]

A Gnostic element also reveals itself in the Pastoral Epistles. The evidence of these three epistles does not present the coherence and elaboration of the Gnostic systems of the second century A.D.[83] Rather, what Paul repudiates is an embryonic or incipient Gnosticism. Proof of this Gnostic element includes: affirmation of one God and one mediator (1 Tim. 2:5) as opposed to the many emanations of the Gnostics; dualistic tendencies which pronounce creation as evil (1 Tim. 4:1-5); docetic Christology which denies the incarnation and resurrection (1 Tim. 3:16; 2 Tim. 2:8, 18); rejection of or tendency to allegorize the Old Testament (1 Tim. 1:7; 1 Tim. 3:15-17; Titus 1:14);[84] and boast of possessing higher esoteric γνῶσις (1 Tim. 6:20). Actually, the element of dualism not only produced an asceticism which forbade marriage and the eating of certain foods, it also promoted immoral behavior or licentiousness (1 Tim. 5:11-15; 2 Tim. 3:1-7).

When the evidence for these two elements—Jewish and Gnostic—is compiled, one concludes that they are actually two sides of a single unorthodox movement. Paul opposes a gnosticizing form of Jewish Christianity in Ephesus.[85] Although there did exist some conflicting tendencies among the false teachings, Paul nowhere indicates the presence of two opposing factions in the church. He does not appeal for church unity as he would have urged two extremist groups as such.[86]

Could any components of the heretical teaching in the Pastoral Epistles stem from the active Artemis cult in Ephesus with its women participants and goddess-orientation?[87] One possible link resides in the fact that Paul does not attack specific unorthodox doctrines but explicit behaviors. The Artemis mystery religion did inspire both ascetic and immoral behaviors. Perhaps what upset whole families (Titus 1:11) included teachings of sexual abstinence for wives and husbands as a means of salvation. The Mother Goddess required such abstinence. She also desired abstaining from certain foods, another heretical notion proposed in Ephesus. There appeared to be a preoccupation with sex on the part of some of the false teachers as previously indicated.[88] This would fit well with the sexual obsession of the Artemis fertility cult. Some heretics might have practiced mysterious rites.[89] The word "γόητες" (2 Tim. 3:13) could suggest this. The word meant sorcerer.[90] Magical practices formed a part of the Artemis cult in Ephesus. Paul characterizes the women entangled with the Ephesian heretics as "led by various impulses." The emotionalism and experience-orientation of the mystery cult reflected this same kind of nonrational motivation. Perhaps the reference to these women being "weighed down with sins" points back to guilty memories of "sacred" sexual misconduct. Undoubtedly, some of the new Christian converts had once been cultic priestesses. One clear parallel between the practitioners of the Artemis cult and the false teachers of the Ephesian congregation centered in their greed for money and use of religion for financial gain.[91]

Conclusion

The understanding of the Pastoral Epistles' context will aid in interpreting 1 Tim. 2:9-15. This context reveals a syncretic tendency—a gnosticizing form of Jewish Christianity which reflects affinities with the Artemis cult. Such syncretism would have felt comfortable in the city of Ephesus with its heightened and accommodating religious interests. These false teachings did contain factors which will aid in understanding Paul's injunctions concerning women in 1 Tim. 2:9-15. The discussion above mentioned the role of women in the heretical movement and already hinted at possible explanations for the passage derived from such participation. This new perception will now be brought to the last context for 1 Tim. 2:9-15—the passage itself.

NOTES

1. Although the "Pastoral Epistles" denote three distinct letters, these may be treated as a unit due to their common interests. See Walter Lock, *A Critical and Exegetical Commentary on the Pastoral Epistles*, in *The International Critical Commentary*, ed. S. R. Driver, A. Plummer, and C. A. Briggs (Edinburgh: T. and T. Clark, 1924), xiii. The discussions of chapters 5 and 6 will treat the Pastoral Epistles as a unit.

2. See the discussion to follow, pp. 106-8.

3. Only minor differences existed between the false teaching in Ephesus (1 and 2 Timothy) and Crete (Titus). The major features seemed to be common to all three epistles. The teachings at Ephesus and Crete represented separate manifestations of a general contemporary tendency. Donald Guthrie, *The Pastoral Epistles*, in *The Tyndale New Testament Commentaries*, gen. ed. R. V. G. Tasker (Grand Rapids: William B. Eerdmans Publishing Co., 1957), 35.

4. Fee, *1 and 2 Timothy*, xix.

5. The ἵνα of verse 15 begins a purpose clause. H. E. Dana and Julius R. Mantey, *A Manual Grammar of the Greek New Testament* (New York: The Macmillan Company, 1955, c.1927), 248. Although the singular εἰδῇς has Timothy as its subject, the verses do have wider application. Paul actually writes to the Ephesian church through Timothy. The letters turn out to be "all business." Fee, *1 and 2 Timothy*, xxiii. Also, verses 1-13 apply to a broader readership. See Guthrie, *PE*, 87.

6. Bassler, "The Widow's Tale," 31; Fee, *1 and 2 Timothy*, 97.

7. David Verner, *The Household of God: The Social World of the Pastoral Epistles* (Chico, Calif.: Scholars Press, 1983), 1. Verner believed that the Pastorals portray the church as the household of God. Consequently, the church's social structure models itself on the household, the basic social unit in the church. Pascual theorized that the metaphor "Casa de Deu" developed from "la situacio religiosa d'Efeso," in particular "el temple efesia d'Artemis." "El temple efesia d'Artemis," 72.

8. Lock, *PE*, xiii; see also William Barclay, *The Letters to Timothy, Titus, and Philemon*, in *The Daily Study Bible* (Philadelphia: The Westminster Press, 1956), 3.

9. Anthony Tyrrell Hanson, *The Pastoral Epistles*, in the *New Century Bible Commentary*, gen. ed. Matthew Black (Grand Rapids: William B. Eerdmans Publishing Co., 1982), 23.

10. Charles J. Ellicott, *The Pastoral Epistles of St. Paul: With a Critical and Grammatical Commentary, and a Revised Translation*, 3d ed. (London: Gman, Green, Longman, Roberts and Green, 1864), xx.

11. Guthrie, *PE*, 53.

12. Richard Kroeger and Catherine Clark Kroeger, "May Woman Teach? Heresy in the Pastoral Epistles," *Reformed Journal* 30 (October 1980): 15.

13. Fee, *1 and 2 Timothy*, xx.

14. The conjunction ἵνα again introduces a purpose clause. Dana and Mantey, *Manual Grammar*, 248.

15. Burton Scott Easton, *The Pastoral Epistles: Introduction, Translation, Commentary and Word Studies* (New York: Charles Scribner's Sons, 1947), 2; Ellicott, *PE*, xx; Bassler, "Widow's Tale," 31.

16. Bartchy, "Power, Submission and Sexual Identity," 70.

17. Titus is similarly instructed. See Titus 1:5, 10-16.

18. Fee, *1 and 2 Timothy*, 5. Other commentators who listed the opposition of heresy as one of several purposes for the Pastoral Epistles included Hanson, *PE*, 23; William Hendricksen, *Exposition of the Pastoral Epistles*, in the *New Testament Commentary* (Grand Rapids: Baker Book House, 1957), 4l; and Norbert Brox, *Die Pastoralbrief*, in the *Regensburger Neues Testament*, ed. Otto Russ (Regensburg: Verlag Friedrich Pustet, 1969), 15.

19. E. F. Scott, *The Pastoral Epistles*, in *The Moffatt New Testament Commentary*, ed. James Moffatt (London: Hodder and Stoughton, 1936), xxv; Hanson, *PE*, 23.

20. Dennis Ronald MacDonald, *The Legend and the Apostle: The Battle for Paul in Story and Canon* (Philadelphia: The Westminster Press, 1983), 14. MacDonald claimed that women in antiquity were prominent in transmitting myths. See 13.

21. The Acts of Paul, included in the apocryphal writings of the New Testament, were a series of stories about Paul's adventures in Syria, Asia Minor, and Greece. MacDonald, *Legend*, 17. Most New Testament scholars held that the purpose of all of the apocryphal Acts

was to supplement the canonical Acts. They were composed during the second and third centuries. Edgar Hennecke, *New Testament Apocrypha*, Vol. II: *Writings Relating to the Apostles; Apocalypses and Related Subjects*, ed. Wilhelm Schneemelcher, Eng. trans. ed. R. McL. Wilson (Philadelphia: The Westminster Press, 1965), 168. Martin Dibelius and Hans Conzelmann indicated that the Acts of Paul do "point to movements similar to those which must be presupposed for the context" of the Pastoral Epistles' author and opponents. *The Pastoral Epistles*, in *Hermeneia*, ed. Helmut Koester, trans. Philip Bultolph and Adela Yarbro (Philadelphia: Fortress Press, 1972), 48.

22. See chapter 2, "The Storytellers behind the Legends," in MacDonald, *Legend*, 34-53.

23. Ibid., 57-59.

24. Ibid., 77; cf. 1 Tim. 4:7.

25. I. Howard Marshall, "Orthodoxy and Heresy in Earlier Christianity," *Themelios* 2 (1976): 8; Verner, *Household of God*, 1.

26. Arland J. Hultgren and Roger Aus, *I-II Timothy, Titus, II Thessalonians*, in the *Augsburg Commentary on the New Testament* (Minneapolis, Minn.: Augsburg Publishing House, 1984), 45; John Parry, *The Pastoral Epistles with Introduction, Text and Commentary* (Cambridge: University Press, 1920), lxxxii; C. K. Barrett, *The Pastoral Epistles in the New English Bible*, in *The New Clarendon Bible* (Oxford: Clarendon Press, 1963), 12; J. N. D. Kelly, *A Commentary on the Pastoral Epistles*, in *Harper's New Testament Commentaries*, ed. Henry Chadwick (New York: Harper and Row, 1963), 12.

27. Marshall, "Orthodoxy and Heresy," 8.

28. Although 2 Tim. 3:1 introduces this passage as relating to "the last days" and the verses which follow (verses 2-5) employ the future tense, Paul actually has in mind the contemporary moment in Ephesus. "The last days" commonly denotes in the New Testament "the period immediately preceding the consummation of the present age." Paul relates this future time to his own time. Guthrie, *PE*, 156. Paul places the presence of the false teachers at Ephesus "into a broader theological perspective—the eschatological reality that the time of the End, the coming of the New Age, has already been set in motion with the coming of Christ." Fee, *1 and 2 Timothy*, 219. "Timothée est invité à voir dans le corruption de la doctrine et des moeurs, dans la pollulation des docteurs hérétiques . . . qui commencent à surgir . . . une manifestation du mal eschatologique. . . ." Celaus Spicq, *Les Épitres Pastorales*, 2 vols., 4th rev. ed. (Paris: J. Gabalda, 1969), 1:772.

29. Lock, *PE*, 105; see also Spicq, *EP*, 1:773.

30. Fee, *1 and 2 Timothy*, 99.

31. The AV has "for filthy lucre's sake."

32. Fee, *1 and 2 Timothy*, 41-42.

33. The heretics had strayed (ἀστοχήσαντες) from a pure heart, a good conscience, and a sincere faith (1 Tim. 1:5-6); rejected (ἀπωσάμενοι) faith and a good conscience thereby suffering shipwreck in regard to their faith (1 Tim. 1:19); fallen away (ἀποστήσονταί) from the faith (1 Tim. 4:1); gone astray (ἠστόχησαν) from the faith (1 Tim. 6:21); gone astray (ἠστόχησαν) from the truth (2 Tim. 2:18); turned away (ἀποστρεφομένων) from the truth (Titus 1:14).

34. See *BAGD*, s.v. "ἀστοχέω," 118.

35. Titus 1:14 describes the genealogies as ᾿Ιουδαϊκοῖς.

36. Expressions depicting "word battles" or "word games" were often associated with the false teachers: controversial questions and disputes about words (ζητήσεις καὶ λογομαχίας, 1 Tim. 6:4; see also 2 Tim. 2:14; 2:23); profane and empty chatter (βεβήλους κενοφωνίας, 1 Tim. 6:20; 2 Tim. 2:16); and, contradictions of falsely-called knowledge (ἀντιθέσεις τῆς ψευδωνύμου γνώσεως, 1 Tim. 6:20).

37. Guthrie, *PE*, 35.

38. Bartchy, "Power, Submission," 74.

39. Douglas J. Moo denied the existence of evidence for a licentious or libertarian element in the Pastorals. "The Interpretation of 1 Timothy 2:11-15: A Rejoinder," *Trinity Journal* 2 (Fall 1981): 215-16.

40. Philip B. Payne, "Libertarian Women in Ephesus: Response to D. J. Moo's Article,' 1 Timothy 2:11-15: Meaning and Significance,'" *Trinity Journal* 2 (Fall 1981): 185.

41. Fee, *1 and 2 Timothy*, xxi; Robert J. Karris, "The Background and Significance of the Polemic of the Pastoral Epistles," *Journal of Biblical Literature* 92 (December 1973): 554. Scholer contended that the heresy Paul is opposing centers on women in particular. "Exegesis," 8. Although women did participate in the heretical movement, they were not the sole culprits. Those Paul specifically names are all men—Hymenaeus, Alexander, and Philetus (1 Tim. 1:20; 2 Tim. 2:17).

42. French L. Arrington, *Maintaining the Foundations: A Study of I Timothy* (Grand Rapids: Baker Book House, 1982), 68-69.

43. Hillard, *PE*, 95; Fee, *1 and 2 Timothy*, 221.

44. In addition to the NASB, the TEV and RSV also translate the word as "weak women." The NIV uses "weak-willed women"; NKJV, "gullible women"; and NEB, "miserable women." Several translations, such as the AV, JB, and Montgomery do choose "silly women."

45. Leslie, "Concept of Woman," 253-54.

46. See J. P. Lilley, *The Pastoral Epistles: A New Translation with Introduction, Commentary, and Appendix* (Edinburgh: T. and T. Clark, 1901), 205.

47. Stanislas de Lestapis, *L'enigme des Pastorales de Saint Paul* (Paris: J. Gabalda, 1976), 278.

48. Fee, *1 and 2 Timothy*, 221.

49. Ibid. See chapter 1 above.

50. Hanson, *PE*, 145.

51. Leslie, "Concept of Woman," 252. In the second century Irenaeus (A.D. 126-202) described the heretic Marcus who "devoted himself especially to women, and those such as are well-bred and elegantly attired, and of great wealth, whom he frequently seeks to draw after him. . . ." Marcus seduced women for their money. *Against Heresies* 1:13:3, in *The Ante-Nicene Fathers*, ed. Alexander Roberts and James Donaldson, rev. A. Cleveland Cox, 10 vols. (Grand Rapids: William B. Eerdmans Publishing Co., 1979, reprint of 1884-86 ed.), 1:334.

52. *TDNT*, s.v. "αἰχμάλωτος, αἰχμαλωτίζω, etc.," by Gerhard Kittel, 1:196.

53. Joseph Henry Thayer, *A Greek-English Lexicon of the New Testament* (New York: American Book Company, 1886), s.v. "ἐνδύνω," 214.

54. See Moffatt's translation.

55. Leslie, "Concept of Woman," 252; Hillard, *PE*, 96.

56. See 2 Tim. 3:13 and Titus 1:10.

57. Hillard, *PE*, 95.

58. Leslie, "Concept of Woman," 254; Hillard, *PE*, 96.

59. The present participle (ἀγόμενα) suggests "continually led astray or from time to time." Robertson, *Word Pictures*, 4:624.

60. Lock, *PE*, 107.

61. Hillard, *PE*, 95.

62. Leslie, "Concept of Woman," 255.

63. Guthrie, *PE*, 159; cf. 1 Tim. 2:4.

64. Newport J. D. White, "The First and Second Epistles to Timothy and the Epistle to Titus," in *The Expositor's Greek New Testament*, 5 vols., ed. W. Robertson Nicoll (New York: George H. Doran Co., n.d.; reprint ed., Grand Rapids: William B. Eerdmans Publishing Co., 1956), 4:104.

65. Robertson, *Word Pictures*, 4:624.

66. Ibid.

67. Lock, *PE*, 107.

68. Leslie, "Concept of Woman," 256.

69. Henry Allan Ironside, *Timothy, Titus, and Philemon* (Neptune, N.J.: Loizeaux Brothers, Inc., 1947), 218.

70. Hillard, *PE*, 96.

71. Fee, *1 and 2 Timothy*, 222-23.

72. Hanson, *PE*, in *New Century Bible Commentary*, 145.

73. 2 Tim. 3:5; Guthrie, *PE*, 158.

74. Lorin Cranford, "Encountering Heresy: Insight from the Pastoral Epistles," *Southwestern Journal of Theology* 22 (Spring 1980): 34.

75. Fee, *1 and 2 Timothy*, xxi; John J. Gunther, *St. Paul's Opponents and Their Backgrounds: A Study of Apocalyptic and Jewish Sectarian Teachings* (Leiden: E. J. Brill, 1973), 12-13.

76. Leslie, "Concept of Woman," 252.

77. Fee, *1 and 2 Timothy*, xxi. Parry noted that one phenomenon of the first-century world was self-appointed teachers who travelled freely from city to city in the Roman Empire. These teachers offered lectures for a fee on every conceivable subject. These numerous and attractive instructors meant danger during the early stages of the development of the Church where freedom of teaching existed. This custom was gradually brought under control. Parry, *PE*, lxxiiiii. Despite this fact, the evidence in the Pastoral Epistles supports the emergence of the false teachers from within the Ephesian congregation.

78. Gunther, *St. Paul's Opponents*, 4-5.

79. See Barrett, *PE*, 13; Kelly, *PE*, 11; Guthrie, *PE*, 36; Marshall, "Orthodoxy and Heresy," 7; Hillard, *PE*, 38; Hultgren, *I-II Timothy*, 46.

80. For a discussion of Jewish genealogical books, tradition, and exegesis as related to the Pastoral Epistles see Gerhard Kittel, "Die Genealogia der Pastoralbriefe," *Zeitschrift für die Neutestamentliche Wissenschaft* 20 (1921): 49-69. F. H. Colson observed that "myths" and "genealogies" represented accepted and leading terms in technical talk for a large, diletante public. Another public, however, despised these terms as frivolous and useless, such as the writer of the Pastoral Epistles, according to Colson. This view sees the Pastoral author regarding these myths and genealogies not as inherently wicked or heretical but as vain, empty, and likely to divert the mind from higher things. Thus, the polemic of the Pastoral Epistles directs itself against an intellectualism which largely consisted of research which was frivolous, useless, and led to strife and irreligion in practice. "'Myths and Genealogies'—A Note on the Polemic of the Pastoral Epistles," *The Journal of Theological Studies* 19 (January-April 1918): 266-68. Whether or not these terms were catchwords of a widely-favored form of learning, Paul would agree that focus on such things was indeed vain and strife-producing.

81. Payne, "Libertarian Women," 185; Gunther, *St. Paul's Opponents*, 101. Jewish legalism would reinforce such abstinence. Barrett, *PE*, 13.

82. Kelly, *PE*, 12.

83. Arrington, *Maintaining the Foundations*, 21; Kroeger and Kroeger, "May Woman Teach?" 15; Guthrie, *PE*, 37; Colson, "Myths and Genealogies," 271; Kelly, *PE*, 12. Easton, *PE*, 3-5, was representative of scholars who viewed this element as the more developed Gnosticism of the second century.

84. "Myths" and "genealogies" relate both to the Jewish and Gnostic tendencies. Allegorization of the Old Testament did characterize Gnostic systems, but this was also found in first-century Jewish speculation. Guthrie, *PE*, 37; Hultgren, *I-II Timothy*, 47.

85. Kelly, *PE*, 12; Moo, "Interpretation," 216; Barrett, *PE*, 13; Hultgren, *I-II Timothy*, 46-48. Such syncretistic Judaism became a well-known feature of the middle of the first-century in Asia Minor. Moo, "Interpretation," 216. The Colossian heresy contains parallels to that suggested in the Pastoral Epistles, but it was more advanced and destructive. One would have no need to look beyond the first century or even the span of Paul's life for the possibilities of such heresies. Kelly, *PE*, 12.

86. Moo, "Interpretation," 215, 217. Payne did see Paul directing his remarks at two extremist poles in the church. "Libertarian Women," 185. According to this view, the two factions, one Judaizing and one libertarian, actually opposed each other.

87. Of Gunther's nineteen identifications, only two indicated a possible connection with any mystery religion: "Jews influenced by Oriental philosophy" and "Jewish-Christian antinomians and Oriental ascetics." *St. Paul's Opponents*, 4-5.

88. See p. 114 of this chapter.

89. A. R. C. Leaney, *The Epistles to Timothy, Titus and Philemon*, om the *Torch Bible Commentaries*, ed. John Marsh and Alan Richardson (London: SCM Press, Ltd., 1960), 26.

90. *BAGD*, s.v. "γόης," 164.

91. Fee, *1 and 2 Timothy*, 99. Paul's encounter with Demetrius the silversmith at Ephesus showed how commercial interests encouraged devotion to Artemis.

CHAPTER VI

EXEGESIS OF 1 TIMOTHY 2:9-15

---

1 Tim. 2:9-15 stands at the center of all the contexts previously examined. This passage implies that some women were teaching in public worship in the Ephesian church.[1] Such activity must have taken place, or Paul would not have forbidden it.[2] Had conflict erupted over this issue?[3] How does Paul perceive women teachers in the Ephesian church? Does the Apostle have more concern with suppressing the deception of false teachers rather than with defining the role of women during worship?[4] Do Paul's injunctions concerning women teachers apply only to the the first-century church in Ephesus because of the problem there with heretics? An answer to these questions obliges a closer examination and exegesis of 1 Tim. 2:9-15.

The previous discussions analyzed the various contexts surrounding 1 Tim. 2:9-15, but what is the immediate context of the passage itself?

The Context of 1 Timothy 2:9-15

A reading of the passage's adjacent parameters, 1 Timothy 1 and 3, discloses a framework which relates to the heretical elders. 1 Timothy 1 includes a statement of the problem of false teachers and ends with the mention of Paul's excommunication of two of these, Hymenaeus and Alexander. 1 Timothy 3 contains descriptions of several church leaders—ἐπίσκοπος, διάκονος, and γυναῖκες. As noted earlier, these delineations detail qualifications of character which stand in sharp contrast to all that the Pastorals say about the false teachers. Within these heretic-oriented boundaries rests chapter two.

1 Tim. 2:1 contains the co-ordinate conjunction οὖν which probably indicates a continuation of Paul's directives to Timothy in chapter one,[5] directives that encouraged him to fight the good fight and oppose the false teachers.[6] This opening paragraph, 1 Tim. 2:1-8, provides guidance for prayer—the objects of prayer, the theological basis for prayer, and the manner of prayer. One can understand these instructions as responses to the presence of the errant elders in the church. These teachers promoted an elitist or exclusivist mentality among their followers. Consequently, Paul teaches that Christians should pray for *all* people (verses 1-2). A tranquil and quiet life results from such praying (verse 2b). The false teachers did not prompt tranquility and quietness but turmoil and strife. The theological basis for prayer centers in a gospel which is universal in its scope (verses 3-7). This again refutes some kinds of heretical exclusiveness.[7] Finally, in verse 8 Paul depicts the manner in which men ought to pray, "without wrath and dissension," that is, without the characteristics of the false teachers.

Part of the Apostle's theological support for his teaching on prayer centers in the uniqueness of God. In the syncretistic religious environment of Ephesus, Paul needs to affirm the oneness of God and the existence of only one mediator between God and humanity (verse 5). This affirmation may here oppose beliefs belonging to the Artemis cult as well as incipient Gnosticism. That this God is a universal God refutes

> les divinités païennes locales qui n'assurent leur protection et n'accordent leur faveur qu'à une cité ou à un groupe de dévôts, telle Artémis qui est la déesse des Éphésiens (Act. xix, 35).[8]

Jesus Christ, the only mediator between the universal God and humankind, is not like any being in the mysteries nor like any Gnostic aeon mediating between God and the creation.[9]

Therefore, 1 Tim. 2:1-8 relates well to the heretical controversy. This paragraph on prayer also establishes the context for the following paragraph on women. Paul is dealing with worship. Most exegetes believe that the discussion of 1 Timothy 2 applies to public worship, that is, a congregational service.[10] Paul's instructions on prayer, however, could apply to private and individual worship as well.[11]

Verses 8 and 9 take a standard feature of the household codes, the pairing of ἄνδρες with γυναῖκες, and develop it in the new context of church worship.[12] Thus, the passage combines rules for conduct in worship services with rules for daily life.[13] Paul starts his treatment on questions related to women from the context of worship, but as one reads from verse 9 to verse 15 his viewpoint seems to broaden into a wider perspective. One approach proposed that

> . . . not all the regulations appear to have been formulated for the situations into which they have here been placed. Thus the argument in 1 Tim. 2:13-15 applies not to the conduct of women in the worship service, but rather to the position of women in general; and even the instructions in 2:9-12 seem, in part at least, not to apply exclusively to the worship service.[14]

Though the passage does contain general principles related to women, the worship context remains important for understanding the meaning of these verses. Even with the utilization of traditional materials[15] from the household tables, the passage represents more than just "a mosaic of catechetical material and miscellaneous sayings on women."[16] A specific purpose exists for the content and inclusion of this paragraph on women in 1 Timothy.

Does the passage concern women in general or wives? The question arises here as it also does in 1 Corinthians 11 and 14 because γυνή may be translated "woman" or "wife."[17] 1 Tim. 2:9-15 has parallels with 1 Cor. 14:34-36[18] and 1 Pet. 3:1-7[19], both of which relate to wives. Also, the allusions to Genesis 2-3 in verses 13-14 relate to a married couple, Eve and Adam. Therefore, a tentative judgment on these verses suggests that Paul's emphasis here concentrates on wives,[20] although some aspects may apply to all women.

Γυναῖκες and Demeanor in Worship
(verses 9-10)

The false notions circulating in the Ephesian church which prompt Paul to offer some correctives for prayer (verses 1-8) now lead him to consider the behavior of women in worship. Evidently, abuses other than that of praying had entered the worship services.[21] ὡσαύτως (verse 9) links the paragraph on women to the preceding verses, showing that public worship still forms the background for the Apostle's words.[22] Paul continues to give guidance on that manner of Christian worship which makes it distinctive from pagan and heretical practices. This centers on comportment in particular for female believers.

The Greek text does not provide a main verb for verse 9. One must supply βούλομαι from verse 8.[23] Paul desires men to pray (προσεύχεσ-θαι). What does he wish the women to do? Are they also to pray, or does Paul merely focus on their dress? In other words, should two verbs be brought down from verse 8—βούλομαι προσεύχεσθαι? Verse 9 does already contain an infinitive, κοσμεῖν, which would complete the meaning of βούλομαι. Whether or not προσεύχεσθαι also complements βούλο-μαι in verse 9 seems, however, a moot issue. Women did pray in public worship (1 Cor. 11:5) just as men did. Paul has just qualified the manner of praying for men. Now he does so for women. The principles he establishes, however, do not apply exclusively to one sex or the other. For instance, women too should pray "without wrath and dissension" (verse 8). According to a number of commentators, verse 9 proves that women should not participate in public praying.[24] The verse actually indicates the manner in which women should pray in public worship.[25]

Paul uses a series of descriptive words and phrases to delineate how women should participate in worship. They should adorn themselves with "proper clothing" (ἐν καταστολῇ κοσμίῳ). καταστολή means "deport-ment, outward, as it expresses itself in clothing, as well as inward."[26] Verse 9 expresses the outward aspect of that deportment—clothing, while verse 10 presents the inward aspect—character. The adjective κόσμιος signifies "well-arranged," "becoming,"[27] "orderly," or "well-behaved."[28] In the worship setting Christian women are to behave themselves in a becoming, orderly manner. This general principle would certainly apply to all women, both married and single. It possesses a universal timelessness as well.

Now the Apostle further clarifies the general principle above. Women should deport themselves outwardly by dressing "modestly and discreetly" (μετὰ αἰδοῦς καὶ σωφροσύνης). Greek literature often paired αἰδώς and σωφροσύνη as virtues of women who exhibit proper reserve and self-control in sexual matters.[29] αἰδώς only appears here in verse 9 in the New Testament. It relates to a moral feeling of reverence, awe, and respect not only for the feelings and opinions of others but also for one's own conscience. Therefore, it can mean "shame" or "self-respect."[30] The use in verse 9 connotes feminine reserve in matters of sex.[31] σωφροσύνη indicates soundness of mind, prudence, discretion, self-control, and moderation in sensual desires.[32] It relates to the self-mastery of one's

physical appetites.³³   The force of these two words encourages modesty
and chasteness in dress on the part of believing women.³⁴   The use of the
words, however, implies that some very inappropriate behavior in terms of
clothing has taken place in the church at Ephesus.   The sexual nature of this
unbecoming dress would appear natural in the religious milieu of Ephesus
with the Artemis fertility cult.   One would only need to look at the
grotesque form of the Goddess herself to see this.   Such inciting dress,
though, is not natural for a Christian worship setting and should be
avoided.³⁵   Self-control represented a problem for some women in the
Ephesian congregation.   Some felt "sensual desires in disregard of Christ"
(1 Tim. 5:11) and were "led on by various impulses" (2 Tim. 3:6).   The
sensuous clothing of some women probably caused male worshippers to lust
rather than worship God.³⁶   Consequently, Paul encourages the women to
exercise good judgment and decency about their clothes.

Verse 9 contains a further specific definition about modest attire: "not
with braided hair and gold or pearls or costly garments."   Hair style again
becomes a matter of concern in the church.   πλέγμασιν points to elaborate
hair styles which involved pleating and braiding one's hair.   This characterized fashionable, wealthy women of the first century.³⁷   Such styles were
often elaborate and artificial and included false hair and jewelry.³⁸   The
arranging of hair could occupy a large part of women's time and thought.³⁹
The adjective πολυτελεῖ indicates that the garments Paul tries to
discourage were very expensive and costly.⁴⁰   All this points to the
existence of a number of wealthy, noble women in the Ephesian church.⁴¹
The condemnation of the focusing on outward attire by these women is
essential.   One "wearing gold or curled hair and other such things customarily done for empty show, or to provide a seductive appearance, is worthy
of reprimand."⁴²   The prophet Isaiah similarly denounced female extrava-
gance (Isa. 3:16-24).   In addition to the possibility of arousing male
worshippers and misplaced priorities, such ostentation might have made the
poorer members feel inconsequential.⁴³

The strong adversative ἀλλ' which begins verse 10 allows Paul by
way of contrast to present the positive and more important adornment for
women—Christian character.   Women should not depend on externals for
their decoration.   True adornment does not consist of what one puts on but
of that which springs from the heart.⁴⁴   Good works stand as the means by
which believing women should clothe themselves—δι' ἔργων ἀγαθῶν.⁴⁵

Verse 10 does not suggest that good deeds allow one to acquire merit
and subsequently procure salvation (cf. Titus 3:5; 2 Tim. 1:9).   Good works
signal the outcome or outworking of one's salvation.⁴⁶   They befit "women

making a claim to godliness." θεοσέβειαν relates to true religion, the worship of the only true God. Perhaps this signifies a comparison with the heathen priestesses. Certainly Paul's whole effort in verses 9-10 pertains to the demarcation of Christian women from pagan.[47] Women who confess the Christian faith must substantiate this confession with their good works.[48] Belief and practice go together.

The instructions of verses 9-10 have relevance beyond public worship and women. Modest and decent dress, which reflects only one aspect of a godly life, should characterize both women and men on all occasions.[49] The problem at Ephesus centered in the worship setting where women's ostentatious and immodest clothing caused disruptions. Paul encourages the demeanor fitting for Christian women. The Gospel should not be compromised by clothing or other externals.

Γυναῖκες and Participation in Worship
(verses 11-12)

In examining verses 11-12 the interpreter must remember that the context for the entire passage focuses on worship.[50] New Testament worship services probably included more than one preacher. Dialogue and discussion transpired among worshippers, especially in the judging of the prophets (cf. 1 Corinthians 14).[51] This type of worship allowed much more congregational participation on the part of individuals than most twentieth-century churches do. It is with this participation in mind that Paul issues his directives.

Verses 11 and 12 parallel one another and are connected by the co-ordinate conjunction δέ. Verse 11 expresses a positive imperative, while verse 12 supplies a negative statement. μανθανέτω as a present permissive imperative implies continuous action: let a woman continue learning. The verb presupposes that women already participated in public worship. They already were learning. μανθάνω means to learn especially by study.[52] These women were to continue to study the truths of the Christian faith. The study of spiritual truths, though, was a new thing for female believers from a Jewish background. A command for women to learn which even acknowledged that this was already occurring indicates an advance on Judaism. Some of the male Jewish converts might have called for the omission of women from doctrinal instruction. Paul opposes this non-Christian conservatism with his command "let a woman keep on learning."[53] Women, as well as men, need to know the essentials of their faith. Their sex does not excuse nor bar them from learning.[54]

μανθάνω occurs more frequently in the Pastorals than διδάσκω. The learning of wrong ideas and behavior had threatened the faith of the Christian community at Ephesus. Heretical elders had promoted an officious and intellectualistic piety that had attracted women. Female believers were learning deceptive teachings.[55] Those women converted from the Artemis cult brought to the worship setting a noisy boisterousness that did not conduce to learning. Between their own former cultic patterns of behavior and the encouragement of wayward elders, these women represented a problem for Christian worship done decently and in order.

Therefore, Paul qualifies the manner in which women should learn: ἐν ἡσυχία and ἐν πάσῃ ὑποταγῇ. The repetition of ἐν ἡσυχία in verse 12 makes this qualification an important one. ἡσυχία means either "quietness," "rest," or "silence."[56] Total silence on the part of women signifies a problem because women could pray and prophesy aloud (1 Cor. 11:5). Women were not to be "silent learners."[57] "Silence," however, is not the primary meaning of ἡσυχία.[58] Neither does it fit the context here. ἡσυχία does not refer to speech,[59] nor to the "quiet of the home,"[60] but to manner, attitude, or demeanor.

The word in fact refers to the Stoic virtue of inward peace and it follows directly upon the injunctions about dress and deportment. It refers to a quietness of spirit, a gentleness of nature and is the exact equivalent of the "meek and quiet (*hesuchios*) spirit" that women are exhorted to show at 1 Pet. 3:4.[61]

Women should learn with a quiet demeanor. A quiet spirit signifies an attitude of receptivity. It implies learning with respect for the teaching one hears and the teacher who instructs. In verses 11-12 ἐν ἡσυχία does not mean "not speaking." If Paul sought to silence women completely, he would have used σιγάω or σιγή. Instead ἡσυχία defines the spirit required of a learner.[62]

Learning should also take place ἐν πάσῃ ὑποταγῇ. For the first time the noun ὑποταγή appears in the γυνή-ἀνήρ context instead of a middle voice form of ὑποτάσσω. Does this imply that depersonalization has occurred? Does this negate the act of submission as a decision by the woman?[63] The nature of the problem at Ephesus demanded strong words and action. Women had to cease participating in behavior uncharacteristic of and opposed to the household of God. To whom is this submission given? The text remains silent at this point. Based on the New Testament evidence as a whole, including Eph. 5:22, Col. 3:18, Titus 2:5, and 1 Cor. 14:34, one would conclude that Paul refers to the submission of wives to husbands. According to the strict notions of morals in the East, married women could only submit to their husbands and not to other men.[64] The difficulty with the "wives-husbands" view resides in the general nature of the passage up to this point. However, verses 13-15 appear to refer specifically to married women. Also the strong parallelism with 1 Cor. 14:34-36 supports the "wives" view for these verses.

Perhaps, however, ὑποταγή does not refer to a person—one's husband—at all. The context deals with how women should learn. They should learn with a quiet attitude. They should learn with submission to *what is taught*. Since the verb form does not appear here, ὑποταγή best relates to what leaders in the congregation teach.[65] Learning involves submission to the sound teaching that Paul has promoted as opposed to the errant notions of the false teachers.[66] The Apostle wants to stem heresy and the conduct it produced on the part of some women.[67] Thus, verse 11 also applies to women in general. Paul certainly would want the younger widows going from house-church to house-church stirring up trouble to learn quietly and with all submission.[68] Women must exercise restraint even when they seek instruction.[69] In fact, this principle of how to learn applies equally to Christian men.

From the positive command to learn in verse 11 one moves to the negative statements of verse 12. Paul introduces the things denied women by using οὐκ ἐπιτρέπω. Does this first person singular present tense verb imply a gnomic, timeless application[70] or a personal, particular instruction for that specific situation?[71] The use of the present tense alone does not restrict this advice to the first century or to the peculiar circumstances at Ephesus.[72] Paul does not use a timeless qualifier here with the present tense such as "in all the churches" (1 Cor. 11:16; 14:33-34) or "in every place" (1 Tim. 2:8).[73] Yet, when Paul does use the present indicative for exhortations, only two of the twelve occurrences have a universal qualifier.[74] There are instances where Paul distinguishes his "personal advice" from a saying from the Lord (1 Cor. 7:6, 10, 12, 25, 40), but even then these words form a part of Scripture.[75] On the other hand, of the nineteen uses of ἐπιτρέπω in the Greek New Testament only three indicate a continuing effect (Matt. 19:8; Mark 10:4; 1 Cor. 14:34). The other occasions refer to a specific time or to a short, limited time duration as indicated by the context.[76]

Consequently, the grammatical and lexical evidence appears evenly divided. Two other factors do exist. The first argument involves the somewhat similar usage of ἐπιτρέπω in the parallel passage 1 Cor. 14:34-36. There Paul does not permit wives to speak. As this study has previously indicated, this meant silence in a particular part of the worship service by a particular group of people. Though given for that peculiar situation, the underlying principle remains timelessly valid—one's ministry should be consistent with and qualified by one's marriage obligations.[77] The second factor resides in the context of verse 12. In 1 Tim. 2:9-15 Paul again deals with a specific worship problem—unpropitious women in dress, speech, and actions. His instructions which follow οὐκ ἐπιτρέπω continue to deal with the rectification of that problem. Though given as a result of a particular first-century situation, these words do contain abidingly relevant principles.

For the first time in this passage verse 12 pairs a form of γυνή (γυναικί) with a form of ἀνήρ (ἀνδρός). This usually indicates a reference to the wife-husband relationship.[78] The numerous similarities with 1 Cor. 14:34-36, in particular a specific prohibition for wives, again underscores the view that Paul now directs his attention not to women in general but to wives in particular. Verses 13-15 will reinforce this interpretation. With the problems caused in Ephesus by disruptive women, the Apostle writes to qualify further the ministry of married women.[79] Wives were not διδάσκειν or αὐθεντεῖν their own husbands in the worship setting.

Paul gives two prohibitions here. οὐδέ simply joins these two words as a negative conjunction.[80] Although the second prohibition explains and qualifies the first, these exist as two separate interdictions. In other words, διδάσκειν does not equal αὐθεντεῖν.[81] Since διδάσκειν and αὐθεντεῖν are linked by a co-ordinate conjunction, ἀνδρός serves as the direct object for both of these verbs. The nature of the two verbs requires a direct object in the genitive case instead of the accusative case.[82]

Teaching figures as one of the problems in the church at Ephesus since the straying elders are teachers (1 Tim. 1:3; 6:3). The use of the present infinitive, διδάσκειν, with its emphasis on continued action could be translated "to be a teacher."[83] "I do not permit a wife to be her husband's teacher." What did "to teach" or "to be a teacher" signify for Christians in the first century? Teaching in the biblical sense focused on the practical. The New Testament teacher did not have to excel as a technical expert. The teacher stood as one called of God to help people "in understanding the meaning of life in a God-centered world, and to guide them in finding, facing, and fulfilling the divine will."[84] Such an instructor directed teaching toward the whole person, especially the will, in order to shape one's life according to God's will. Every leader of the primitive church was a teacher because of the indispensable nature of this function. Paul ranks teaching as one of the preeminent gifts (1 Cor. 12:28-29; Eph. 4:11; Rom. 12:7). As a charismatic function any believer—female or male—could receive this gift because the Spirit distributes "to each one individually just as He wills" (1 Cor. 12:11).

As the Christian movement spread, the need for this charismatic endowment grew. Also there increased a sense of possessing a Christian past and tradition. The early believers discerned that different persons possessed different gifts of leadership including teaching. This caused certain gradations of prestige and differences of endowment to emerge that did not depend entirely on formal election or official installation. The first-century teacher challenged persons' hearts and wills as well as their minds. Part of the teacher's task included the interpretation and clarification of Scripture.[85] The references to teaching in the Pastoral Epistles seem to possess the sense of the handing down of a fixed body of doctrine or tradition which must be mastered and preserved intact.[86] Paul directs this sound doctrine against the heretical ideas of some leaders in Ephesus.

Did those the church recognized as teachers possess any authority? The answer is yes. The most important basis for this authority resided in its charismatic endowment.[87] Also, the content of New Testament teaching itself—Christian tradition and Scripture interpretation—gave an inherent authority to the instructor.[88] The New Testament does not indicate that the teaching ministry had authority because it was restricted to particular individuals.[89] It does recognize that teaching belongs to the ministries of certain leaders, such as the ἐπίσκοπος (1 Tim. 3:2) and πρεσβύτερος (1 Tim. 5:17). Yet, Paul also identifies the ability to teach as a characteristic of the δοῦλος (2 Tim. 2:24) which represents a designation of Christian leaders in general.

What relevance does this discussion on teaching have for wives in public worship? Women too received the charisma of teaching in the early church. It would be questionable to assume that Priscilla's teaching of Apollos in Ephesus represented an exception. Women participated vocally in mixed worship assemblies in an authoritative manner as prophets (1 Cor. 11:5).[90] Both the prophet and teacher in early Christianity possessed authority. Either both roles were acceptable for women or neither was.[91] In explaining Paul's injunction in verse 12 it does not suffice to say that the role of the teacher in New Testament days represented an authoritative office[92] of one who declared doctrine, and therefore, the New Testament denied women such responsibility. The majority of commentators held the view that teaching in the church was and is to be done by men.[93] Some of them based this view on some doubtful grounds: "Usually a woman's guide is her feelings, and therefore being a creature of impulse, she is disqualified from taking the lead or dominion over the man."[94] Many of these interpreters would allow women to teach other women or children but not men.[95]

The problem with the above approach centers in its neglect of the various contexts for this passage. The religious context for Christian women varied depending on whether or not their conversion was from the Jewish or a pagan religion. The Jews did not even entertain the possibility of women speaking in a synagogue service. At the other extreme, women played a very vocal role in the mystery religion of Artemis.[96] Although some rabbis would not permit women even to teach small children,[97] the Old Testament contexts reveal women who taught and exercised authority over men, such as Deborah and Huldah. The New Testament portrays many women in leadership roles in the church. Paul gives specific instructions for such women in public worship. One would have to conclude that the interpretation held by most commentators based on an official significance for διδάσκειν in verse 12 contradicts the above evidence.

Even more significant for this verse, however, is the context of the Pastoral Epistles themselves. As indicated earlier, women had become involved in the unorthodox teachings. Some had failed to grasp Christian truth and maintain sound doctrinal balance. With their new sense of freedom these women had gone too far. They acquired the arrogant attitude of the false teachers. They were creating confusion.[98] Marriage represented one area of attack by the heretical elders. Paul reminds women of the importance of the marital bond between wife and husband. Being a Christian or a Spirit-endowed teacher does not negate marriage responsibilities. Wives still were to recognize their husbands as κεφαλή and submit themselves. Thus, married women should not teach in public worship when the exercise of that ministry compromises their relation to their husbands.[99]

What does αὐθεντεῖν mean and how does it relate to the above discussion of διδάσκειν? According to standard lexicons, αὐθεντέω means "to have full power or authority over,"[100] "to domineer,"[101] or "to commit a murder."[102] Two closely related nouns are αὐθέντης ("master, autocrat, murderer, suicide, perpetrator") and αὐθεντία ("absolute sway, authority").[103] In a negative sense the latter noun means "irresponsibility, license, high-handedness, and tyranny."[104] Although αὐθεντέω occurs only once in the New Testament, it does appear in the popular vocabulary of its time.[105]

Debate has arisen recently over the meaning of αὐθεντεῖν due to the appearance of an article whose author suggested a unique meaning for the word: "to engage in fertility practices."[106]   This writer presented evidence from ancient texts by writers such as Antiphon, Philo, Euripides, the Wisdom of Solomon, and Chrysostom.   She concluded that "to bear rule" and "to usurp authority" do not appear as meanings for αὐθεντεῖν until the third or fourth century A.D.   What does appear earlier are meanings related to murder or sexual behavior.   She contended that this latter significance relates well to the context of 1 Tim. 2:12. Paul is prohibiting the promulgation of licentious doctrines and practices. Women converts from the cult of Artemis had much to unlearn. Previously they had believed that sexual intercourse brought worshippers into direct communication with their deity. Paul does not want this pagan idea to advance into the church. Also, female teachers among the Greeks were courtesans who made themselves available for a "second occupation" after their lectures. With all this in mind, verse 12 would then read: "I forbid a woman to teach or engage in fertility practices with a man."[107]

Although the above argument "sounded good" relative to the Ephesian context, it did not fare well against scholarly attack.[108] Basically the evidence cited for "to engage in fertility practices" was undocumented and taken out of context. The passages so cited do not require or support a sexual or erotic connotation.[109] Two of the earliest extant occurrences of αὐθεντεῖν in pre-Christian vocabulary do indeed possess the meaning of "to exercise authority."[110] Hence, one must reject this novel translation.

Why does αὐθεντεῖν offer such a problem? Several reasons exist: it is a *hapax legomena* in the New Testament; only a paucity of occurrences prevail in ancient literature; and, scholars do not agree on its etymology. Etymologically, it means either "to murder" or "to exercise authority," as the lexical meanings above have already suggested.[111]   Since these two meanings are so diverse, one must examine the context of the uses. An evaluation of the linguistic data for αὐθεντεῖν indicates the presence of the broad concept of "authority" almost everywhere.[112] The data suggests that the word has a positive connotation without having any overtone of misuse of one's position or power. First centuries B.C. and A.D. documents attest the meaning "to have authority over" with a positive nuance. One concludes that αὐθεντεῖν refers to authority as a neutral concept without any necessary negative connotation.[113] In other words, nothing in the word itself suggests "usurp authority" or "dictatorial rule."[114]

This conclusion does fit the context of 1 Tim. 2:12. The verse links διδάσκειν and αὐθεντεῖν. The former word refers to the activity of teaching without any inherent negative implication. Thus, the same emphasis would also apply to αὐθεντεῖν. Consequently, the preferred translation would be "to have authority over." Both διδάσκειν and αὐθεντεῖν would then be given "neutral" translations. Now, however, one must interpret what "to have authority over" means in the context of the passage and the Pastoral Epistles. It may remain inherently neutral without negative or positive nuances, but the context may dictate either of these connotations.

Several clues suggest a less-than-positive emphasis for αὐθεντεῖν in this context. Verse 11 encourages women, including wives, to learn with a quiet, receptive spirit and with submission to sound doctrine. Being submissive and having authority suggest opposite concepts. Verse 12 repeats the idea of ἐν ἡσυχίᾳ. These qualifiers imply that the opposite, disruptive behavior was taking place in the Ephesian congregation. Just as Paul prohibited wives from teaching their husbands in public worship, so he also forbids them to have authority over their husbands in that same context. "The relationship and function of a woman in the congregation is to be seen in the light of the relationship between man and woman in the family."[115] Wives should participate in worship in a manner consonant with voluntary submission to their husbands.[116]

That Paul finds it necessary to give these directives must mean that the opposite behavior was taking place in Ephesus among some believing wives. At this point one can see the relationship between διδάσκειν and αὐθεντεῖν. Teaching in the first century did contain the idea of authority for both Jews and pagans. For wives to teach their husbands gave the impression that they were "lording it over them."[117] The problem intensified in Ephesus because of the attitude of the false teachers—arrogant and highhanded.[118] Some women, including wives, unfortunately adopted this unchristian disposition. A further complication resided in the fact that the heretics forbade marriage. As a result, some wives publicly demeaned their husbands.[119] Ephesian Christian wives had overstepped their bounds.[120] This behavior had to cease. Paul's instructions in this entire passage reveal his pastoral concern[121] at this point to maintain not only order in church worship but also healthy family relationships in an environment hostile to the same.

Although αὐθεντεῖν remains a neutral word, the context here supplies it with a negative connotation.[122] In and of itself, the word does not mean "to exercise illegitimate authority."[123] Here wives have abused the authority they possess in worship (1 Cor. 11:10) as well as their spiritual gifts and functions. They have dishonored their marriage relationship.

Christian marriage relationships, according to the Apostle, should not reflect the post-Fall discord between woman and man. Verse 12 affirms the same principle underlying 1 Cor. 14:34-36: a wife's marital obligations qualify her ministry in the church. This is not to say, however, that this verse prohibits all women from ever teaching or having authority over men.[124] Biblical precedents, such as Deborah, Huldah, Phoebe, and Priscilla, refute this view.

Γυναῖκες and the Theological Basis for Their Participation in Worship (verses 13-14)

The conjunction γάρ follows verse 12 linking it to verses 13-15. What does γάρ indicate? Scholars have suggested two possible uses here: in the illative sense to express the reason[125] for the injunctions of verses 11-12 or in the explanatory sense to provide an illustration.[126] γάρ most frequently occurs in the illative sense. In this passage it does answer the "why" question.[127] Why does Paul give these instructions? In other passages dealing with women in worship Paul has also utilized the creation accounts to affirm the relationship between wives and husbands (1 Cor. 11:7-9; 14:34). Yet, Paul uses more than the creation narratives here. In verse 14 he also uses the Genesis 3 account of the Fall. Would the Apostle base Christian relationships on the Fall? The approach which views γάρ as explanatory emphasizes Eve as an historical example. She illustrates how serious consequences result when women deceived by heresy convey it to others.[128] A better way of viewing Eve as an illustration focuses on her role as wife. She acted independently at a critical moment in a personal decision that ultimately involved her husband as well.[129] In this sense, γάρ does mean "for example."[130] Eve serves as a negative example of what some Christian wives in Ephesus were probably doing. Consequently, one best sees the conjunction here as serving a dual function—reason and illustration. Whether γάρ is illative or explanatory, verses 13-14 express theological conditions which prohibit wives from teaching and having authority over their husbands in worship.

In using the Genesis narratives, does Paul "distort the Yahwist account"[131] or develop a "bizarre exegesis of Genesis?"[132] The following discussion will answer these questions.

The Apostle employs Eve and Adam as historical figures as well as archetypes for humanity.[133] He points to the creation account as recorded in Genesis 2. With the use of πρῶτος Paul seems to attribute significance to the "order of creation." πρῶτος, in reference to time, means "first, earliest, or earlier."[134]   Instead of viewing this as mere temporal priority, many commentators interpreted this precedence in time as precedence in rank and indicative of Adam's (the husband's) superiority in place and power.   This proves Eve's (the wife's) inferiority and subordination.[135] As one scholar stated it,

> . . . the order in which God created man and woman (Adam and Eve) expresses and determines the relationship God intended and the order of authority. The one formed first is to have dominion, the one formed after and from him is to be in subjection.[136]

Any attempt on the woman's part to assume the role of leader or guide reverses this primal order of creation.[137]

The problem with the above interpretation resides in its contradiction of what the Genesis narratives do teach. Although verse 13 alludes to the Genesis 2 narrative, this does not necessarily minimize the Genesis 1 account which asserts the simultaneous creation of female and male as well as their shared responsibilities in the created world. Genesis 2 does indicate Adam's precedence in time as πρῶτος and εἶτα[138] in verse 13 substantiate. The entire account, Gen. 2:18-25, does not indicate man's superiority. Instead it reveals man's need for the woman, her equality with the man ("fit for him," "bone of my bone"), and the man's responsibility toward the woman ("cleave to his wife"). Adam's precedence places upon him responsibility more than anything else.[139] Paul's teaching on the husband as κεφαλή in the marriage relationship underscores such responsibility. ἀγάπη informs κεφαλή—not ἐξουσία. This understanding also harmonizes better with Jesus' teaching on leadership in Mark 10:43-45.

Why then does Paul employ πρῶτος and εἶτα, thus emphasizing the creation order? The context may offer a clue. All of the topics in 1 Timothy 2 have been given as correctives—the correct objects, basis, and manner of prayer; the appropriate dress and demeanor of worship; the proper attitude for learning; and maintaining the legitimate marital relationship in the exercise of gifts in worship. Does the rationale in verse 13 also serve as a corrective to false understandings in Ephesus? Some wives' disregard of their marriage roles and responsibilities as well as adoption of the haughty attitudes of the heretics necessitated a firm reminder of their duties in marriage. In a religious environment saturated with the "feminine principle" due to the Artemis cult, attitudes of female exaltation or superiority existed. Verse 13 attempts to correct such an emphasis. God formed Adam first, then Eve. This truth would certainly deflate ideas of female superiority. Also, the myths of Cybele and Attis from which the Ephesian Artemis sprang emphasized the creation of the Goddess first, then her male consort.[140] Paul could be affirming the biblical narratives based on historical reality and exposing these fiction-based myths.

Now the Apostle turns to the account of the Fall in Genesis 3. "Adam was not deceived." In Rom. 5:12-21 Paul places the responsibility for the Fall on Adam. 1 Tim. 2:14 does not exculpate Adam but shows that the man deliberately chose to sin.[141] Some interpreters have arrived at some unwarranted conclusions based on verse 14. "Adam is here declared to be without fault in the matter."[142] This contradicts the Romans 5 passage. "It is undoubtedly implied here that man in general has a power of resisting certain kinds of temptation superior to that possessed by woman. . . ."[143] How can this be implied from three Greek words? There also exists the view that Adam exhibited chivalry in his Fall. He fell into transgression out of his love for Eve, preferring to be with her in the place of disapproval than to be alone without her in the place of blessing.[144] This strikes one as the same imaginative reading between the lines of which some feminists are guilty. One other view holds that verse 14a may have represented a saying used by Judaizers to indicate male superiority.[145] One doubts that Paul's use here intends that purpose.

The Apostle has two emphases in verse 14. His use of two forms of ἀπατάω shows a focus on deception. Deception characterized the false teachers in Ephesus (2 Tim. 3:13; Titus 1:10). His second emphasis falls on the woman. "Adam was not deceived" provides the contrast for what is now stated about Eve.

Again, biblical expositors have suggested a number of meanings for verse 14b. One view proposes that this verse reflects a Jewish-Christian tradition. Contemporary Judaism did blame Eve for sin and death entering the human race.[146] Sirach 25:24 states, "From a woman sin had its beginning, and because of her we all die" (RSV). Despite the assertion of Adam's responsibility in Romans 5, Christian writers through the centuries have similarly blamed Eve. Ambrose (fourth century) credited woman as the originator of man's wrongdoing.[147] Chrysostom (fifth century) wrote:

> For the woman taught the man once, and made him guilty of disobedience and wrought our ruin. . . . The woman taught once, and ruined all. On this account therefore he saith, let her not teach . . . for the sex is weak and fickle. . . .[148]

Therefore let her descend from the professor's chair! Those who know
not how to teach, let them learn, he says. If they don't want to learn but
rather want to teach, they destroy both themselves and those who learn
from them. This is the very thing that occurred through the woman's
agency.[149]

Augustine (fifth century) asserted that through Eve the man became guilty
of transgression.[150] Calvin (sixteenth century) believed that the cause and
source of transgression proceeded from Eve.[151] Wesley (eighteenth
century) contended that Eve persuaded Adam.[152] This view has continued
into the twentieth century.[153] These interpretations neglect Adam's
culpability. Adam seems to have the greater fault, for he sinned "with his
eyes open." He was not deceived.

Another theory contends that verse 14b refers to sexual seduction.
This bases itself on a Jewish speculative tradition which suggests that the
serpent indulged in unchaste practices with Eve.[154] Some second century
A.D. references to ἐξαπατάω do have the sense of sexual seduction.[155]
This becomes an attractive option in view of the sexual-oriented environment of Ephesus with its Mother Goddess. However, the Genesis 3
narrative of the Fall does not portray any sexual orientation for the act of
disobedience. None of the other five uses of ἐξαπατάω in the Pauline
letters have a sexual sense.[156] In fact, Paul uses this same illustration of
the deception of Eve in 2 Cor. 11:3 to speak of both female and male
believers being deceived.[157] There he clearly writes of their "minds"
being led astray—an intellectual deception.

Many commentators found support in verse 14 for the "myth of
feminine weakness and gullibility."[158] Women are more easily deceived
than men due to their openness and susceptibility to spiritual influences.[159]
God does not appoint women as spiritual leaders in the home, and therefore
he has not given them the ability to discern. Eve had no capability of
discerning the serpent's lies.[160] Temptation makes a stronger impression
on a woman.[161] Women have the tendency to follow.[162] Women, by
nature, are not suited for some activities (such as teaching and ruling).[163]
Verse 14 proves women's gullibility, and consequently explains the
prohibition for them not to teach in verse 12.

The problem with these views centers in the fact that they do not find
support in the biblical materials. Neither does the opposite extreme
interpretation: Eve's inquisitiveness, adventurous spirit, and willingness to
risk led her to the moment of temptation. She evaluated and made her own
decision.[164] This approach glorifies Eve's sinful act. The witness of the

Genesis narratives as well as the New Testament proclaims the spiritual equality, capability, and culpability of both women and men. Verse 14 does indicate the differences between Eve and Adam in the Fall. Adam sinned openly. Eve sinned because of the serpent's deception.

The problem with all of the above approaches to verse 14 centers in their neglect of the context. Saying that a woman's gullibility prohibits her from teaching hardly does justice to the context. The Ephesian church had problems during worship. False teachers had encouraged some women, including wives, to flaunt respected behavior and traditional roles. Some women dressed indecently. Some wives exalted their Christian freedom and denigrated their husbands in public. They had been deceived by the wayward elders. Paul has interest in the fact of Eve's deception because it illustrates the current problem among the Ephesian believers.[165] Wives who did not submit to sound doctrine but to unorthodox notions and instructed their husbands in public reminds one of Eve's behavior. Paul wants to break a similar pattern at Ephesus.[166] He speaks of the false teachers as those who want to be teachers of the Law "even though they do not understand either what they are saying or the matters about which they make confident assertions" (1 Tim.1:7). These instructors were deceived just like Eve.[167] Paul therefore stressed that women and men so deceived should not teach in the church.

Another approach which takes the context into consideration observes that some later Gnostic sects revered Eve as the mediatrix who brought divine enlightenment to mankind. Perhaps some of the "gnosticizing" elders in the Ephesian church argued in a similar manner, especially if they had come out of the Artemis cult where the female principle dominated. With Artemis glorified as the giver of life and knowledge, it would not be too surprising if former devotees overturned the Genesis accounts and similarly glorified Eve. Later gnostics did this.[168] 1 Tim. 2:13-14 refutes such an argument. Eve was not the paradigmatic revealer of truth to mankind. Such a doctrinal system based on the primacy of revelation made to Eve could not stand up to the test of biblical orthodoxy.

Γυναῖκες—A Positive Encouragement
(verse 15)

A superficial reading of verse 15 contradicts salvation by grace through faith in Jesus Christ (Eph. 2:8; Rom. 10:9). Does this verse teach eternal salvation from sin and death διὰ τῆς τεκνογονίας? Why is σωθήσεται singular and μείνωσιν plural? How does this verse relate to verses 9-14? The following discussion will attempt to resolve these issues.

Verse 15 begins with a contrast to verses 13-14 due to the use of the adversative δέ. Eve's prominent place in the Fall and the connotation of permanency suggested by the perfect tense γέγονεν present a dismal, hopeless view of the spiritual condition of women.[169] But—δέ—Paul contends that their situation does have hope. Women do not lie under God's "permanent displeasure."[170] The promise of this verse alleviates the severity of verses 13-14. Women are not degraded and abandoned.[171] Women do have the hope of salvation.

What does σωθήσεται διὰ τῆς τεκνογονίας mean? Commentators have offered at least five interpretations of this statement. The first approach sees verse 15a as a reference to the Incarnation, Christ's birth.[172] 1 Tim. 2:14-15 does have parallels with Gen. 3:13-15, especially the affirmation that salvation comes through the woman. This balances the criticism of her deception and Fall. Also, διὰ plus the ablative case refers to agency. Christ is the only agent by means of whom God offers salvation. The definite article indicates a definite, particular event. Finally, σῴζω in the Pastoral Epistles always means redemption from sin for eternal life, that is, spiritual salvation.[173] Despite these arguments, difficulties arise for this view. Primarily, this is an ambiguous and obscure way of referring to the Incarnation. The noun τεκνογονία refers to the activity of bearing children, not to the event of a single birth.[174] This interpretation also raises a question about the role of Mary. Is her role in the birth of Christ the means of salvation?[175] Also, the Incarnation alone does not provide salvation. Christ himself saves through his atoning death and resurrection, not just his birth.[176] One must reject this explanation.

The second interpretation views verse 15a as referring to physical deliverance during childbirth.[177] σωθήσεται διὰ τῆς τεκνογονίας would be translated "she will be kept safe through childbirth" or "she will be preserved through childbirth."[178] 1 Cor. 3:15 represents a possible parallel to this use of σῴζω. This approach interprets the διὰ plus the genitive case as indicating either circumstance of action ("through")[179] or condition ("even though she must bear children").[180] Since a woman's τεκνογονία represents the area in which the curse of Gen. 3:16 finds its operation, the Apostle promises her exemption from that curse's worst and heaviest effects.[181] Although σῴζω may refer to physical health or healing,[182] in the Pastoral Epistles it speaks of spiritual salvation as noted above.[183] The major weaknesses of this view reside in its failure to account for the godly women who have died in childbirth[184] and its failure to fit the context.

The third interpretation affirms that the Christian woman still receives salvation from the eternal judgment against sin in spite of experiencing the temporal judgment of the curse. The continued pain suffered in childbearing does not contradict salvation through Jesus Christ for Christian mothers. διά thus means "through the midst of" rather than "by means of."[185] This view remains consistent with New Testament soteriology. In some respects, it is similar to the second interpretation yet maintains a spiritual meaning for σῴζω. This sense does balance the thrust of verse 14. Woman became (permanently) a transgressor, but she will be saved eternally. A major problem with this view centers in its complexity. One has to "read into" the words of verse 15a and recall the curse of Gen. 3:16. This criticism could also be applied to the second approach.

The fourth interpretation gives a nontheological connotation to σωθήσεται. It contends that verse 15a refers to salvation from the condition which demands the churchly silence of woman. In this respect, it is the only approach so far to deal with the larger context, verses 11-15 and not verses 13-14 alone. "Woman will be saved through childbearing, not from death, but from the theological condition which outlaws her teaching. She shall be saved into ecclesiastical wholeness."[186] How does τεκνογονία achieve this kind of "salvation?" Childbearing counterbalances man's prior creation. The woman's ability to give birth cancels the ramifications of her being created second. ". . . if there exists a male-headed hierarchy in nature because God first created man, then equally there exists a female-headed hierarchy because God created woman to give birth."[187] This follows the argument of 1 Cor. 11:8-9, 12. Verse 15a implies the interdependence and reciprocity between the sexes. The hierarchical terms of verses 13-14 do not stand alone. Childbearing thus avenges woman's deception and transgression. Although this view makes some valid points, it gives an unnatural meaning to σῴζω. Also, after the author of this interpretation developed it, he concluded that verse 15a refers to the birth of the Messiah after all. His arguments have simply shown that the verse implies a different kind of salvation and does not contradict Pauline soteriology. The verse deals with a woman's earthly restoration and not her means of eternal salvation.[188] This seems a recondite way to speak of churchly restoration. This approach also misunderstands the reason for the silence of the wives in the Ephesian congregation.

The final interpretation, and the one held by most commentators, has many variations. Basically, this view contends that woman will be saved and will find her greatest fulfillment by faithfulness to her proper role—

motherhood.[189] In other words, the teaching and ruling activities of the church do not represent woman's proper sphere.[190] In this approach διά plus the genitive case indicates attendant circumstances. Childbearing represents the milieu in which woman finds "wholeness"; motherhood is not the means of salvation.[191] One writer suggested that the bearing and rearing of children keep woman out of the public life. Nature fits woman for the home where she lives safe from the temptations of the world.[192] Another contended that woman's function centers in the physical, not the intellectual. The "religious treatment" of this concept softens its "brutality."[193] One variation insists that the embracing of a woman's proper function saves her from the error of usurping authority and wrongly seizing man's roles.[194] Several believed that verse 15a expresses a Hebrew maxim retrieved from Jewish parenetic materials. The ἐάν clause adds the Christian element.[195]

This fifth view has appeal due to its simplicity. It takes the words of verse 15a at face value and does try to relate them to the immediate context, verses 11-15. In terms of the larger context, one emphasis of the Pastorals shows the need for Christian women to devote themselves to the home as an antidote to the false teaching (1 Tim. 5:9-10, 14; Titus 2:4-5).[196] This approach also gives a good explanation for διά. The difficulty with this view rests in the danger of making motherhood meritorious for salvation.[197] Also, where does this view leave the childless or single woman?[198] This interpretation ignores the presence of women in the biblical witness who were active outside the home in leadership roles in the the church.

In trying to understand σωθήσεται διὰ τῆς τεκνογονίας one needs to ask several questions: Why does Paul relate salvation to childbearing? How would this provide encouragement to women? The entirety of 1 Timothy 2 up to this verse has aimed itself at correcting abuses or ideas of the wayward elders. One must also see verse 15 in this light. It too serves as a corrective. This verse contradicts the ascetic, antisexual beliefs of Paul's opponents who have rejected marriage (1 Tim. 4:3). The heretics proclaimed the evil nature of marriage, sexual intercourse, and procreation.[199] This verse promises Christian women—wives—that they can bring children into the world without endangering their own salvation in Christ. It refutes the heretical claims. Some scholars believed that verse 15 represents an antignostic polemic.[200] Others pointed to the opposite views in the apocryphal Acts of the Apostles which emphasize sexual continence, as did some of the Ephesian heretics. A religion which teaches that the essential worth of a person is determined by one's ability to lead a chaste life negates the usual social norm that identifies a woman's worth by her ability to bear children.[201]   Earlier discussion has indicated that the Artemis cult encouraged sexual continence.[202]   Whatever the background of this heretical notion, verse 15a affirms that bearing children and, by implication, sexual relations should be accepted as a part of Christian marriage. These do not hinder salvation. Wives needed this corrective and encouragement. The religious milieu of Ephesus confronted them with both asceticism and promiscuity. The temptation also existed to elevate their religious functions to the neglect of "the drudgery" of home and family responsibilities.

Verse 15b adds a condition to this affirmation of marital life, for it cannot be separated from verse 15a. A problem exists, however, because σωθήσεται is singular while μείνωσιν is plural. Since γυνή serves as the subject of the first verb and applies to wives, μείνωσιν also refers to wives. It is not unusual for Greek to move from the singular to the plural, especially when the singular represents a generic term as it does here.[203] Verse 15b corrects any misunderstanding of salvation that verse 15a might convey. In essence it states, "Provided of course that she is already a truly Christian woman."[204]   Childbearing itself neither procures salvation nor hinders it. Faith serves as the means of salvation. The Apostle lists πίστει first in this list of Christian virtues and follows with ἀγάπη and ἀγιασμῷ. Verse 15 ends where verse 9 begins—the need for σωφροσύνη. The word again reminds the Christian wives in Ephesus of areas in which they need to exercise self-control as believers. Paul urges them to persevere in the Christian faith.[205]   By implication, they should stop following the heretics and return to those beliefs and behavior which not only foster healthy marital relationships but which also reflect positively on the household of God.

Conclusion

1 Tim. 2:9-15 does relate to the problem of heresy in the church at Ephesus. Women's ostentatious and even seductive clothing reflected the influence of the Artemis cult and disrupted Christian worship (verses 9-10). The acceptance of ascetic tendencies which prohibited marriage disrupted Christian marital relationships (verses 11-12, 15). False understandings of the role of Eve linked to the primacy of the feminine principle in the Mother Goddess religion denied the teachings set forth by the Genesis narratives (verses 14-15). Paul includes this passage in 1 Timothy for the purpose of

refuting these false ideas. He wants believing women to know how they should behave as members of the household of God.

NOTES

1. Verner, *Household of God*, 171.

2. Leslie, "Concept of Woman," 292. Moo denied the possibility that any women were teaching at Ephesus, especially in light of the Jewish element. Moo, "1 Timothy 2:11- 15," 82.

3. Verner, *Household of God*, 171.

4. Leslie, "Concept of Woman," 292-93.

5. 1 Tim. 1:5, 15, 18.

6. See Lock, *PE*, 14; White, "First Timothy," 102. This marks a continuative or resumptive use of οὖν. Dana and Mantey, *Manual Grammar*, 253.

7. Fee, *1 and 2 Timothy*, 25-28.

8. Spicq, *EP*, 1:366.

9. Lock, *PE*, 28. Women served as mediators between God and humans in some ancient religions. These religions thought of women as possessing a special affinity for the divine. Some Gnostics of the second century and later would base their gnosis on special revelations given to a woman. Kroeger and Kroeger, "May Woman Teach?" 15-16. Several Gnostic texts mention the revelation received by a woman, such as the following example:
> "Peter said to Mary, 'Sister, We know that the Savior loved you more than the rest of women. Tell us the words of the Savior which you remember—which you know (but) we do not nor have we heard them.' Mary answered and said, 'What is hidden from you I will proclaim to you.'"

The Gospel of Mary, 10.1-9, in *The Nag Hammadi Library in English*, ed. James M. Robinson (San Francisco: Harper and Row, 1977), 472.

10. For example, see Moo, "1 Tim. 2:11-15," 63; Brox, *Pastoralbrief*, 131, 134; Spicq, *EP*, 1:375; Hommes, "Let Women Be Silent," 7; Russell C. Prohl, *Woman in the Church* (Grand Rapids: William B. Eerdmans Publishing Co., 1957), 34; J. Leipoldt, *Die Frau in der antiken Welt und im Urchristentum* (Leipzig: Koehler und Amelang, 1954), 188-89.

11. B. W. Powers suggested that one should not restrict verses 1-8 to public worship alone. ἐν παντὶ τόπῳ could signify more than every place the church gathered for worship. Paul might have intended the wider connotation of family worship and, consequently, the sphere of family relationships. "Women in the Church: The Application of 1 Timothy 2:8-15," *Interchange* 17 (1975): 56-57.

12. Verner, *Household of God*, 166.

13. Dibelius and Conzelmann, *PE*, 48.

14. Ibid., 5.

15. Ellis noted the similarities between 1 Cor. 14:34-35 and 1 Tim. 2:11-3:1a. This suggests the indebtedness of both passages to a common tradition or existing regulation as opposed to a direct literary relationship to each other. The formula of 1 Tim. 3:1a, "faithful

is the word," which probably includes the preceding pericope, offers support to this pre-existing piece. In the Pastoral Epistles "faithful is the word" signals a traditional teaching-piece or a biblical exposition of Christian prophets or inspired teachers. See also 1 Tim. 4:8-9 and Titus 3:3-8a. "Silenced Wives of Corinth," 214-15. See also Ellis, "Traditions in the Pastoral Epistles," 242. The appearance of words in 1 Peter 3:1-5 which parallel those in 1 Tim. 2:9-15 also support the use of a preformed tradition.

16. See Leslie, "Concept of Woman," 271.

17. 1 Cor. 11:2-16 deals with wife-husband relationships but also contains principles for women in general. The context and content of 1 Cor. 14:34-36 limit the application of those verses to wives. See chapter 4, pp. 88-90.

18. See n. 15 above, and Guthrie, *PE*, 75. Ellis noted these similarities between the two passages: ἐπιτρέπεσθαι; silence (σιγᾶν, ἡσυχία); subjection (ὑποτάσσεσθαι, ὑποταγή); μανθάνειν; and, a common allusion to Gen. 3:16. Few exact parallels of words and phrases exist. Ellis, "Silenced Wives of Corinth," 214.

19. Clark, *Man and Woman in Christ*, 193; Balch, *Let Wives Be Submissive*, 95-105.

20. Those interpreting γυνή as "wife" included: Lock, *PE*, 32; Barrett, *PE*, 55; Hommes, "Let Women Be Silent," 14; Powers, "Women in the Church," 57; Margaret D. Gibson, "Let the Woman Learn in Silence," *The Expository Times* 15 (1903-1904): 380; G. Engel, "Let the Woman Learn in Silence," *The Expository Times* 16 (1904-1905): 189; Prohl, *Woman in the Church*, 32, 35. Fee believed γυνή refers to women in general, especially since it lacks the definite article. *1 and 2 Timothy*, 34. Moo also followed this broader meaning. "1 Tim. 2:11-15," 63.

21. Joseph Reuss, *The First Epistle to Timothy and the Second Epistle to Timothy*, trans. Benen Fahy (New York: Herder and Herder, 1969), 32.

22. Kelly, *PE*, 66; Homer A. Kent, Jr., *The Pastoral Epistles: Studies in I and II Timothy and Titus* (Chicago: Moody Press, 1958), 110.

23. Ellicott, *PE*, 34. Else Kähler argued that the use of βούλομαι points to an author other than Paul. In the uncontested Pauline writings θέλω is used for the Apostle's authoritative will. *Die Frau in den Paulinischen Briefen* (Zürich: Gotthelf-Verlag, 1960), 147-48.

24. Those holding this view included: Henry Alford, *The Epistles to the Galatians, Ephesians, Philippians, Colossians, Thessalonians, Timotheus, Titus and Philemon*, in *The Greek New Testament: With a Critically Revised Text: A Digest of Various Readings: Marginal References to Verbal and Idiomatic Usage: Prolegomena: And a Critical and Exegetical Commentary*, 3rd ed. (London: Rivingtons, 1862), 318; Alfred Barry, A. J. Mason, and H. D. M. Spence, *The Epistles to the Colossians, Thessalonians and Timothy*, in the *Layman's Handy Commentary*, ed. Charles John Ellicott (reprint ed., Grand Rapids: Zondervan Publishing House, 1957; 1st ed., 1877), 208; R. F. Horton, *The Pastoral Epistles: Timothy and Titus*, in *The Century Bible*, gen. ed. W. F. Adeney (Edinburgh: T. C. and E. C. Jack, 1901,), 100; Ryrie, *Role of Women*, 76; Foh, *Women and the Word of God*, 122; Kelly, *PE*, 66; Scott, *PE*, 25.

25. Representatives of this view were: Barrett, *PE*, 55; Lock, *PE*, 29-30; Fee, *1 and 2 Timothy*, 33-34; John Calvin, *Commentaries on the Epistles to Timothy, Titus, and Philemon*, trans. William Pringle (Grand Rapids: William B. Eerdmans Publishing Co., 1948), 65; Verner, *Household of God*, 168; Spicq, *EP*, 1:375.

26. *BAGD*, s.v. "καταστολή," 419.

27. Robertson, *Word Pictures*, 4:569.

28. *LS*, s.v. "κόσμιος," 984.

29. Verner, *Household of God*, 168; Grant R. Osborne, "Hermeneutics and Women in the Church," *Journal of the Evangelical Theological Society* 20 (December 1977): 346.

30. *LS*, s.v. "αἰδώς," 36. The AV translates αἰδώς as "shamefacedness." This could mislead one to think more of "shamefulness" than "modesty." See Charles R. Erdman, *The Pastoral Epistles of Paul* (Philadelphia: The Westminster Press, 1923), 35.

31. Kelly, *PE*, 66.

32. *LS*, s.v. "σωφροσύνη," 1751.

33. Kelly, *PE*, 66.

34. "Chastity" is the "main object in view." J. L. Houlden, *The Pastoral Epistles: I and II Timothy, Titus*, in *Pelican New Testament Commentaries* (New York: Penguin Books, 1976), 70.

35. Brox, *Pastoralbrief*, 132.

36. Osborne, "Hermeneutics and Women," 346.

37. Kelly, *PE*, 67.

38. Leslie, "Concept of Women," 272; Easton, *PE*, 127.

39. Balsdon, *Roman Women*, 255. For a description and pictures of hair styles, see Balsdon, "Women in Imperial Rome," 24-31.

40. *LS*, s.v. "πολυτελής," 1444.

41. See Alan Padgett, "Wealthy Women at Ephesus: 1 Timothy 2:8-15 in Social Context," *Interpretation* 41 (January 1987): 23.

42. Augustine *Letter 262*, cited in Elizabeth A. Clark, ed. *Women in the Early Church: Message of the Fathers of the Church* (Wilmington, Del.: Michael Glazier, 1983), 68.

43. Leslie, "Concept of Women," 272.

44. Guthrie, *PE*, 75; Ironside, *Timothy*, 66-67; Kent, *PE*, 111. 1 Pet. 3:3-4 contains this same principle. The contrast of outward and inward adornment for women represents a common Hellenistic topos. Unique in this passage is the specific application to worship. Verner, *Household of God*, 168-69.

45. "Good deeds" represents a recurring theme in the Pastoral Epistles with twelve references. Paul has concern for the behavior of all Christians. Here he focuses on women. His concern arises in a situation where bad deeds and behavior characterize those who follow heretical ideas. See Houlden, *PE*, 70. References to conduct include: 1 Tim. 2:10; 3:1; 5:10, 25; 6:18; 2 Tim. 2:21; 3:17; Titus 2:7, 14; 3:1, 8, 14.

46. Barrett, *PE*, 55; Kelly, *PE*, 67. Kelly observed that "good deeds" do surface in the acknowledged Paulines yet with less frequency. See Rom. 2:7; 2 Cor. 11:8; Eph. 2:10; Col. 1:10.

47. Lock, *PE*, 31.

48. *TDNT*, s.v. "θεοσεβής," by George Bertram, 3:126.

49. Arrington, *I Timothy*, 65; Powers, "Women in the Church," 57.

50. See discussion above, 124-25. See also Dibelius and Conzelmann, *PE*, 47; Guthrie, *PE*, 75; Fee, *1 and 2 Timothy*, 35; Ironside, *Timothy*, 67; Houlden, *PE*, 71; and Moo, "1 Tim. 2:11-15," 62.

51. Hommes, "Let Women Be Silent," 7.

52. *LS*, s.v. "μανθάνω," 1078.

53. Easton, *PE*, 124; Williams, *Apostle Paul and Women*, 111-12.

54. Matthew Henry, *Romans to Revelation*, in *An Exposition of the Old and New Testaments* (London: James Nisbet and Co., 1873), 451.

55. *TDNT*, s.v. "μανθάνω," by Karl H. Rengstorf, 4:410; Aida Dina Besancon Spencer, "Eve at Ephesus (Should Women Be Ordained as Pastors According to the First Letter to Timothy 2:11-15?)" *Journal of the Evangelical Theological Society* 17 (Fall 1974): 216. See also chapter 5, 111-14.

56. *BAGD*, s.v. "ἡσυχία," 349; *LS*, s.v. "ἡσυχία," 779. 1 Cor. 14:34 does not use this word but the verb σιγάω, which indicates the absence of sound. There Paul speaks of a specific instance of silence—in the judging of one's husband who has prophesied. See chapter 4, pp. 89-90.

57. Contra H. Harvey, *Commentary on the Pastoral Epistles: First and Second Timothy and Titus; and the Epistle to Philemon* (Valley Forge: Judson Press, 1890), 34.

58. Payne, "Libertarian Women," 169. Some scholars did accept "silence" as the best translation and meaning here, such as: Moo, "1 Tim. 2:11-15," 64; idem, "Interpretation of 1 Tim. 2:11-15," 198; Herbert W. Williams, "Let the Woman Learn in Silence," *The Expository Times* (1904-1905): 188; and Ellicott, *PE*, 36. Hurley noted that ἡσυχία means silence but carries with it the connotation of quiet receptivity. *Man and Woman*, 200. Spencer contended that learning in silence is not a derogatory command. Wise people learn in silence (Prov. 17:27-28). "Eve at Ephesus," 218.

59. "For the [female] sex is naturally somewhat talkative: and for this reason he restrains them on all sides." Chrysostom *Homily 9 on 1 Tim. 2:11-15* in *Nicene and Post- Nicene Fathers of the Christian Church*, 11:435.

60. Engel, "Let the Woman Learn in Silence," 189.

61. Howard, "Neither Male Nor Female," 40.

62. A number of scholars adhered to this position. These included: Bartchy, "Power, Submission and Sexual Identity," 72-73; Scholer, "Exegesis," 7; Leslie, "Concept of Woman," 276-77, 294; Payne, "Libertarian Women," 170; Gibson, "Let the Woman Learn in Silence," 380; Josephine Massyngberde Ford, "Biblical Material Relevant to the Ordination of Women," *Journal of Ecumenical Studies* 10 (Fall 1973): 683; Fee, *1 and 2 Timothy*, 35; Hillard, *PE*, 22; and Clark, *Man and Woman in Christ*, 195.

63. Leslie would answer "yes" to both these questions. "Concept of Woman," 281-82.

64. Engel, "Let the Woman Learn in Silence," 189.

65. Dibelius and Conzelmann, *PE*, 47. Padgett concluded the submission was to teachers. "Wealthy Women at Ephesus," 24.

66. See Moo, "1 Tim. 2:11-15," 64. Moo thought the word possesses a dual reference: submission to sound teaching and submission to men.

67. Leslie, "Concept of Woman," 284.

EXEGESIS OF 1 TIMOTHY 2:9-15 149

68. Fee, *1 and 2 Timothy*, 35.

69. *TDNT*, s.v. "μανθάνω," by Rengstorf, 4:410.

70. Moo, "1 Tim. 2:11-15," 65; idem, "Interpretation of 1 Tim. 2:11-15," 199-200; Hurley, *Men and Women*, 201.

71. Payne, "Libertarian Women," 170-73; Williams, *Apostle Paul and Women*, 112; Fee, *1 and 2 Timothy*, 35; Arrington, *I Timothy*, 69.

72. Moo, "1 Tim. 2:11-15," 65.

73. Payne, "Libertarian Women," 171.

74. Moo, "Interpretation of 1 Tim. 2:11-15," 199.

75. Ibid. One would have to agree with Moo that Payne indeed overstated his case at this point. Simply because Paul identifies his own personal advice does not mean it is not a valid instruction from the Lord. See Payne, "Libertarian Women," 170. Paul does affirm, "I give an opinion as one who by the mercy of the Lord is trustworthy" (1 Cor. 7:25).

76. For a listing of these references, see Smith, *Greek-English Concordance*, 146, word 2010, "ἐπιτρέπω." Payne indicated that every occurrence of ἐπιτρέπω in the LXX refers to permission for a specific situation and never for a universally applicable permission. "Libertarian Women," 172.

77. See Ellis, "Silenced Wives of Corinth," 217.

78. There are 221 references for γυνή as listed by Smith, *Greek-English Concordance*, 75, word 1135, "γυνή." Of these, fifty-one references in forty verses (excluding 1 Tim. 2:12) have γυνή directly appearing with ἀνήρ (or in five instances with ἄνθρωπος): Matt. 19:5, 10; Mark 10:2, 7; Luke 8:3; Acts 5:1; Rom. 7:2; 1 Cor. 7:1, 2, 3, 4, 10, 11, 13, 14, 16, 39; 11:3, 7, 8, 9, 11, 12; 14:35; Eph. 5:22, 23, 24, 25, 28, 31, 33; Col. 3:18, 19; 1 Tim. 3:2, 12; 5:9; Titus 1:6; 1 Pet. 3:1, 5. Of these fifty-one references, twelve refer to women in general while the remaining thirty-three refer to wives. Ten references relating to wives do not use the article with γυνή.

79. See Ellis, "Silenced Wives of Corinth," 214-17. See n. 20 above for others who saw γυνή as "wife" here. Patrick Fairbairn referred to these verses in 1 Timothy as an "abbreviated reinforcement of the instruction in 1 Cor. 14:34." *Commentary on the Pastoral Epistles: I and II Timothy, Titus* (Grand Rapids: Zondervan Publishing House, 1956; reprint of 1874 ed.), 127.

80. *BAGD*, s.v. "οὐδέ," 591.

81. Moo, "1 Tim. 2:11-15," 68.

82. This is the genitive of direct object or root idea. Here it describes or defines who is being taught and ruled—ἀνδρός. See James A. Brooks and Carlton L. Winbery, *Syntax of New Testament Greek* (Washington, D.C.: University Press of America, 1978), 19. This genitive is used with verbs of ruling. A. T. Robertson, *A Grammar of the Greek New Testament in the Light of Historical Research* (Nashville: Broadman Press, 1934), 510.

83. Kenneth S. Wuest, *The Pastoral Epistles in the Greek New Testament for the English Reader* (Grand Rapids: William B. Eerdmans Publishing Co., 1952), 48.

84. Floyd V. Filson, "The Christian Teacher in the First Century," *Journal of Biblical Literature* 60 (September 1941): 318.

85. Ibid., 318-19, 322-24.

86. *The New International Dictionary of New Testament Theology*, 3 vols., gen. ed. Colin Brown (Grand Rapids: Zondervan Publishing House, 1975-1978), s.v. "Teach, Instruct," by Klaus Wegenast, 3 (1978): 765. See also Moo, "1 Tim. 2:11-15," 65.

87. Bengt Holmberg, *Paul and Power: The Structure of Authority in the Primitive Church as Reflected in the Pauline Epistles* (Lund: Gleerup, 1978), 198.

88. Moo, "1 Tim. 2:11-15," 65; Osborne, "Hermeneutics and Women," 346; Clark, *Man and Woman in Christ*, 196.

89. Contra Moo, "1 Tim. 2:11-15," 65, and Clark, *Man and Woman in Christ*, 196. See Payne, "Libertarian Women," 173-74. It is a questionable assumption that "authority" and "office" within the early Christian congregations were expressed and experienced as they were then and are now "among the Gentiles." This contradicts the servant emphasis of Mark 10:42-45. Bartchy, "Power, Submission and Sexual Identity," 75.

90. See chapter 4, p. 88.

91. Sigountos, "Public Roles for Women," 286.

92. "Office" has no equivalent in the New Testament. It represents an "analytical concept used to summarize a cluster of functions. . . ." Permanency, recognition by the church, regular commission, authority, and dignity characterize "office." Some "functions" in the New Testament came to be termed as "offices." See Holmberg, *Paul and Power*, 110-13.

93. These included: Kent, *PE*, 113; Wuest, *PE*, 48-49; Ironside, *Timothy*, 67-69; Lilley, *PE*, 93-94; Ellicott, *PE*, 36-37; Parry, *PE*, 15; Kelly, *PE*, 68; Scott, *PE*, 26; Hanson, *Pastoral Letters*, 36-37; Harvey, *PE*, 34; Calvin, *Timothy*, 67; Hurley, *Man and Woman*, 201; Howard, "Neither Male Nor Female," 40-41; Robert G. Bratcher, *A Translator's Guide to Paul's Letters to Timothy and to Titus* (New York: United Bible Societies, 1983), 25; J. P. Greene, *The Pastoral Epistles* (Nashville: Sunday School Board, SBC, 1915), 37; R. C. H. Lenski, *The Interpretation of St. Paul's Epistles to the Colossians, to the Thessalonians, to Timothy, to Titus and to Philemon* (Minneapolis: Augsburg Publishing House, 1937), 562-64; Otis W. Yates, *A Good Soldier of Christ Jesus: An Interpretation of I Timothy* (Kansas City, Kans.: Central Seminary Press, 1946), 60-61; and Spicq, *EP*, 1:380.

94. Yates, *I Timothy*, 60-61. See also Ironside, *Timothy*, 70.

95. Kent, *PE*, 113; Charles B. Cunningham, *Simple Studies in Timothy, Titus, and Philemon* (Grand Rapids: Baker Book House, 1964), 23; Wuest, *PE*, 49.

96. Leaney, *Timothy*, 53. See also Hillard, *PE*, 22-23.

97. Guthrie, *PE*, 76.

98. Bartchy, "Power, Submission and Sexual Identity," 73-74; Arrington, *I Timothy*, 66-67; Guthrie, *PE*, 75-76; Fee, *1 and 2 Timothy*, 36.

99. Hommes, "Let Women Be Silent," 13-14. Engel believed that wives should not teach in public due to their special relation of submission to their husbands. "Let the Woman Learn in Silence," 190.

100. *LS*, s.v. "αὐθεντέω," 275; G. W. H. Lampe, ed., *A Patristic Greek Lexicon* (Oxford: Clarendon Press, 1961), s.v. "αὐθεντέω," 262; *BAGD*, s.v. "αὐθεντέω," 121.

101. *BAGD*, s.v. "αὐθεντέω," 121.

102. *LS*, s.v. "αὐθεντέω," 275.

103. Ibid.

104. Lampe, *Patristic Greek Lexicon*, s.v. "αὐθεντία," 263.

105. *MM*, s.v. "αὐθεντέω," 91. See also Adolf Deissmann, *Light from the Ancient East*, 4th ed., trans. Lionel R. M. Strachan (New York: Harper and Brothers, 1922), 89. Deissmann refuted the view that αὐθεντέω is only a biblical and patristic word. He told of one Atticist, Moeris, who warns his pupil to use the Attic αὐτοδικεῖν because αὐθεντεῖν was vulgar (κοινή). Ibid.

106. Catherine Clark Kroeger, "Ancient Heresies and a Strange Greek Verb," *Reformed Journal* 29 (March 1979): 13.

107. Ibid., 12-15.

108. The following articles all criticized Kroeger's work: Armin J. Panning, "ΑΥΘΕΝΤΕΙΝ—A Word Study," *Wisconsin Lutheran Quarterly* 78 (July 1981): 185-91; Carroll D. Osburn, "ΑΥΘΕΝΤΕΩ (1 Tim. 2:12)," *Restoration Quarterly* 25 (1982): 1-12; and George W. Knight, III, "ΑΥΘΕΝΤΕΩ in Reference to Women in 1 Timothy 2:12," *New Testament Studies* 30 (January 1984): 143-57.

109. Panning, "ΑΥΘΕΝΤΕΙΝ," 187-91.

110. Osburn, "ΑΥΘΕΝΤΕΩ," 6.

111. See also Knight, "ΑΥΘΕΝΤΕΩ," 143 and Panning, "ΑΥΘΕΝΤΕΙΝ," 86. Panning gave the best etymological discussion.

112. Knight listed and discussed occurrences of αὐθεντεῖν from the fifth century B.C. to the fifteenth century A.D. To this documentary evidence he added the evaluation of linguistic experts of earlier and later periods. "ΑΥΘΕΝΤΕΩ," 144-49.

113. Ibid., 150-52, 154.

114. Moo, "1 Tim. 2:11-15," 67, and Hurley, *Man and Woman*, 202. Bartchy differed with this interpretation. He contended that αὐθεντεῖν bears the nuance of absolute power in a destructive manner. It describes the activity of a person who acts for her or his own advantage without considering the needs or interests of others. "Power, Submission and Sexual Identity," 71-72.

115. Powers, "Women in the Church," 59

116. George H. Gilbert, "Women in Public Worship in the Churches of Paul," *The Biblical World* 2 (July 1893): 46.

117. Osborne, "Hermeneutics and Women," 346. Lenski expressed this in an extreme way: to teach means to act as an αὐθεντής over all those taught, that is, as a self-doer, a master, an autocrat. *Timothy*, 563. Robert Falconer expressed a similar vein of thought when he stated that αὐθεντεῖν means to come forward and challenge what a man says in public worship. "1 Timothy 2:14-15: Interpretative Notes," *Journal of Biblical Literature* 60 (December 1941): 375.

118. See Bartchy, "Power, Submission and Sexual Identity," 74.

119. Clark, *Man and Woman in Christ*, 197.

120. Osburn, "ΑΥΘΕΝΤΕΩ," 11.

121. Jerome H. Neyrey believed Paul's concern for women "probably represents a genuine pastoral concern which was unfortunately smothering and unenlightened." *First Timothy, Second Timothy, Titus, James, First Peter, Second Peter, Jude* (Collegeville, Minn.: The Liturgical Press, 1983), 16.

122. Most translators have supplied a negative term for the word. It has been translated: "to have authority" (RSV, NIV, TEV, NKJV, Beck); "to exercise authority" (NASB, New World Trans., Montgomery); "to usurp authority" (AV); "to domineer" (NEB, Goodspeed, Berkeley, Vulgate [*dominari*]); "to have dominion" (ASV, Moulton); "to dominate" (Fenton); "to have the mastery" (Westminster); "to lord it over" (LB); "to tell a man what to do" (JB); "to rule over" (Alford); "to dictate" (Moffatt); "to boss" (Jordan). Of those surveyed only two translations indicated that verse 12 refers to "wives:" "domineering over a husband" (Williams) and "to issue commands to her husband" (Knox).

123. Scholer, "Exegesis," 8.

124. See Payne, "Libertarian Women," 175.

125. See Moo, "Interpretation of 1 Tim. 2:11-15," 203; Robert J. Karris, *The Pastoral Epistles* (Wilmington, Del.: Michael Glazier, Inc., 1979), 67.

126. See Payne, "Libertarian Women," 176; Williams, *Apostle Paul and Women*, 112-13; Padgett, "Wealthy Women at Ephesus," 25.

127. Dana and Mantey, *Manual Grammar*, 243.

128. Payne, "Libertarian Women," 176-77.

129. Prohl, *Woman in the Church*, 39.

130. Dana and Mantey, *Manual Grammar*, 243.

131. Karen W. Hoover, "Creative Tension in 1 Timothy 2:11-15," *Brethren Life and Thought* 22 (Summer 1977): 163.

132. Neyrey, *First Timothy*, 16.

133. Martin E. Marty, *Good News in the Early Church: 1 and 2 Timothy, Titus, James, 1 and 2 Peter, 1, 2 and 3 John and Jude in Today's English Version* (Cleveland, Ohio: Williams Collins and World Publishing Co., 1976), 36; Kelly, *PE*, 68; Spicq, *EP*, 1:380; Padgett, "Wealthy Women at Ephesus," 26

134. *BAGD*, s.v. "πρῶτος," 725.

135. Fairbairn, *PE*, 128; Kent, *PE*, 114; Hillard, *PE*, 23; Harvey, *PE*, 34; John Wesley, *Explanatory Notes upon the New Testament* (London: John Mason, 1842), n.p.; Kelly, *PE*, 68; Moo, "1 Tim. 2:11-15," 68.

136. Knight, *New Testament Teaching*, 31.

137. Yates, *I Timothy*, 61.

138. εἶτα is used to denote sequence in time. *LS*, s.v. "εἶτα," 498.

139. See Erdman, *PE*, 35.

140. See Showerman, *Great Mother*, 20-24; Cavendish, *Mythology*, 152; Vermaseren, *Cybele*, 90-91.

141. See Payne, "Libertarian Women," 189; Moo, "1 Tim. 2:11-15," 70; Ellicott, *PE*, 210; Scott, *PE*, 27; Hurley, *Man and Woman*, 214-15; Zerbst, *Office of Woman*, 54. This rebukes those views which perceive Adam as inept and belly-oriented. See chapter 3, 57. Kähler contended that verse 14 portrays Eve as the only sinner and therefore does not harmonize with Genesis 3. *Frau*, 157.

142. Bratcher, *Timothy*, 25.

143. Albert Barnes, *Thessalonians, Timothy, Titus, and Philemon* in *Notes on the New Testament: Explanatory and Practical* (London: Blackie and Son, Ltd., 1868), 137.

144. Ironside, *Timothy*, 71; Yates, *I Timothy*, 61. Horton said this view derives from Milton. *PE*, 102.

145. Payne, "Libertarian Women," 189.

146. See ibid.; Moo, "1 Tim. 2:11-15," 69; Hultgren, *I-II Timothy*, 69.

147. Ambrose *On Paradise* 32.1.316, 329, in Clark, *Women in the Early Church: Message of the Fathers*, 41.

148. Chrysostom *Homily 9 on 1 Tim. 2:11-15*, in *Nicene and Post-Nicene Fathers*, 13:435-36.

149. Chrysostom *Discourse 4 on Genesis* 54.594, in Clark, *Women in the Early Church: Message of the Fathers*, 44.

150. Augustine *Literal Commentary on Genesis* 28.1.376, in Clark, *Women in the Early Church: Message of the Fathers*, 40.

151. Calvin, *Timothy*, 69.

152. Wesley, *Explanatory Notes*, n.p.

153. For example, see Falconer, "1 Tim. 2:14-15," 375-76. See also the article by Higgins, "The Myth of Eve: The Temptress."

154. Dibelius and Conzelmann, *PE*, 48. See also Hanson, *PE*, in the *New Century Bible Commentary*, 72.

155. Houlden, *PE*, 71. *LS* lists "to seduce a woman" as one of the meanings of ἐξαπατάω. S.v. "ἐξαπατάω," 586.

156. Rom. 7:11, 16:18; 1 Cor. 3:18; 2 Cor. 11:3; 2 Thess. 2:3.

157. Evans, *Woman in the Bible*, 104; Scholer, "Exegesis," 8.

158. Leslie, "Concept of Woman," 287.

159. Clark, *Man and Woman in Christ*, 203; Green, *PE*, 38; Easton, *PE*, 124; Harvey, *PE*, 34; Wesley, *Explanatory Notes*, n.p.

160. Hurley, *Man and Woman*, 216.

161. Barnes, *Timothy*, 137.

162. Hendricksen, *PE*, 109.

163. Moo, "1 Tim. 2:11-15," 70.

164. Hoover, "Creative Tension in 1 Tim. 2:11-15," 164.

165. Fee, *1 and 2 Timothy*, 40.

166. Spencer, "Eve at Ephesus," 219; Arrington, *I Timothy*, 70.

167. Williams, *Apostle Paul and Women*, 113.

168. For example, in *The Apocalypse of Adam*, V.5.64.9- 14, (Robinson, *Nag Hammadi Library*, 256-57), Adam says this about Eve: "I went about with her in a glory which she had seen in the aeon from which we had come forth. She taught me a word of knowledge of the eternal God." In *On the Origin of the World*, II.5.115.31-116.9, (Robinson, *Nag Hammadi Library*, 172), Eve, the "instructor," gives Adam life. See the discussion in Kroeger and Kroeger, "May Women Teach?" 16-17. Even Moo acknowledged that such a tradition may

be partially responsible for the statements of verse 14 though this position is "hypothetical, problematic, and inadequate" for the verse's entire explanation. "Interpretation of 1 Tim. 2:11-15," 204 n. 10.

169. Although the singular αὐτή is the assumed subject of σωθήσεται, this refers to "woman" or "women" in general despite the fact that Εὖα represents the closest antecedent. Eve, after all, stands as an archetypal figure. Verses 11-12 use the singular γυνή. Verse 15 resumes Paul's discussion after the break caused by the Old Testament support for his arguments. See Hultgren, *I Timothy*, 69; Houlden, *PE*, 72; Fee, *1 and 2 Timothy*, 37. Several translations use "women" as the subject of σωθήσεται: NASB, NIV, TCNT, LB, Williams, and Moffatt.

170. Kelly, *PE*, 69.

171. Barnes, *Notes on the New Testament*, 137; Calvin, *Timothy*, 70.

172. Those holding this view included: Payne, "Libertarian Women," 177-81; Spencer, "Eve at Ephesus," 220; Kent, *PE*, 118-20; Ellicott, *PE*, 39; Lock, *PE*, 33; Arrington, *I Timothy*, 71; Spence, *Timothy*, 211; Bushnell, *God's Word to Women*, sections 342-44; Williams, *Apostle Paul and Women*, 113. See also the Montgomery and Amplified translations. Falconer reported that the Latin Fathers preferred this approach, but the Greek Fathers gave no place to this interpretation. "1 Tim. 2:14-15," 376.

173. For a discussion of the arguments, see Payne, "Libertarian Women," 177-81, and Kent, *PE*, 118-20.

174. Fee, *1 and 2 Timothy*, 38.

175. Moo, "Interpretation of 1 Tim. 2:11-15," 205.

176. Roberts, "Woman Shall Be Saved," 5.

177. Those who supported this view included: Powers, "Women in the Church," 58; Ironside, *Timothy*, 72; Hillard, *PE*, 24; Alford, *Timotheus*, 320; Wesley, *Explanatory Notes*, n.p.; Scott, *PE*, 28; John R. Rice, *Bobbed Hair, Bossy Wives and Women Preachers* (Wheaton, Ill.: Sword of the Lord Publishers, 1941), 42.

178. See these versions: NASB, NIV, New Berkeley, Moffatt, and Phillips.

179. Hillard, *PE*, 24.

180. Scott, *PE*, 28.

181. Alford, *Timotheus*, 320; Wesley, *Explanatory Notes*, n.p.

182. See Wuest, *PE*, 49.

183. Fee, *1 and 2 Timothy*, 37; Kent, *PE*, 119.

184. Leslie, "Concept of Woman," 291-92.

185. Robert H. Gundry, *A Survey of the New Testament* (Grand Rapids: Zondervan Publishing House, 1970), 325.

186. Roberts, "Woman Shall Be Saved," 6.

187. Ibid.

188. Ibid., 5-6.

189. Among those adhering to this view were: Greene, *PE*, 39; Lilley, *PE*, 94-95; Wuest, *PE*, 50; Hultgren, *I Timothy*, 70; Yates, *I Timothy*, 62; Calvin, *Timothy*, 71; Barrett, *PE*, 56; Hendricksen, *PE*, 111; White, *Timothy*, 110; Spence, *Timothy*, 211; Russell Bradley Jones, *The*

Epistles to Timothy: A Study Manual (Grand Rapids: Baker Book House, 1959), 24; E. K. Simpson, *The Pastoral Epistles: The Greek Text with Introduction and Commentary* (London: The Tyndale Press, 1954), 49; E. Glenn Hinson, "1-2 Timothy and Titus," in *The Broadman Bible Commentary*, 12 vols., ed. Clifton J. Allen (Nashville: Broadman Press, 1971), 11:316. See also the sources cited in n. 190. The following translations appear to follow this view: TEV, RSV, ASV, TCNT, NEB, JB, AV, Williams, and Knox. P. Altfrid Kassing was extreme in his expression of this approach: "Bereitschaft zur Empfangnis ist ein Hingeben und Einsetzen seiner selbst." The woman who bears children practices Christlike, giving love. "Das Heil der Mutterschaff: 1 Tim. 2,15 in biblischen Zusammenhängen," *Litergie und Monchtum* 23 (1958): 60-61.

190. Moo, "1 Tim. 2:11-15," 71; Barclay, *Timothy*, 79; Parry, *PE*, 15; Marty, *1 and 2 Timothy*, 36; Reuss, *Timothy*, 34; Kelly, *PE*, 69-70; Robert H. Mounce, *Pass It On: A Bible Commentary for Laymen—First and Second Timothy* (Glendale, Calif.: Regal Books, 1979), 34.

191. Leslie, "Concept of Paul," 292; Robertson, *Word Pictures*, 4:571; Spicq, *EP*, 1:383.

192. Greene, *PE*, 39.

193. Easton, *PE*, 124-25.

194. S. Jebb, "A Suggested Interpretation of 1 Tim. 2:15," *Expository Times* 81 (1970): 221; Hurley, *Man and Woman*, 222.

195. Falconer, "1 Tim. 2:14-15," 377-78; Dibelius and Conzelmann, *PE*, 48.

196. Paul did not want the Gospel discredited by Christian misbehavior.
"If those regarded as having the highest moral code among both Gentiles and Jews valued woman's presence in the home and if her 'gadding about' only produced difficulties, one can see how the Pastor, anxious to avoid putting Christianity in the wrong light, as well as avoiding possible scandal, would encourage the young women to concentrate on ordering their households."
Leslie, "Concept of Woman," 265.

197. Ibid., 290. Some commentators discussed διά as if it were indicative of agency or means.

198. Moo explained that τεκνογονία also means "child-rearing." "1 Tim. 2:11-15," 72. Neither *BAGD* (s.v. "τεκνογονία," 808) nor *LS* (s.v. "τεκνογονία," 1768) lists this as an option.

199. Reuss, *Timothy*, 34; Karris, *PE*, 67-68; Kelly, *PE*, 70; Mounce, *1 and 2 Timothy*, 34; Bartchy, "Power, Submission and Sexual Identity," 74; Hommes, "Let Women Be Silent," 21. Brox stated that since verse 15a describes childbearing as a redemptive function, "das . . . Eheverbot einer Lasterung gleichkommt." *Pastoralbrief*, 138.

200. See Blum, "Office of Women," 184; Dibelius and Conzelmann, *PE*, 49-50; Brox, *Pastoralbrief*, 136.

201. Ross Shepard Kraemer, "Ecstatics and Ascetics: Studies in the Functions of Religious Activities for Women in the Greco-Roman World" (Ph.D. dissertation, Princeton University, 1976), viii.

202. See chapter 2, pp. 33, 40.

203. Bratcher, *Timothy*, 26. Spicq noted that "la substitution du pluriel impersonnel . . . au singulier est conforme a la mentalite hebraique qui passe aisement de l'individuel au collectif. . . ." *EP*, 1:384. Others who saw "they" as women included: Parry, *PE*, 15; Kent,

PE, 120; Barnes, *Notes on the New Testament*, 139; Calvin, *Timothy*, 71; Roberts, "Woman Shall Be Saved," 6; Kelly, *PE*, 70; and, Falconer, "1 Tim. 2:14-15," 377. Some believed "they" refers to the wife and husband: Powers, "Women in the Church," 58; Wuest, *PE*, 51; and Ironside, *Timothy*, 72. Others contended "they" indicates the children of these women: Houlden, *PE*, 72; Jones, *Timothy*, 25; and Brox, *Pastoralbrief*, 137.

204. Fee, *1 and 2 Timothy*, 38.

205. Roberts believed that the failure of the Ephesian women to continue in faith, not their femaleness, demands their silence. "Woman Shall Be Saved," 6.

CONCLUSION

The thesis of this book stated that the prohibition of women in regards to teaching and exercising authority over men as expressed in 1 Tim. 2:9-15 resulted from the particular situation in the primitive Ephesian church, a situation complicated by pagan influences from the beliefs and practices of the cult of the Mother Goddess Artemis in Ephesus which had infiltrated the church through false teachers. Has the research of the previous six chapters confirmed this statement?

The discussions have shown that the Artemis cult was a major factor in the religious milieu of Ephesus. Its pervasiveness did influence the Christian church, perhaps through those converted out of this pagan mystery religion.[1] Some of the heretical tenets and behaviors mentioned in the Pastoral Epistles reflect similarities to the worship of the Mother Goddess. Some Christian women did participate with the false teachers who espoused these heretical notions.

In light of the relationship of this passage to the religious situation in Ephesus, is 1 Tim. 2:9-15 "culturally conditioned" or "culturally bound" thus restricting its meaning to the early church and not to the twentieth century? The answer is no. The local situation did occasion the inclusion of this passage in 1 Timothy.[2] The temporary situation at Ephesus, for instance, explains the difficulty in understanding verse 15. The meaning of the passage, however, remains relevant for and applicable to believers today. The problems created by these verses diminish when one realizes that Paul is dealing with the relationship between wives and husbands. After all, the

157

marriage of believers, cemented by mutual submission and ἀγάπη, should portray the relationship of Christ and the church. The Apostle responds to the troubles stirred up by the heretics among the women of the Ephesian congregation by utilizing traditional materials already accepted by the church.[3] This fact reinforces both the validity of these instructions for contemporary Christians and the view that the passage relates to wives and husbands.[4]

Therefore, a better translation of 1 Tim. 2:12 is: "I do not allow a wife to teach or exercise authority over her husband but to remain quiet." This interpretation eliminates any contradiction between this passage and other biblical materials. It restates the teaching of 1 Cor. 14:34-36.[5] It also permits the exercise of spiritual gifts by all women, both married and single. Thus, 1 Tim. 2:9-15 does not contradict Jesus' relationship with and teachings about women nor Paul's relationship with women coworkers and his affirmation of their participation in the worship of the church (1 Cor. 11:2-16). All women do have the right to enter the ministry as God so calls and equips them. The New Testament examples verify this. The normative principle underlying 1 Tim. 2:9-15 is that marriage qualifies a married woman's ministry. A wife's commitment and obligations to her husband should shape her public ministry.[6]

NOTES

1. This area needs further study as this book has only dealt with it in a limited manner. The Mother Goddess cult persisted in its influence in Ephesus. After all, it was the council of Ephesus (A.D. 431) which declared Mary to be what the Goddess had been from the beginning, θεοτόκος, the Mother of God. Mary became the true counterpart to Artemis. See Barth, "Traditions in Ephesians," 16, and Joseph Campbell, "Joseph Campbell on the Great Goddess," *Parabola* 5 (Fall 1980): 84. For further discussions on the cult of Mary and Mariolotry as reflections of the Goddess, see Engelsman, *Feminine Dimension of the Divine*, 122, and Carol Ochs, *Behind the Sex of God: Toward a New Consciousness Transcending Matriarchy and Patriarchy* (Boston: Beacon Press, 1977), 68-81.

2. Contra Moo who contended that nothing in the passage suggests Paul issued his instructions due to the local situation of societal pressure. "1 Tim. 2:11-15," 82.

3. Ellis, "Traditions in the Pastoral Epistles," 242; idem, "Silenced Wives of Corinth," 214-15; Dibelius and Conzelmann, *PE*, 48.

4. The traditional parenetic material deals with family and household relationships as the term "household codes" suggests.

5. Contra Leslie who believed the 1 Timothy passage is more restrictive than 1 Cor. 14:34-36. "Concept of Women," 294-96.

6. See Charles D. Cerling, "Women Ministers in the New Testament Church?" *Journal of the Evangelical Theological Society* 19 (Summer 1976): 214, and Ellis, "Silenced Wives of Corinth," 217.

ABBREVIATIONS

BAGD

Bauer, Walter. *Greichisch-Deutsches Wörterbuch zu den Schriften des Neuen Testaments und der übrigen urchristlichen Literatur.* Adapted by William F. Arndt, Wilbur F. Gingrich, and Frederick W. Danker. *A Greek-English Lexicon of the New Testament.* 2nd ed. Chicago: University of Chicago Press, 1979.

IDB

The Interpreter's Dictionary of the Bible. Edited by George Arthur Buttrick. Nashville: Abingdon Press, 1962-1976.

LCL

The Loeb Classical Library

LS

Liddell, Henry George and Robert Scott. *A Greek-English Lexicon.* 9th ed. Revised by Henry Stuart Jones and Roderick McKenzie. Oxford: Clarendon Press, 1940.

MM

Moulton, James Hope and George Milligan. *The Vocabulary of the Greek Testament Illustrated from the Papyri and Other Non-literary Sources.* 1930. Reprint. Grand Rapids: William B. Eerdmans Publishing Co., 1963.

PE

Pastoral Epistles

TDNT

Theological Dictionary of the New Testament. 10 vols. Edited by Gerhard Kittel and Gerhard Friedrich. Translated by Geoffrey W. Bromiley. Grand Rapids: Williams B. Eerdmans Publishing Co., 1964-1974.

TDOT

Theological Dictionary of the Old Testament. 5 vols. Edited by G. Johannes Botterweck and Helmer Ringgren. Translated by John T. Willis. Grand Rapids: William B. Eerdmans Publishing Co., 1974.

TWOT

Theological Wordbook of the Old Testament. 2 vols. Edited by R. Laird Harris. Chicago: Moody Press, 1980.

SELECTED BIBLIOGRAPHY

This bibliography represents only a portion of the works consulted and cited in this book. Its entries focus primarily on understanding the biblical materials on women. The one exception is the first division which provides the background for the biblical study. The bibliography is divided into the following sections: (1) Cultural and Religious Contexts, (2) Old Testament Context, (3) New Testament Context, (4) Pastoral Epistles' Context, (5) Women and the Bible—General, and (6) Women, the Bible, and Hermeneutics. The reader is urged to consult the chapter endnotes for bibliographic data on other sources.

1. Cultural and Religious Contexts

Books

Adams, J. McKee. *Biblical Backgrounds*. Revised by Joseph A. Callaway. Nashville: Broadman Press, 1965.

Angus, Samuel. *The Mystery-Religions and Christianity: A Study in the Religious Background of Early Christianity*. New York: Charles Scribner's Sons, 1925.

Balsdon, J. P. V. D. *Roman Women: Their History and Habits*. London: Bodley Head, 1962.

Bauer, Jr., Richard A. *Philo's Use of the Categories Male and Female*. Leiden: E. J. Brill, 1970.

Coburn, Camden M. *The New Archeological Discoveries*. 9th ed. New York: Funk and Wagnalls, Co., 1929.

Cumont, Franz. *The Oriental Religions in Roman Paganism*. Chicago: The Open Court Publishing Co., 1911.

Deissmann, Adolf. *Light from the Ancient East*. 4th ed. Translated by Lionel R. M. Strachan. New York: Harper and Brothers, 1922.

Farnell, Lewis Richard. *The Cults of the Greek States*. 5 vols. New Rochelle, N.Y.: Caratzas Brothers, Publishers, 1977.

Ferguson, John. *The Religions of the Roman Empire*. Ithaca, N.Y.: Cornell University Press, 1970.

Finegan, Jack. *Light from the Ancient Past*. Princeton, N.J.: Princeton University Press, 1946.

Fleischer, Robert. "Artemis Ephesia und Aphrodite von Aphrodisias." In *Die Orientalischen Religionen im Römerreich*, edited by Maarten J. Vermaseren, 298-315. Leiden: E J. Brill, 1981.

Frazer, James George. *Adonis, Attis, and Osiris: Studies in the History of Oriental Religion*. 2nd ed. London: Macmillan and Co., Ltd., 1907.

Guthrie, W. K. C. *The Greeks and Their Gods*. London: Methuen and Co., Ltd., 1950.

Heyob, Sharon Kelly. *The Cult of Isis among Women in the Graeco-Roman World*. Leiden: E. J. Brill, 1975.

James, E. O. *The Cult of the Mother-Goddess*. New York: Frederick A. Praeger, Inc., Publishers, 1959.

Kramer, Samuel Noah. *The Sacred Marriage Rite: Aspects of Faith, Myth, and Ritual in Ancient Sumer*. Bloomington: Indiana University Press, 1969.

Lefkowitz, Mary L., and Maureen B. Fant. *Women's Life in Greece and Rome*. Baltimore: Johns Hopkins University Press, 1982.

Lohse, Eduard. *The New Testament Environment*. Translated by John E. Steely. Nashville: Abingdon Press, 1976.

Machen, J. Gresham. *The Origin of Paul's Religion*. Grand Rapids: William B. Eerdmans Publishing Co., 1947.

Meeks, Wayne A. *The First Urban Christians: The Social World of the Apostle Paul*. New Haven: Yale University Press, 1983.

Nash, Ronald H. *Christianity and the Hellenistic World*. Grand Rapids: Zondervan Publishing House, 1984.

Palmer, Robert E. A. *Roman Religion and Roman Empire: Five Essays*. Philadelphia: University of Pennsylvania Press, 1974.

Pomeroy, Sarah B. *Goddesses, Whores, Wives, and Slaves: Women in Classical Antiquity*. New York: Schocken Books, 1975.

Ramsay, William M. *The Church in the Roman Empire before A.D. 170*. London: Hodder and Stoughton, 1897; reprint ed., Grand Rapids: Baker Book House, 1954.

_____. *The Cities of St. Paul: Their Influence on His Life and Thought*. London: Hodder and Stoughton, 1907; reprint ed., Grand Rapids: Baker Book House, 1960.

_____. *The Historical Geography of Asia Minor*. London: John Murray, 1890.

_____. *Letters to the Seven Churches of Asia and Their Place in the Plan of the Apocalypse*. London: Hodder and Stoughton, 1904.

Seibert, Ilse. *Woman in Ancient Near East*. Translated by Marianne Herzfeld. Revised by George A. Shepperson. Leipzig: Edition Leipzig, 1974.

Showerman, Grant. *The Great Mother of the Gods*. 1901. Reprint. Chicago: Argonaut, Inc., Publishers, 1969.

Stone, Merlin. *When God Was a Woman*. New York: Harcourt-Harvest Press, 1978.

Swidler, Leonard. "Goddess Worship and Women Priests." In *Women Priests: A Catholic Commentary on the Vatican Declaration*, edited by Leonard Swidler and Arlene Swidler, 167-75. New York: Paulist Press, 1977.

_____. "Greco-Roman Feminism and the Reception of the Gospel." In *Traditio-Krisis-Renovatio*, edited by Bernd Jaspert and Rudolf Mohr. Marburg: N. G. Elwert Verlag, 1976.

Vermaseren, Maarten J. *Corpus Cultus Cybelae Attisdisque*. Leiden. E. J. Brill, 1977.

_____. *Cybele and Attis: The Myth and the Cult*. Translated by A. M. H. Lemmers. London: Thames and Hudson, Ltd., 1977.

_____. *Mithras, the Secret God*. New York: Barnes and Noble, Inc., 1963.

Willoughby, Harold R. *Pagan Regeneration: A Study of Mystery Initiations in the Graeco-Roman World*. Chicago: University of Chicago Press, 1929.

Wood, John Turtle. *Modern Discoveries on the Site of Ancient Ephesus*. Oxford: The Religious Tract Society, 1890.

Articles

Balsdon, J. P. V. D. "Women in Imperial Rome." *History Today* 10 (1960): 24-31.

Campbell, Joseph. "Joseph Campbell on the Great Goddess." *Parabola* 5 (Fall 1980): 74-85.

Case, Shirley Jackson. "Christianity and the Mystery Religions." *The Biblical World* 43 (January 1914): 3-16.

Farnell, Lewis Richard. "Sociological Hypotheses Concerning the Position of Women in Ancient Religion." *Archiv für Religionswissenschaft* 7 (1904): 70-94.

Filson, Floyd V. "Ephesus and the New Testament." *The Biblical Archaeologist* 8 (September 1945): 73-80

Finley, M. I. "Archaeology and History." *Daedalus* 100 (1971): 168-86.

Grant, Frederick C. "Greek Religion in the Hellenistic-Roman Age." *Anglican Theological Review* 34 (January 1952): 11-26.

Hardy, E. R. "Priestesses in the Graeco-Roman World." *Churchman* 84 (1970): 264-70.

Hawkins, Peter S. "From Mythography to Myth-Making: Spenser and the Magna Mater Cybele." *Sixteenth Century Journal* 12 (1981): 50-64.

Hinnells, John R. "Christianity and the Mystery Cults." *Theology* 71 (January 1968): 20-25.

House, H. Wayne. "Tongues and the Mystery Religions of Corinth." *Bibliotheca Sacra* 140 (April-June 1983): 134-50.

Kraemer, Ross S. "Ecstasy and Possession: The Attraction of Women to the Cult of Dionysos." *Harvard Theological Review* 72 (January 1979): 55-80.

Metzger, Bruce M. "Considerations of Methodology in the Study of the Mystery Religions and Early Christianity." *Harvard Theological Review* 48 (January 1955): 1-20.

Parvis, Merrill M. "Archaeology and St. Paul's Journeys in Greek Lands: Part IV—Ephesus." *The Biblical Archaeologist* 8 (September 1945): 62-73.

Seiterle, Gérard. "Artemis, die grosse Göttin von Ephesus." *Antike Welt* 10 (1979): 3-16.

Sokolowski, F. "A New Testimony on the Cult of Artemis of Ephesus." *Harvard Theological Review* 58 (October 1965): 427-31.

Unpublished Materials

Falwell, Jr., Reuben H. "The Place of Ephesus in the Propagation of Christianity in New Testament Times." Ph.D. dissertation, Southern Baptist Theological Seminary, 1978.

Greenlaw, Alton Whitman. "Some Factors Contributing to the Distinctiveness of the Philippian Church." Th.D. dissertation, Southern Baptist Theological Seminary, 1944.

Kraemer, Ross Shephard. "Ecstatics and Ascetics: Studies in the Functions of Religious Activities for Women in the Greco-Roman World." Ph.D. dissertation, Princeton University, 1976.

2. Old Testament Context

Books

Bird, Phyllis. "Images of Women in the Old Testament." In *Religion and Sexism*, edited by Rosemary Radford Ruether. New York: Simon and Schuster, 1974.

Carmichael, Calum M. *Women, Law, and the Genesis Traditions*. Edinburgh: University Press, 1979.

Mace, David R. *Hebrew Marriage: A Sociological Study*. London: The Epworth Press, 1953.

Otwell, John. *And Sarah Laughed: The Status of Woman in the Old Testament*. Philadelphia: The Westminster Press, 1977.

Patai, Raphael. *The Hebrew Goddess*. New York: KTAV Publishing House, Inc., 1967.

Reed, William L. *The Asherah in the Old Testament*. Fort Worth: Texas Christian University Press, 1949.

Tischler, Nancy M. *Legacy of Eve: Women of the Bible*. Atlanta: John Knox Press, 1977.

Trible, Phyllis. *God and the Rhetoric of Sexuality*. Philadelphia: Fortress Press, 1978.

_____. *Texts of Terror: Literary-Feminist Readings of Biblical Narratives*. Philadelphia: Fortress Press, 1984.

Vaux, Roland de. *Ancient Israel: Its Life and Institutions*. Translated by John McHugh. New York: McGraw-Hill Book Co., Inc., 1961.

Vos, Clarence J. *Women in Old Testament Worship*. Delft: Judels und Brinkman, 1968.

Wright, G. Ernest. "Women and Masculine Theological Vocabulary in the Old Testament." In *Grace upon Grace*, edited by James I. Cook. Grand Rapids: William B. Eerdmans Publishing Co., 1975.

Articles

Bailey, John A. "Initiation and the Primal Woman in Gilgamesh and Genesis 1-3." *Journal of Biblical Literature* 89 (June 1970): 137-50.

Breyfolge, Caroline M. "The Social Status of Women in the Old Testament." *Biblical World* 35 (February 1910): 107-16.

_____. "The Religious Status of Women in the Old Testament." *Biblical World* 35 (June 1910): 405-19.

Brooks, Beatrice A. "Fertility Cult Functionaries in the Old Testament." *Journal of Biblical Literature* 60 (September 1941): 227-53.

Brueggemann, Walter. "Of the Same Flesh and Bone." *The Catholic Biblical Quarterly* 32 (October 1970): 532- 42.

Busenitz, Irvin A. "Woman's Desire for Man: Genesis 3:6 Reconsidered." *Grace Theological Journal* 7 (Fall 1986): 203-12.

Clark, Gordon H. "The Image of God in Man." *Journal of the Evangelical Theological Society* 12 (Fall 1969): 215-22.

Ellingworth, Paul. "They Were Both Naked, the Mensch and His/Her Woman." *Église et Théologie* 9 (1978): 505-6.

Feinberg, Charles L. "The Image of God." *Bibliotheca Sacra* 129 (July-September 1972): 235-46.

Foh, Susan T. "What Is the Woman's Desire?" *Westminster Theological Journal* 37 (1974): 376-83.

Higgins, Jean M. "The Myth of Eve: The Temptress." *Journal of the American Academy of Religion* 44 (December 1976): 639-47.

Knight, III, George W. "Male and Female Related He Them. "*Christianity Today,* 9 April 1976, 13-17.

Meyers, Carol. "The Roots of Restriction: Women in Early Israel." *Biblical Archeologist* 41 (September 1978): 91-103.

Oden, Jr., R. A. "The Persistence of Canaanite Religion." *Biblical Archeologist* 39 (March 1976): 31-36.

Peritz, Ismar J. "Women in the Ancient Hebrew Cult." *Journal of Biblical Literature* 17 (1898): 111-48.

Phipps, William E. "Adam's Rib: Bone of Contention." *Theology Today* 33 (October 1976): 263-73.

Stitzinger, Michael F. "Genesis 1-3 and the Male/Female Role Relationship." *Grace Theological Journal* 2 (Spring 1981): 23-44.

Terrien, Samuel. "Toward a Biblical Theology of Womanhood." *Religion in Life* 42 (1973): 322-33.

Trible, Phyllis. "Biblical Theology as Women's Work." *Religion in Life* 44 (1975): 7-13.

Vogels, Walter. "It Is Not Good that the 'Mensch' Should Be Alone; I Will Make Him/Her a Helper Fit for Him/Her." *Église et Théologie* 9 (1978): 9-35.

3. New Testament Context

Books

Allworthy, T. B. *Women in the Apostolic Church: A Critical Study of the Evidence in the New Testament for the Prominence of Women in Early Christianity.* Cambridge: W. Heffer and Sons, Ltd., 1917.

Balch, David L. *Let Wives Be Submissive: The Domestic Code in 1 Peter.* Chico, Calif.: Scholars Press, 1981.

Bartchy, S. Scott. "Power, Submission and Sexual Identity among the Early Christians." In *Essays on New Testament Christianity: A Festschrift in Honor of Dean E. Walker,* edited by C. Robert Wetzel, 50-80. Cincinnati: Standard Publishing, 1978.

Boldrey, Richard and Joyce Boldrey. *Chauvinist or Feminist? Paul's View of Women.* Grand Rapids: Baker Book House, 1976.

Brooten, Bernadette. "Junia . . . Outstanding among the Apostles (Romans 16:7)." In *Women Priests: A Catholic Commentary on the Vatican Declaration,* edited by Leonard Swidler and Arlene Swidler, 141-44. New York: Paulist Press, 1977.

————. *Women Leaders in the Ancient Synagogue: Inscriptional Evidence and Background Issues.* Chico, Calif.: Scholars Press, 1982.

Crouch, J. E. *The Origin and Intention of the Colossian Haustafel.* Göttingen: Vandenhoeck and Ruprecht, 1972.

Daniélou, Jean. *The Ministry of Women in the Early Church.* 2nd ed. Translated by Glyn Simon. Leighton Buzzard, England: The Faith Press, 1974.

Ellis, E. Earle. "The Silenced Wives of Corinth (I Cor. 14:34-5)." In *New Testament Textual Criticism: Its Significance for Exegesis,* edited by Eldon Jap Epp and Gordon D. Fee, 213-20. Oxford: Clarendon Press, 1981.

Faxon, Alicia Craig. *Women and Jesus.* Philadelphia: United Church Press, 1973.

Fiorenza, Elisabeth Schüssler. "The Apostleship of Women in Early Christianity." In *Women Priests: A Catholic Commentary on the Vatican Declaration,* edited by Leonard Swidler and Arlene Swidler, 135-40. New York: Paulist Press, 1977.

————. *In Memory of Her: A Feminist Theological Reconstruction of Christian Origins.* New York: Crossroad Publishing Co., 1983.

————. "The Twelve." In *Women Priests: A Catholic Commentary on the Vatican Declaration,* edited by Leonard Swidler and Arlene Swidler, 114-23. New York: Paulist Press, 1977.

————. "Word, Spirit and Power: Women in Early Christian Communities." In *Women of Spirit: Female Leadership in the Jewish and Christian Traditions,* edited by Rosemary Ruether and Eleanor Mclaughlin. New York: Simon and Schuster, 1979.

Jeremias, Joachim. *Jerusalem in the Time of Jesus: An Investigation into Economic and Social Conditions during the New Testament Period.* Philadelphia: Fortress Press, 1969.

Kähler, Else. *Die Frau in den paulinischen Briefen.* Zürich: GotthelfVerlag, 1960.

Knight, III, George W. *The New Testament Teaching on the Role Relationship of Men and Women.* Grand Rapids: Baker Book House, 1977.

Kroeger, Richard, and Catherine Clark Kroeger. "An Inquiry into Evidence of Maenadism in the Corinthian Congregation." In *SBL Seminar Papers,* edited by Paul J. Achtemeier, 2:331-38. Missoula, Mont.: Scholars Press, 1978.

————. "St. Paul's Treatment of Misogyny, Gynephobia, and Sex Segregation in 1 Cor. 11:2-16." In *SBL Seminar Papers,* edited by Paul J. Achtemeier, 2:213-21. Missoula, Mont.: Scholars Press, 1979.

Leipoldt, Johannes. *Die Frau in der antiken Welt und im Urchristentum.* Leipzig: Koehler and Amelang, 1954.

Martin, W. J. "1 Cor. 11:2-16: An Interpretation." In *Apostolic History and the Gospel: Biblical and Historical Essays Presented to F. F. Bruce on His 60th Birthday,* edited by W. W. Gasque and R. P. Martin, 31-34. Grand Rapids: William B. Eerdmans Publishing Co, 1970.

Mercadante, Linda. *From Hierarchy to Equality: A Comparison of Past and Present Interpretations of 1 Corinthians 11:2-16 in Relation to the Changing Status of Women in Society.* Vancouver, B.C.: Regent College, 1978.

Moltmann-Wendel, Elisabeth. *The Women around Jesus.* New York: Crossroad Publishing Co., 1982.

Stagg, Frank and Evelyn Stagg. *Woman in the World of Jesus.* Philadelphia: Westminster Press, 1978.

Swidler, Leonard. *Women in Judaism: The Status of Women in Formative Judaism.* Metuchen, N.J.: The Scarecrow Press, Inc., 1976.

Wahlberg, Rachel Conrad. *Jesus and the Freed Woman.* New York: Paulist Press, 1978.

Williams, Don. *The Apostle Paul and Women in the Church.* Glendale, Calif.: Regal Books, 1977.

Witherington, III, Ben. *Women in the Ministry of Jesus: A Study of Jesus' Attitudes to Women and Their Roles as Reflected in His Earthly Life.* New York: Cambridge University Press, 1984.

Articles

Allmen, Daniel von. "L'homme et la femme dans les textes pauliniens." *Foi et Vie* 70 (May 1971): 157-81.

Bedale, Stephen. "The Meaning of *Kephalē* in the Pauline Epistles." *Journal of Theological Studies* 5 (October 1954): 211-15.

Blum, Georg Gunter. "The Office of Women in the New Testament." *The Churchman* 85 (Autumn 1971): 175-89.

Boucher, Madeleine. "Some Unexplored Parallels to 1 Corinthians 11:11-12 and Galatians 3:28." *The Catholic Biblical Quarterly* 31 (January 1969): 50-58.

Brown, Raymond E. "Roles of Women in the Fourth Gospel." *Theological Studies* 36 (1975): 688-99.

Caird, G. B. "Paul and Women's Liberty." *Bulletin of the John Rylands Library* 54 (Spring 1972): 268-81.

Cerling, Charles D. "Women Ministers in the New Testament Church?" *Journal of the Evangelical Theological Society* 19 (Summer 1976): 209-15.

Chilton, Bruce D. "The Gospel of Jesus and the Ministry of Women." *The Modern Churchman* 22 (1978-79): 18-21.

Clark, Gillian. "The Women at Corinth." *Theology* 85 (July 1982): 256-62.

Cope, Lamar. "1 Corinthians 11:2-16: One Step Further." *Journal of Biblical Literature* 97 (September 1978): 435-36.

Davis, John Jefferson. "Some Reflections on Galatians 3:28, Sexual Roles and Biblical Hermeneutics." *Journal of the Evangelical Theological Society* 19 (Summer 1976): 201-8.

Detrick, Mary C. "Jesus and Women." *Brethren Life and Thought* 22 (Summer 1977): 155-61.

Fennema, David. "Unity in Marriage: Ephesians 5:21-33." *Reformed Review* 25 (Autumn 1971): 62-71.

Feuillet, André. "La dignité et le rôle de la femme d'après quelques textes pauliniens: comparison avec l'ancien testament." *New Testament Studies* 21 (January 1975): 157-91.

_____. "L'homme 'glorie de Dieu' et la femme 'glorie de l'homme.'" *Revue Biblique* 81 (April 1974): 161-82.

Fiorenza, Elisabeth Schüssler. "The Biblical Roots for the Discipleship of Equals." *The Duke Divinity School Review* 45 (Spring 1980): 87-97.

_____. "Women in the Pre-Pauline and Pauline Churches." *Union Seminary Quarterly Review* 33 (Spring and Summer 1978): 153-66.

Fitzmyer, J. A. "A Feature of Qumran Angelology and the Angels of I Corinthians XI:10." *New Testament Studies* 4 (October 1957): 48-58.

Flanagan, Neal M. "Did Paul Put Down Women in 1 Corinthians 14:34-36?" *Biblical Theology Bulletin* 11 (1981): 10-12.

Gartner, Bertil. "Didaskolos: The Office, Man and Woman in the New Testament." *Concordia Journal* 8 (March 1982): 52-60.

Gilbert, George H. "Women in Public Worship in the Churches of Paul." *The Biblical World* 2 (July 1893): 38-47.

Goodspeed, Edgar J. "Phoebe's Letter of Introduction." *Harvard Theological Review* 44 (January 1951): 55-57.

Hommes, N. J. "Let Women Be Silent in Church: A Message Concerning the Worship Service and the Decorum to Be Observed by Women." *Calvin Theological Journal* 4 (1969): 5-22.

Hooker, Morna D. "Authority on Her Head: An Examination of 1 Corin-thians 11:10." *New Testament Studies* 10 (April 1964): 410-16.

House, H. Wayne. "Paul, Women and Contemporary Evangelical Feminism." *Bibliotheca Sacra* 136 (January-March 1979): 40-53.

Howard, J. Keir. "Neither Male Nor Female: An Examination of the Status of Women in the New Testament." *Evangelical Quarterly* 55 (January 1983): 31-42.

Hurley, James B. "Did Paul Require Veils or the Silence of Women? A Consideration of 1 Cor. 11:2-16 and 1 Cor. 14:33b-36." *Westminster Theological Journal* 35 (1973): 190-220

Jaubert, Annie. "Le voile des femmes (1 Cor. XI:2-16)." *New Testament Studies* 18 (July 1972): 419-30.

Kroeger, Richard and Catherine Clark Kroeger. "Pandemonium and Silence at Corinth." *The Reformed Journal* 28 (June 1978): 6-11.

Kurzinger, Josef. "Frau und Mann nach 1 Kor. 11,11f." *Biblische Zeitschrift* 22 (1978): 270-75.

Layman, Fred D. "Male Headship in Paul's Thought." *Wesleyan Theological Journal* 15 (Spring 1980): 46-67.

Maly, Eugene H. "Women and the Gospel of Luke." *Biblical Theology Bulletin* 10 (1980): 99-104.

Meeks, Wayne A. "The Image of the Androgyne: Some Uses of Symbol in Earliest Christianity." *History of Religions* 13 (1974): 165-208.

Meier, John P. "On the Veiling of Hermeneutics." *The Catholic Biblical Quarterly* 40 (April 1978): 212-26.

Murphy-O'Connor, Jerome O. "The Non-Pauline Character of 1 Corin-thians 11:2-16?" *Journal of Biblical Literature* 95 (December 1976): 615-21.

_____. "Sex and Logic in 1 Corinthians 11:2-16." *The Catholic Biblical Quarterly* 42 (October 1980): 482-500.

Pagels, Elaine H. "Paul and Women: A Response to Recent Discussion." *Journal of the American Academy of Religion* 42 (September 1974): 538-49.

Reynolds, Stephen A. "On Head Coverings." *Westminster Theological Journal* 36 (Fall 1973): 90-91.

Scroggs, Robin. "Paul and the Eschatological Woman." *Journal of the American Academy of Religion* 40 (September 1972): 283-303.

————. "Paul and the Eschatological Woman Revisited." *Journal of the American Academy of Religion* 42 (September 1974): 532-37.

Sigountos, James G. and Myron Shank. "Public Roles for Women in the Pauline Church: A Reappraisal of the Evidence [1 Cor. 11:2-16; 1 Cor. 14:33-36; 1 Tim. 2:15]." *Journal of the Evangelical Theological Society* 26 (Spring 1983): 283-95.

Swidler, Leonard. "Jesus Was a Feminist." *South East Asia Journal of Theology* 13 (1971): 102-10.

Thomas, W. Derek. "The Place of Women in the Church at Philippi." *Expository Times* 83 (1972): 117-20.

Trompf, Garry W. "On Attitudes toward Women in Paul and Paulinist Literature: 1 Cor. 11:3-16 and Its Context." *The Catholic Biblical Quarterly* 42 (April 1980): 196-215.

Walker, William O. "1 Corinthians 11:2-16 and Paul's Views regarding Women." *Journal of Biblical Literature* 94 (1975): 94-100.

Waltke, Bruce K. "1 Corinthians 11:2-16: An Interpretation." *Bibliotheca Sacra* 135 (January-- March 1978): 46-57.

Weeks, Noel. "Of Silence and Head Covering." *Westminster Theological Journal* 35 (Fall 1972): 21-27.

Witherington, III, Ben. "On the Road with Mary Magdalene, Joanna, Susanna, and Other Disciples—Luke 8:1-3." *Zeitschrift für die neutestamentliche Wissenschaft und die Kunde der alteren Kirche* 70 (1979): 243-48.

————. "Rite and Rights for Women—Galatians 3:28," *New Testament Studies* 27 (October 1981): 593-604.

Zens, Jon. "Aspects of Female Priesthood: A Focus on 1 Cor. 11:2-16 and 1 Cor. 14:34-35." *Baptist Reformation Review* 10 (1981): 3-18.

Unpublished Material

Leslie, William Houghton. "The Concept of Woman in the Pauline Corpus in Light of the Social and Religious Environment of the First Century." Ph.D. dissertation, Northwestern University, 1976.

4. Pastoral Epistles' Context

Books

Ellis, E. Earle. "Traditions in the Pastoral Epistles." In *Early Jewish and Christian Exegesis: Studies in Memory of William Hugh Brownlee*, edited by C. A. Evans. Decatur, Ga.: Scholars Press, 1987.

MacDonald, Dennis Ronald. *The Legend and the Apostle: The Battle for Paul in Story and Canon.* Philadelphia: Westminster Press, 1983.

Pascual, Bartomeu. "El temple efesià d'Artemis i la primera carta a Timoteu." In *Analecta sacra Tarraconensia*, 77-82. Barcelona: n.p., 1925.

Verner, David. *The Household of God: The Social World of the Pastoral Epistles.* Chico, Calif.: Scholars Press, 1983.

Articles

Bassler, Jouette M. "The Widow's Tale: A Fresh Look at 1 Timothy 5:3-16." *Journal of Biblical Literature* 103 (March 1984): 23-41.

Colson, F. H. "'Myths and Genealogies'—A Note on the Polemic of the Pastoral Epistles." *Journal of Theological Studies* 19 (January and April 1918): 265-71.

Cranford, Lorin. "Encountering Heresy: Insight from the Pastoral Epistles." *Southwestern Journal of Theology* 22 (Spring 1980): 23-40.

Engel, G. "Let the Woman Learn in Silence." *The Expository Times* 16 (1904-1905): 189-90.

Falconer, Robert. "1 Timothy 2:14-15: Interpretative Notes." *Journal of Biblical Literature* 60 (December 1941): 375-79.

Gibson, Margaret D. "Let the Woman Learn in Silence." *The Expository Times* 15 (1903-1904): 379-80.

Hoover, Karen W. "Creative Tension in 1 Timothy 2:11-15." *Brethren Life and Thought* 22 (Summer 1977): 163-66.

Jebb, S. "A Suggested Interpretation of 1 Timothy 2:15." *The Expository Times* 81 (April 1970): 221-22.

Karris, Robert J. "The Background and Significance of the Polemic of the Pastoral Epistles." *Journal of Biblical Literature* 92 (December 1973): 549-64.

Kassing, P. Altfrid. "Das Heil der Mutterschaft: 1 Tim. 2, 15 in biblischen Zusammenhängen." *Litergie und Mönchtum* 23 (1958): 39-63.

Kittel, Gerhard. "Die Genealogia der Pastoralbriefe." *Zeitschrift für die Neutestamentliche Wissenschaft* 20 (1921): 49-69.

Knight, III, George W. "AUΘENTEΩ in Reference to Women in 1 Timothy 2:12." *New Testament Studies* 30 (January 1984): 143-57.

Kroeger, Catherine Clark. "Ancient Heresies and a Strange Greek Verb." *Reformed Journal* 29 (March 1979): 12-15.

Kroeger, Richard, and Catherine Clark Kroeger. "May Woman Teach? Heresy in the Pastoral Epistles." *Reformed Journal* 30 (October 1980): 14-18.

Moo, Douglas J. "1 Timothy 2:11-15: Meaning and Significance." *Trinity Journal* 1 (Spring 1980): 62-83.

_____. "The Interpretation of 1 Timothy 2:11-15: A Rejoinder." *Trinity Journal* 2 (Fall 1981): 198-222.

Osburn, Carroll D. "AUΘENTEΩ (1 Timothy 2:12)." *Restoration Quarterly* 25 (1982): 1-12.

Padgett, Alan. "Wealthy Women at Ephesus: 1 Timothy 2:8-15 in Social Context." *Interpretation* 41 (January 1987): 19-31.

Panning, Armin J. "AUΘENTEIN—A Word Study." *Wisconsin Lutheran Quarterly* 78 (July 1981): 185-91.

Payne, Philip B. "Libertarian Women in Ephesus: Response to D. J. Moo's Article, '1 Timothy 2:11-15: Meaning and Significance.'" *Trinity Journal* 2 (Fall 1981): 169-97.

Powers, B. W. "Women in the Church: The Application of 1 Timothy 2:8-15." *Interchange* 17 (1975): 55-59.

Roberts, Mark D. "Woman Shall Be Saved: A Closer Look at 1 Timothy 2:15." *TSF Bulletin* 5 (November/December 1981): 4-7.

Scholer, David M. "Exegesis: 1 Timothy 2:8-15." *Daughters of Sarah* 1 (May 1975): 7-8.

Spencer, Aida Dina Besancon. "Eve at Ephesus (Should Women Be Ordained as Pastors According to the First Letter to Timothy 2:11-15)?" *Journal of the Evangelical Theological Society* 17 (Fall 1974): 215-22.

Williams, Herbert W. "Let the Woman Learn in Silence." *The Expository Times* 16 (1904-1905): 188-89.

5. Women and the Bible—General

Books

Bushnell, Katherine C. *God's Word to Women*. 1923. Reprint. North Collins, N.Y.: n.p., 1978.

Clark, Stephen B. *Man and Woman in Christ: An Examination of the Roles of Men and Women in Light of Scripture and the Social Sciences*. Ann Arbor, Mich.: Servant Books, 1980.

Ermarth, Margaret Sittler. *Adam's Fractured Rib: Observations on Woman in the Church*. Philadelphia: Fortress Press, 1970.

Evans, Mary J. *Woman in the Bible: An Overview of All the Crucial Passages on Women's Roles*. Downers Grove, Ill.: InterVarsity Press, 1983.

Foh, Susan T. *Women and the Word of God: A Response to Biblical Feminism*. Grand Rapids: Baker Book House, 1979.

Gerstenberger, Erhard S., and Wolfgang Schrage. *Woman and Man*. Translated by Douglas W. Stott. Nashville: Abingdon Press, 1981.

Gundry, Patricia. *Heirs Together*. Grand Rapids: Zondervan Publishing House, 1980.

Harkness, Georgia. *Women in Church and Society: A Historical and Theological Inquiry*. Nashville: Abingdon Press, 1972.

Howe, E. Margaret. *Women and Church Leadership*. Grand Rapids: Zondervan Publishing House, 1982.

Hurley, James B. *Man and Woman in Biblical Perspective*. Grand Rapids: Zondervan Publishing House, 1981.

Jewett, Paul K. *Man as Male and Female*. Grand Rapids: William B. Eerdmans Publishing Co., 1975.

Maertens, Thierry. *The Advancing Dignity of Woman in the Bible*. De Pere, Wis.: St. Norberts Abbey Press, 1969.

Mollenkott, Virginia Ramey. *Women, Men and the Bible*. Nashville: Abingdon Press, 1977.

Prohl, Russell C. *Woman in the Church*. Grand Rapids: William B. Eerdmans Publishing Co., 1957.

Rice, John R. *Bobbed Hair, Bossy Wives and Women Preachers*. Wheaton, Ill.: Sword of the Lord Publishers, 1941.

Ruether, Rosemary Radford. *Religion and Sexism*. New York: Simon and Schuster, 1974.

Ruether, Rosemary, and Eleanor McLaughlin, eds. *Women of Spirit: Female Leadership in the Jewish and Christian Traditions*. New York: Simon and Schuster, 1979.

Ryrie, Charles C. *The Role of Women in the Church*. Chicago: Moody Press, 1958.

Scanzoni, Letha and Nancy Hardesty. *All We're Meant to Be: A Biblical Approach to Women's Liberation*. Waco, Tex.: Word Books, 1974.

Stanton, Elizabeth Cady et al. *The Woman's Bible*. New York: European Publishing Co., 1898.

Starr, Lee Anna. *The Bible Status of Woman*. New York: Fleming H. Revell Co., 1926.

Swidler, Leonard. *Biblical Affirmations of Woman*. Philadelphia: The Westminster Press, 1979.

Zerbst, Fritz. *The Office of Woman in the Church: A Study in Practical Theology*. Translated by Albert B. Merkens. St. Louis: Concordia Publishing House, 1955.

Articles

Ford, Josephine Massyngberde. "Biblical Material Relevant to the Ordination of Women." *Journal of Ecumenical Studies* 10 (Fall 1973): 669-94.

Sakenfeld, Katharine D. "The Bible and Women: Bane or Blessing?" *Theology Today* 32 (October 1975): 222-33.

6. Women, the Bible, and Hermeneutics

Books

Fiorenza, Elisabeth Schüssler. "Interpreting Patriarchal Traditions." In *The Liberating Word: A Guide to Nonsexist Interpretation of the Bible*, edited by Letty Russell, 39-61. Philadelphia: The Westminster Press, 1976.
_____. "Toward a Feminist Biblical Hermeneutics: Biblical Interpretation and Liberation Theology." In *The Challenge of Liberation Theology*, edited by Brian Mahan and L. Dale Richesin, 91-112. Maryknoll, N.Y.: Orbis Books, 1981.
Stendahl, Krister. *The Bible and the Role of Women: A Case Study in Hermeneutics*. Translated by Emilie Sander. Philadelphia: Fortress Press, 1966.
Swartley, Willard M. *Slavery, Sabbath, War and Women: Case Issues in Biblical Interpretation*. Scottdale, Pa.: Herald Press, 1983.

Articles

Fiorenza, Elisabeth Schüssler. "Feminist Theology and New Testament Interpretation." *Journal for the Study of the Old Testament* 22 (February 1982): 32-46.
Osborne, Grant R. "Hermeneutics and Women in the Church." *Journal of the Evangelical Theological Society* 20 (December 1977): 337-52.
Ruether, Rosemary. "Feminism and Patriarchal Religion: Principles of Ideological Critique of the Bible." *Journal for the Study of the Old Testament* 22 (February 1982): 54-66.
Tolbert, Mary Ann. "Defining the Problem: The Bible and the Feminist Hermeneutics." *Semeia* 28 (1983): 113-26.
Trible, Phyllis. "Feminist Hermeneutics and Biblical Studies." *Christian Century*, February 1982, 116-18.

INDEX OF BIBLICAL REFERENCES

INDEX OF NAMES

179

INDEX OF SUBJECTS